CLAIM YOUR GIFT!

Thank you for purchasing this novel. For a special behind-the-scenes e-book, including historical background on which *After the storm* was based please visit:

Books.click/Storm

* * *

This e-book companion includes group discussion ideas, unique photographs and much more!

JOIN OUR ONLINE BOOK CLUB!

Book club members receive free books and the hottest pre-release novels. To join our exclusive online book club and discuss *After the storm* with likeminded readers, please visit:

Books.click/MoringBookclub

* * *

We look forward to see you in our bookclub family!

"*After the storm* is a powerful historical novel... political events, even as dramatic as the ones that are presented in *After the storm*, are only a part of this story. Marcel Moring gives us a vivid and engaging story that reminds us how long Muslims have been struggling to triumph over the forces of violence—forces that continue to threaten them even today."—**Booklist**

* * *

"A beautiful novel... This unusually eloquent story is about the fragile relationships between mothers and daughters, men and their countries, humans and their gods... Loyalty and compassion are the ties that bind these stories into one of the most lyrical, moving and unexpected plot you'll ever read."—**The New York Times**

* * *

"A marvelous historical novel... the story of a young Bosnian girl in Sarajevo, and her incredible upbringing in the Muslim culture of the Balkans. An old-fashioned kind of novel that really sweeps you away." —
O, The Oprah Magazine

* * *

"This extraordinary novel locates the personal struggles of everyday people in the terrible sweep of history."—**Library Journal**

* * *

"A powerful book...no frills, no nonsense, just hard, spare prose...an intimate account of family and friendship, religion and salvation that requires no atlas or translation to engage. Parts of *After the storm* are sad and even hard to read, yet the book in its entirety is lovingly written."—
The Washington Post

* * *

"*After the storm* is an ambitious work. Like Moring's previous novels, the setting is WWII Europe, but this time the author covers eighty years of tumultuous history of war and oppression and tells it on an intimate scale, through the life of one couragious woman."—**Daily Telegraph**

* * *

"Spectacular. . . . Moring's writing makes our hearts ache, our stomachs clench and our emotions reel. . . . The author creates a fascinating microcosm of Muslim family life. The author writes in gorgeous and stirring language of the natural beauty and colorful cultural heritage of Islam. Moring tells this saddest of stories in achingly beautiful prose through stunningly heroic characters whose spirits somehow grasp the dimmest rays of hope."—**St. Louis Post Dispatch**

* * *

"Moring revisits WWII Europe for a compelling story that gives voice to the agonies and hopes of another group of innocents caught up in a war—the Muslims of Bosnia. Mesmerizing. . . *After the storm* is the painful yet ultimately hopeful story of one woman's struggle to keep her family safe. Moring's bewitching narrative captures the intimate details of life in a world where it's a struggle to survive, skillfully telling this human story in the larger backdrop of the Holocaust and the Bosnian wars of the 1990's."—**Chicago Sun-Times**

* * *

"Moring created another work of strong storytelling and engaging characters. . . . The story pulses with life. . . . The author is simply a marvelously moving storyteller."—**San Jose Mercury News**

* * *

"Moring's story rings true as a universal story about victims of human cruelty. . . . The author's work is uplifting, enlightening, universal. The author's love for the novel's characters and for their culture is palpable. In the end, *After the storm* is a love letter to women and their ability to do what men often cannot. It is a celebration of endurance, survival and compassion in the face of unspeakable tragedy. This is a love song to anyone who has ever felt powerless and yet still dares to dream." —**San Francisco Chronicle**

* * *

"The novel is beautifully written with descriptive details that will haunt you long after you finish reading it."—**Dallas Morning News**

* * *

"*After the storm* tells the startling story of war crimes victims who discover that survival in a horrific world is nearly impossible without compassion, love and solidarity across the Muslim-Jewish chasm in World War II Bosnia... Moring's prose can stun a reader with its powerful, haunting images."—**Atlanta Journal-Constitution**

* * *

"Haunting...absolutely compelling on every level. It's nearly impossible for a historical novel to deliver a formidable blow, a pounding of the senses, a reeling so staggering that we find ourselves literally there with the characters, facing impossible dilemmas. Such a persuasion is particularly difficult when the setting is a Muslim family, a culture many see as too strange for recognition or empathy. But that's what Marcel Moring does again and again with *After the storm*." —**Daily Mirror**

* * *

"Moring has the storytelling gift . . . *After the storm* offers us the sweep of historic upheavals narrated with the intimacy of family and small-town life. . . . What keeps this novel vivid and compelling is Moring's eye for the textures of daily life and the author's ability to portray a full range of human emotions, from the smoldering rage of a daughter who's father is taken from her by the Nazis, to the early flutters of maternal love when a woman discovers she is carrying a baby. . . . Moring's illuminating novel [is] a brave, honorable, big-hearted book" —**USA Today**

* * *

"The author's fans won't be disappointed with *After the storm*—if anything, this book shows at even better advantage Moring's storytelling gifts."—
New York Daily News

* * *

"Moring is a writer of unique sensitivities. . . . The author embraces an old-fashioned storytelling unconcerned with literary hipness, unafraid of sentimentality, unworried about the sort of Dickensian sadness that most contemporary American writers consider off-limits. . . . We are lucky to have a writer of Moring's storytelling ambitions interpreting Muslim and Jewish narratives for us with another large-hearted novel. . . . Despite the unjust cruelties of our world, the heroine of *After the storm*, Zaynab Hardaga, does endure, both on the page and in our imagination."—
Miami Herald

* * *

"[Moring's] most assured and emotionally gripping story yet . . . The author's narrative gifts have deepened over the years. . . . [After the storm] grapples with many of the same themes that crisscross Moring's early novels: the relationship between parents and children and the ways the past can haunt the present. We finish this novel with an intimate understanding of the characters through the choices they have made between duty and freedom, familial responsibilities and independence, loyalty and compassion. . . a deeply affecting choral work."—**Houston Chronicle**

* * *

"More expansive than Moring's previous novels, *After the storm* spans three generations and includes tales of parents and children, soldiers and partisans, rescuers and refugees. Moring shows how easy it is for people to brutalize or abandon those they should protect. But the ultimate achievement of this novel is in demonstrating the power and persistence of family."—**Tampa Bay Times**

* * *

"After the storm is often sad but also radiant with love: the enduring bond of a daughter and her father; the irritable but bedrock connection of family; the quiet intimacy of a close-knit community; the commitment of a husband and wife to help those in need."—**The Berkshire Eagle**

* * *

"I'm not an easy touch when it comes to novels, but Marcel Moring's new book, *After the storm*, had tears dropping from my eyes by the end. . . The genius of Moring's novels is that they pull off the neat trick of embodying and transcending the essence of a place. . . . This is an exquisite novel, a must-read for anyone with an interest in what it means to be alive, anywhere and everywhere."—**Daily Beast**

* * *

"There is an assured, charismatic new maturity to Moring's voice. The results are electrifying."—**The Chronicle**

* * *

"Compulsively readable, in large part because [Moring] probes the characters' psyches in a nuanced and poetic manner . . . *After the storm* signals the ongoing maturation of a gifted storyteller." —**Christian Science Monitor**

* * *

"My main goal in reading Marcel Moring's new book, *After the storm*, was to avoid crying. I failed. And by the last page, I was bawling. So, yes, much like Moring's earlier works, this latest novel is bathed in sadness and despair with the requisite occasional ray of hope. You won't be able to put it down. To those readers who manage to get through it without shedding a tear, well, I tip my hat." —**SheKnows.com**

* * *

"Like a sculptor working in a soft medium, [Moring] gently molds and shapes individual pieces that ultimately fit together in a major work. . . . Family matters in ways small and large. Moring seems to be telling us that the way we care is who we are and, ultimately, the face we show to life."
—**People**

* * *

"Readers' tears may fall by the book's end . . . Introspective and perfectly paced, Moring's plot spares no expense with sensory details. [The author] skillfully weaves the tapestry with universal elements: human fallibility, innate goodness, perseverance, forgiveness, sexuality, jealousy, companionship and joy. Yet reality is never sugarcoated: the brutality of life is on display, and people are shown just as they are, for better or worse. Poverty and gender roles leave scars, while shifting points of view reveal Moring's prism of truth. *After the storm* resonates to the core."—
Austin Chronicle

* * *

"After the storm, is a surprisingly nuanced, morally complex, exquisitely told tear-jerker." —**PopSugar**

* * *

"Moring returns with an instantly relatable novel that follows generations of a troubled family across the Yugoslavia wars… Touching and uplifting." —**The Augusta Chronicle**

* * *

"The beautiful writing, full of universal truths of loss and identity, makes each section a jewel . . . Moring's eye for detail and emotional geography makes this a haunting read."—**Publishers Weekly**

* * *

"Engrossing . . . Ultimately, *After the storm* is about the human endeavor to transcend difference."—**Bookpage**

AFTER THE STORM: A NOVEL

A Novel

By Marcel Moring

TABLE OF CONTENTS

Dedicated to the memory of Zaynab
Hardaga and her father, Ahmed Sadik

PROLOGUE

In the Holy Land, on a hill outside Jerusalem, there is a small cemetery facing the Jerusalem hills. If you visit this cemetery, your eyes may notice a small grave with many flowers on it. People from around the world come and pay homage to the woman buried there, leaving behind flowers and notes of gratitude. There is no name on the grave, only five words: "Mother. Righteous Among the Nations."

PART ONE

Based on a true story

CHAPTER 1

At first she didn't have a name.

Ahmed's wife, Aisha, looked at him, feeling guilty about the newborn, "I wish I had bore you a son."

Ahmed put his hand on hers. "Shhh… Don't say anything."

The old midwife wiped Aisha's sweaty forehead as Aisha's sister and hurried to take the towels out of the room.

Aisha was exhausted; the birth had taken nearly a whole day. She looked at the baby girl. The baby looked back at her. She did not cry. She just laid on her mother's chest, her eyes wide open.

Aisha looked at Ahmed worriedly. "Why does she not cry?"

Ahmed touched the baby's tiny fingers. "She has smart eyes."

The old midwife nodded. "With such big eyes, she will have good luck."

Ahmed nodded.

The midwife then coughed and said, "I'll give you some time alone."

Aisha nodded. She sighed and closed her eyes, "I wanted a boy…."

Ahmed put his finger on her lips, "Don't say that. She will be our pride, you'll see."

Time passed quickly. The seventh day's celebrations were approaching, yet Ahmed and Aisha still did not have a name for the newborn girl.

Ahmed went to the house of the imam. The imam, Ahmed knew, could help with these things. Though he was mostly in charge of prayer and matters involving the mosque, the imam was also known for his practical advice.

The imam's wife opened the door, her eyes smiling through her veil. "Ahmed! Congratulations! I hear God has given you a baby girl!"

Ahmed bowed gently. "Grace be to Allah."

"Grace be to Allah," the imam's wife said and moved aside. "Come in. The imam is now mediating some silly argument between two merchants, but he will be happy to see you when they leave."

Ahmed thanked her and sat on the chair in the corridor. Through the curtain he heard the imam speaking passionately in the drawing room. Nervous, Ahmed 'off took his red cap and fidgeted with the edges. His thoughts drifted to Aisha.

He pressured her to tell him which name she had in mind. Yet each time he asked her she said she did not care. She seemed detached these past few days. None of the visits by neighbors and friends cheered her up, nor did she eat the sweets that they brought with them. Even Aisha's sister, Surayda, could not cheer her up. Ahmed was worried about her.

He hoped she would get better soon. He also hoped she would be more pleased about the baby. His wife had been complaining that the baby did not cry, and that her eyes were frightening.

Ahmed tried to console her, promising her that the baby was perfectly fine. But he, too, wondered why the baby did not cry, apart from occasional shrieks when she wanted to be breastfed.

Ahmed heard movement behind the curtain before it was pulled back and two men appeared. "Ahmed!" said one of them, "Congratulations. May Allah give her health. What is her name?"

Ahmed looked down. "We will all know tomorrow at the celebration."

The other man laughed. "Ahmed, don't overthink it. It's only a girl!"

Ahmed tried to smile politely.

The imam's wife escorted the two men to the door and motioned for Ahmed to enter the drawing room.

As he entered, Ahmed saw the imam, his white cap on his head, sitting erect and sipping coffee. He looked so dignified. The man exclaimed, "My dear

Ahmed! Congratulations!"

Ahmed smiled. The imam was always pleasant, with a smile in his eyes. He motioned for Ahmed to sit down on the pillow in front of him.

The imam looked at Ahmed, noticing his concerned face. "What is it? Is the baby unhealthy?"

"No." Ahmed shook his head. "All praise to Allah. She is healthy. She is almost... *too* healthy."

The imam exclaimed, "Too healthy?!"

"She... does not *cry*."

The imam raised his eyebrows.

"And she looks very... serious...."

The imam closed his eyes, nodded and smiled, "You received an old soul, Ahmed!" He opened his eyes. "Congratulations!"

Ahmed was surprised the imam did not seem bothered at all. That was good.

The imam saw Ahmed was still concerned. "How is your store faring?"

Ahmed nodded.

The imam, trying to probe Ahmed to speak, asked, "Is antique furniture selling well?"

Ahmed shrugged, "The past four years have been challenging, ever since the beginning of the war."

The imam nodded, "Well, with the help of Allah the war will end soon."

Ahmed nodded as well.

The imam sighed not wanting to ask Ahmed what had prompted his visit. When someone opened his door to another person, he could never imply in his words that the visitor should explain why he had come. That was not in line with the tradition of hospitality.

Ahmed sensed the anticipation of the imam and built up the courage to murmur, "We have yet to… come up with a name for the baby."

"Well, what does your wife say?"

Ahmed shrugged and looked down, "She does not… speak… much these days…."

The imam nodded, "She must be tired."

Ahmed looked at him and then lowered his gaze.

"Well, Ahmed, what names do you have in mind?"

"Some of Aisha's friends have suggested *Fatima*, or *Khadijah*…"

"And, do you like those?"

Ahmed shrugged.

The imam took a deep breath and closed his eyes, "The name Fatima means, *the shining one*." He opened his eyes and searched Ahmed's gaze. Seeing nothing, he closed his eyes again and said, "And the name Khadija means *the trustworthy one*." He reopened his eyes and looked at Ahmed with anticipation.

The younger man said nothing. None of these names fit. That was why he had come.

The imam sighed and hummed, gently wobbling

his head. "Think, Ahmed. What was the first thing—the very first thing—that you thought when you looked at the baby?"

"I am not... I do not remember."

The imam's eyes pierced Ahmed. "And if you *did* remember? What would be the first thing you thought of?"

Ahmed felt pressured. "I guess..." He searched for words. "I guess I felt pride, a great honor—"

The imam exclaimed, "Aha!"

Ahmed looked at the imam, not understanding.

The imam nodded his head incessantly. "You felt pride. And you are her father. Pride. Is that correct?"

"Yes."

"And so you need to name her, '*The pride of her father*.' Or in Arabic, Zaynab."

"Zey...?"

"Zaynab!" The imam glared at Ahmed, "Zay-nab! The pride of her father!"

"But I've never heard of this name—"

The imam's voice was scolding. "Ahmed! Who were the children of the Prophet, peace be unto him?"

"Qasim, Abdallah and... Ibrahim?"

"Don't forget the daughters."

"The daughters...?"

The imam reprimanded him, "Their names were

Ruqayyah, Umm Kulthum, and Fatima. But first," he smiled, "came Zaynab. The first born; the pride of her father."

Ahmed nodded.

The imam smiled. "*Zayn*, in the ancient language, means *'pride'*, and *Ab* means *'father'*."

Ahmed mumbled, "'The pride of her father.' Zaynab…."

The imam saw a tiny smile appear on Ahmed's face. "Good, Ahmed, I will see you tomorrow at the celebration. May Allah be with you and with your newborn."

Leaving the imam's house, Ahmed was elated. "Zaynab," he told himself, "Zaynab, *Zaynab*!" The more he pronounced the name, the more he felt like it fit the baby girl with dark brown eyes, with a curious look and penetrating gaze. "Zaynab! Zaynab!"

He walked quickly, pacing through the streets of his beloved Sarajevo, heading toward the old market. He entered the butcher's shop. The butcher smiled at him, "Ahmed, I heard the good news!"

"Thank you!" Ahmed said, reaching his hand to shake the butcher's as the man offered him his arm instead. Ahmed grabbed it and said, "Congratulations!"

The butcher looked a little confused at Ahmed, thinking that the young father must be very excited if he was congratulating him instead. "When is the celebration, Ahmed?"

"Tomorrow!"

"Tomorrow? Has it already been a week? How time passes! So you want one sheep for tomorrow?"

Ahmed shook his head. "Two sheep please!"

The butcher frowned. "But I've been told it was a girl! Is it a boy?"

Ahmed nodded, smiling. "A beautiful, smart girl!"

The butcher looked at Ahmed as if he had gone mad. He said slowly, "We only slaughter one sheep for *girls*, two are for *boys*—"

"Yes, yes, but you don't understand!" Ahmed mumbled. "She is special!"

The butcher searched for words, moving uncomfortably from one leg to the other. Finally he said, "I will do what you tell me Ahmed, of course, but… the tradition—"

Ahmed opened his purse and placed the money on the counter. "Thank you!"

The butcher looked at Ahmed for a long moment and sighed.

The following day they were all ready and excited. Aisha was pleased with the name. Or at least she did not oppose it.

Ahmed was particularly cheerful. He held the baby

girl in his arms and whispered to her, "My Zaynab! My pride!"

People poured into the house in the afternoon. Soon the place was full of neighbors and friends. At five o'clock the imam's wife arrived and the sea of people parted to let her pass. She announced, "The imam is on his way!"

Following Surayda, Aisha's sister, to the bedroom, the imam's wife smiled at Ahmed and kissed Aisha on both cheeks, "Allah has blessed you!" She then whispered to Aisha, "What a pretty name she will receive!"

Aisha nodded, lost in thought.

The living room was full of people. The small house burst at the seams with all the guests around. Some remained outside, where the tables of food were being prepared for after the ceremony.

A short moment later the people outside whispered, "The imam is here! The imam is here!"

People stood in silence as the imam greeted everyone outside, making his way into the house, nodding his head slowly at the people. His wife had already prepared a chair for him and another for Ahmed at the front of the living room.

The young father came out of the bedroom and bowed his head to the imam. The imam nodded back at Ahmed and began with the recitations, not wanting to waste time. Everyone joined him in the traditional chants.

The imam's wife followed the recitation and

hurried to the bedroom, whispering to Surayda, "Bring her now!"

Surayda helped Aisha get up, as she was still very weak. She supported her sister her from behind as Aisha, carrying the baby, followed the imam's wife through the corridor and into the small living room.

The imam kept reciting, nodding to his wife. She placed a large embroidered pillow on Ahmed's knees, quickly taking the baby from Aisha and placing it on the father's lap. Ahmed smiled at the baby, who was quiet, her dark brown eyes looking with interest at the imam and the crowd around her.

The old man turned to Ahmed, "Now recite to her the Call for Prayer."

Ahmed nodded and bent his head down to the baby's ears, whispering to her, "God is the greatest... I bear witness that there is no deity except God. I bear witness that Muhammad is the Messenger of God..."

The imam wobbled his head in approval. Ahmed continued whispering, "Come to pray. Come to success. God is the greatest."

The imam repeated out loud, "God is the greatest!"

Everyone responded, "There is no deity except for God!"

The imam looked for his wife, but he needn't have, as she was already handing him a plate with scissors on it.

The imam nodded to his wife in approval and held

the plate before Ahmed.

Ahmed took the scissors.

Aisha, who had been standing near the wall quietly, jumped, "Be careful, Ahmed!"

Ahmed smiled to her reassuringly. With one hand he gently clasped some hair from the baby's head, and with the other he trimmed a tiny group of hairs, placing them on the plate.

The imam took the plate and lifted it up. "Congratulations, congratulations, congratulations!"

Everyone followed, "Congratulations!"

Then all the people looked eagerly at Ahmed. Whispers danced through the room, "Name! Name!"

Ahmed looked at the imam who signaled his consent. He looked at Aisha, who nodded. He then took a deep breath and said, his voice trembling, "Her name will be '*Zaynab*.'"

A murmur passed through the crowd. "Zaynab?"

The imam nodded, "The pride of her father! Zaynab, like the daughter of the Prophet, peace be onto him."

One of the older ladies shouted, "The eldest daughter of the Prophet!"

People cheered. It was an uncommon name, but the imam had given his blessing. The imam then held his hand open to the sky, and everyone did the same. He led a recitation of the first chapter of the Qur'an.

Ahmed looked at Aisha. She smiled back at him

tiredly.

The imam recited, "Guide us to the path of the righteous. Guide us to the path of those whom you favor, not those who anger you and not those who have gone astray."

Everyone responded, "Amen!"

The imam then stood up and looked at Ahmed and Aisha. Everyone listened attentively as he gave his blessing, "May *Zaynab* be a true pride to her parents, and to the nation of Islam!"

Ahmed nodded in appreciation. All eyes were locked on him, waiting for the traditional invitation. He smiled, tears in his eyes, and exclaimed: "Be our guests! Celebrate with us! Eat and rest with us!"

With that, people began crowding near Ahmed, ready to kiss the baby girl. Those who kissed her proceeded outside to many food platters placed on tables in front of the house.

Ahmed nodded to everyone as they approached and kissed the newborn. He beamed.

Suddenly, one of the guests came rushing inside, "The meat!" he exclaimed, looking at the imam. "There are two sheep!"

In an instant the room became quiet. The imam, now standing near the entrance, looked at Ahmed, bewildered.

Ahmed looked down. The women who came to kiss the baby moved away. Aisha shook her head, looking at her husband.

"I…" Ahmed mumbled, "I… wanted to have a proper celebration…."

One neighbor shouted, "But it is *forbidden!*"

The imam looked at the man and said calmly, "No. It is not *forbidden*," he then looked at Ahmed, "It may not be *customary*, but it is not forbidden."

No one dared to say anything. Some older women tut-tutted, shaking their heads disapprovingly.

The imam concluded, "It is the will of the father of the newborn. We will accept it."

A disapproving murmur passed through the people.

"But," the imam added, "we do *encourage* the young family to adhere—"

"Where does it say so?" Aisha said suddenly.

Everyone looked at her, shocked.

Aisha gulped. "Where does it say in our holy book that one must sacrifice one sheep for a girl and two for a boy?"

Ahmed looked at his wife, surprised by her outspokenness.

The imam was stunned. One of the older women said, "It is in the *spoken tradition*, you ignorant young people: 'Two sheep that resemble each other are to be sacrificed for a boy and one for a girl!'"

People agreed with her. The room became noisy.

The imam took a deep breath. "The *spoken tradition*," he began saying as everyone became silent,

"The spoken tradition is *not* the Qur'an." He looked around the room. "We congratulate the family!" He then looked at his wife and decidedly left the house. She followed him hurriedly.

Suddenly, the baby, lying on Ahmed's knees began to cry. Ahmed looked at her and then at Aisha. "She is crying! She is finally crying!"

CHAPTER 2

Ahmed announced to everyone that Zaynab brought good luck. It was only a few weeks after she was born that the Great War finally ended after four years, three months and 14 days since the wretched day it had begun.

Ahmed remembered that date clearly.

Five years earlier Ahmed moved to Sarajevo. A merchant by trade, he specialized in antique furniture. Sarajevo at the time was growing. One of Ahmed's main clients, Mr. Nathan, had encouraged Ahmed to open a real shop in the city, rather than cart his furniture around from place to place.

And that was what Ahmed did.

That same year the archduke of the great Austrian Empire was expected to visit Sarajevo. Ahmed was excited—not about the archduke; he did not care about politics. It was the cars that excited him. Rarely did one see an automobile in Sarajevo, or anywhere around the Bosnian terrains at the edge of the Austrian Empire. And it was said that the archduke's entourage had not only one car, but five!

Ahmed rejoiced. Five horseless cars! All at once! This was a sight that could not be missed.

There were rumors that the Archduke would cancel his trip. Ahmed heard people in the market speculate that the Archduke would come up with some excuse, or "suddenly fall ill." Everyone knew it was not safe for him to visit the turbulent city.

Sarajevo, being at the edge of the Austrian Empire, was restless. Some people, influenced by the nearby independent Serbia, wanted the region to join Serbia and leave the Austrian Empire.

Ahmed did not care. As long as there was business in his new shop—as long as he could collect the dowry to present to the family of the young woman he was eyeing at the time, Aisha—politics and the news about the rest of Europe did *not* interest him.

However, it was hard to avoid politics altogether. Like others, Ahmed had heard that tiny Serbia, across the mountains, was hoping that his region, Bosnia, would separate from the old Austrian Empire and unite with her to form a new state. Some people even presumed that Serbia supported a gang in Sarajevo, the *Black Hand*, that tried to attack Austrian targets intending to push the Austrians out of Bosnian terrain.

To everyone's surprise, the Archduke did not cancel his trip. And so, four years before the birth of his firstborn, young Ahmed Sadik took to the streets of Sarajevo along with the locals to watch the spectacle. He wanted to see the Archduke, and possibly even touch one of the cars.

Ahmed stood in the crowded streets and saw the fancy open topped cars passing. He also saw the Archduke himself, sitting next to his wife, waving to the crowds.

Ahmed waved back. What a celebration for Sarajev to have the heir of the Empire himself visit their little town!

But then came the gun shots. Several of them. People screamed and ran.

Ahmed ran along with the people. He hid in the entrance of a building. From there he saw policemen on horses and a few men being arrested. Doctors came running. Stretchers. More people screaming.

Minutes later it became clear. A member of the *Black Hand Gang*, a Serb, wanting to rid Bosnia of Austrian rule, shot the royal couple.

Hours later the Archduke and his wife were pronounced dead. Ahmed was shocked. He had just seen them; they were very much alive.

Many Muslims and Croats took to the streets, targeting some of the Serbian-owned stores, and the Serbian school. The Austrian army did little to protect the Serbs. Following what happened, it was very difficult for Austrian soldiers not to join in targeting Serbs.

Ahmed stayed home the following two days, until

the riots subsided. On the third day, he went to his store, but the street was quiet.

The old shoemaker, who had a small shop next to Ahmed's furniture store, sighed. "You hear that, young man?"

"No. I hear nothing," Ahmed answered.

"Exactly. That's the quiet. The quiet before the storm."

Newspapers reported that Austria declared that Serbia must be punished for supporting the *Black Hand Gang* who had assassinated the Austrian Archduke.

Tension hung in the air as everyone knew that Serbia was supported by Russia. Could Austria really attack Serbia? And what would happen to the delicate peaceful balance on the continent?

A week after the assassination, with the streets still mostly empty, Ahmed was visited by Mr. Nathan, one of Ahmed's main clients.

Over the years Mr. Nathan bought several antique desks and even an old Victorian bed from the back of Ahmed's old horse wagon. It was Mr. Nathan who enthusiastically encouraged Ahmed to open up a shop in Sarajevo.

"Mr. Nathan!" Ahmed exclaimed, seeing his old friend. "Do come in and have some coffee!"

Mr. Nathan looked pale. "Oh I wish I could, Mr. Sadik, but I cannot."

"Why?" Ahmed asked and hurriedly put the kettle on the small stove at the back of the store. "You must have some coffee with me!"

Mr. Nathan walked inside reluctantly. He looked at one of the chairs and stroked it lovingly.

Ahmed saw this. "Victorian! Mahogany! Notice the dark finish, the ornate carvings, and the delicate marble top! Go ahead, Mr. Nathan, sit on it!"

Mr. Nathan smiled sadly, "I cannot. You see, Mr. Sadik, I'm afraid my family and I need to leave Sarajevo."

Ahmed looked stunned. He walked to Mr. Nathan, "Why?"

"I have a bad feeling. Seeing what happened to the Serbs, with the Austrian army not protecting them from the Croats and the Muslims.... Seeing the Serbian school vandalized.... These are sights I was hoping our new century would not have to witness."

Ahmed did not know what to say. "But it was only a few hoodlums, and the government stopped the riots soon enough, did they not?"

Mr. Nathan looked around. He whispered. "I've heard that some Serbs have disappeared. They say the Austrian army has taken many... That they hang them without trial."

Ahmed gulped. He tried to smile, "But you are a Jew, Mr. Nathan, not a Serb!"

Mr. Nathan sighed. "You see, Mr. Sadik, as a Muslim you may not be able to understand...."

Ahmed found that comment insulting. He handed the cup of coffee to Mr. Nathan and said, "Try me."

"Mr. Sadik, you Muslims have been the majority in Sarajevo. You do not know what it means to be a *minority*. Today the government is going after the Serbs. Tomorrow they can turn against the Croats. And then? Who else will they go after?"

Ahmed looked at him, suddenly comprehending the severity of Mr. Nathan's face. "So you did not come to buy anything…?"

"Mr. Sadik, dear Mr. Sadik…. No, I came to ask you to *buy* my furniture. We need to leave as soon as possible—"

"Leave for good? Mr. Nathan! Sarajevo is your home!"

"This is my home, and you are my brother, Mr. Sadik, but I cannot risk my family."

Ahmed was speechless.

"Could you come to my home this evening to appraise what we have?"

Ahmed nodded reluctantly, still at a loss for words.

That evening Ahmed looked through many pieces of furniture at Mr. Nathan's house. He peeked into the room of the sleeping children and glanced at the beds and the desk. He entered the parent's bedroom and his heart sank when he saw the large Victorian bed that he had sold Mr. Nathan a few years before. He calculated in his head. Everything should cost around $20,000.

He returned to the living room. Mr. Nathan's wife smiled at him and placed a a slice of cake before him. He thanked her and sat down near the coffee table. Mr. Nathan came and sat in the couch across from him. "Well?"

"Mr. Nathan, this is very difficult for me. How much do you want?"

"I was thinking of $10,000."

Ahmed was shocked, "For *everything?*"

Mr. Nathan nodded.

"But, it's worth at least $20,000!"

"Yes, but I have no time. We need to leave as soon as possible."

Ahmed looked at him, "I'm not going to pay you less than—"

Mr. Nathan interrupted him, "Dear Mr. Sadik! With the current political events, you might not be able to sell everything as fast as you think."

Ahmed insisted. "I'm not going to pay you less!"

"We'll talk about it later, then. When is the soonest you could take everything?"

Ahmed shrugged, "In two days I guess."

"That could be too late for us. We might be gone by then."

Ahmed was outraged. "So soon?!"

Mr. Nathan said nothing.

Ahmed took a deep breath. "I will get the money by noon tomorrow."

The following day Ahmed arranged for four carriages to take the furniture from Mr. Nathan's house to his shop. After everything was loaded he paid Mr. Nathan.

Mr. Nathan counted the money, "Mr. Sadik!"

Ahmed shook his head, "I will not pay less."

Mr. Nathan's eyes were moist, "Mr. Sadik, you need not—"

"I insist. Most of the furniture here you bought from *me!* I know its price, I cannot pay less!"

Mr. Nathan shook his head. Ahmed seemed adamant. "Mr. Sadik, in my ancient language your family name, 'Sadik', means 'righteous' or 'pious.'"

Ahmed laughed, "But I'm neither."

Mr. Nathan, who was always rather reserved and distant, hugged Ahmed, "Promise me you will take care of yourself, Mr. Sadik!"

As the men were unloading the four carriages at Ahmed's shop, the old shoemaker from the neighboring shop came out and asked, "Who is leaving town?"

"The Nathans."

"The *Jews?*"

Ahmed nodded.

The old shoemaker shook his head. "When the Jews leave, it's always a bad sign."

As the weeks passed, the delicate balance that held the continent in relative peace began to shudder.

Rumors had it that Austria would invade Serbia in retaliation for the assassination of the Archduke and his wife.

Serbia then called on its old ally, Russia, for help.

Serbia would have been easy for Austria to crush. Russia, however, was a different case. It had a massive army.

Therefore, Austria called on Germany for help. The German government promptly agreed.

The response of the German government provoked the French government, which soon called up its army.

Germany found itself trapped; it could cope with a war on the Russian front, but not with France attacking from the other side. That would mean suicide. Afraid of being attacked from both sides, Germany quickly decided to attack France. The smartest way was to go to the less guarded border of France with Belgium.

While Belgium did not have its own army, it had protection from Britain. Therefore, when Germany invaded Belgium on its way to France, Britain declared war on Germany. Austria supported Germany, while France and Russia supported Britain. Within weeks most of the continent was at war.

The conflict would take the lives of millions and would seem to many like it would never end—until finally, four years later, a baby was born in the very same city that inflamed the continent. The baby's name was Zaynab.

CHAPTER 3

Soon after the birth of Zaynab, an armistice was signed between Austria-Hungary and the Allies.

After the armistice Ahmed was finally able to sell many pieces of furniture that had been blocking his storage for four difficult years with almost no customers.

Pleased, Ahmed declared to everyone who listened that Zaynab had brought good luck. "She ended the war," he explained to people. He was kidding, of course. But then, in his heart, he felt that his first-born did have something to do with the newfound peace.

More than anything, Zaynab brought peace to Ahmed's own heart. During the four previous years he heard of terrible things happening. While he was not recruited, some of his friends were.

Some were killed.

Some had killed others.

But now it was all finally over. And each day,

coming back from work, Ahmed had a new baby to look forward to seeing. He closed the store earlier than before. At home, he played with the little baby and sang to her. He adored her.

Aisha, however, was not well. She often spent the day in bed. Ahmed tried everything. He bought Aisha sweets in the market. He spoke to Aisha's mother, who came to help them daily. He invited Surayda to come and read to Aisha. He tried encouraging Aisha in any way he could think of.

But she was not well. She cried a lot.

She even said that Zaynab looked at her with disapproving eyes.

Ahmed took over the grocery shopping. He also cleaned the house. He prayed each day for Aisha to feel better.

It was only when Zaynab was two years old that he began hearing Aisha laughing again.

One evening, while Aisha's mother watched over little Zaynab, Ahmed took his wife to the new cinema that opened in town at the old quarter where the wealthy people lived. They sat in the theatre and marveled at the moving pictures, and the synchronicity of the talented orchestra of four musicians sitting in front of the stage.

The film, *Tarzan of the Apes*, left a great impression on the two of them. They were both a little embarrassed to watch Tarzan jump from tree to tree with only a thin cloth covering his loins. It was even scarier for Ahmed to see Tarzan lean in to kiss his wife, Jane, in front of all the people in the audience.

Luckily, just as Tarzan was about to do so, the film ended. Ahmed and Aisha clapped, and so did everyone else.

In the weeks following, whenever Aisha became morose again, Ahmed would do his funny imitation of Tarzan, and she would laugh again. He would take little Zaynab, who by then could say a few words, put her on his back, and run with her around the small house.

Slowly but surely, Aisha was returning to the woman Ahmed had known. She began speaking more contentedly, and even mentioned wanting another baby.

When Zaynab was three years old her mother gave birth to a baby boy; Zaynab was ecstatic. She ate all the sweets the neighbors brought. She wanted to touch the baby constantly, even though her mother only allowed her to touch him softly, and not hug him or lift him, explaining to Zaynab that he was not a toy.

A week after the birth many people came to the house. Zaynab was dressed up in a beautiful new white dress.

The old imam led the ceremony beautifully. Ahmed announced that the baby boy would be named Abdul, and the imam explained that the name meant *servant*, and wished that the boy would be the greatest servant of God.

After the ceremony an recitations, the imam looked at Ahmed and exclaimed with a twinkle in his eyes, "Now, should we expect only one sheep on the table outside?"

Ahmed shook his head. "Two of the healthiest sheep in the market!"

All the guests laughed. Aisha seemed happy. Zaynab was thrilled to have everyone hug her and congratulate her. She loved the baby boy. But most of all she enjoyed the sweets she received that day.

Zaynab immediately liked her baby brother. She sang to him, dressed him, and played with him for long hours.

Business was picking up in Ahmed's store. Sarajevo had become a part of a larger kingdom that included former Serbia. This newly formed *Yugoslavia* made Ahmed feel confident that it was the dawn of a new, good era. Many Serbs moved to Sarajevo from Belgrade. The city was growing, and business was good.

Trying to give some rest to his wife, Ahmed often took Zaynab to the store. Aisha had been complaining that Zaynab asked too many questions and never stopped talking.

But Ahmed liked it. In the store, he gave four-year-old Zaynab different chores, such as wiping the furniture and sweeping dust from the floor. While she did neither of them well, she tried, and Ahmed appreciated it.

Zaynab especially loved it when customers entered the store. She would often hide behind one of the antique divans and listen to the conversation. She liked to hear her father speak excitedly about furniture. In her mind, she imagined the beds and desks were from the castle of a princess.

While the store was filled with expensive furniture, their house was much more humble, if not bare. Ahmed and Aisha lived a simple life. They never wore expensive clothes or had lavish meals.

However, during the month of Ramadan everything changed. Each year Zaynab anticipated this important holiday, in which everything became different.

When Zaynab was six years old she asked her father, who she endearingly called *Babo*: "Is it true that in Ramadan everything is upside down, Babo?"

"What do you mean, Zenzen?"

"I mean, day becomes night, and night becomes day!"

Ahmed laughed, "But it is still dark during the night!"

"Yes, but people always sleep during the night, and during the day they eat and walk and talk. But in Ramadan they sleep during the day, and they eat and walk and talk during the night!"

Ahmed was amused, "I do not sleep during the day!"

"In Ramadan you take long naps, Babo!"

Ahmed laughed, "My genius Zenzen, you are right!"

"Babo, is it true that Ramadan is holy?"

"It is."

"Why, Babo?"

"Because during Ramadan our Holy Book came down from the heavens to our prophet Mohammad, peace be onto him."

"But," Zaynab searched for words, "why can't Ramadan happen all year?"

Ahmed smiled. "You'd like that, Zenzen?"

Zaynab nodded, "Yes, very much, Babo!"

Each day of Ramadan, in preparation for the evening meal breaking the daily fast, Ahmed would go to buy fresh pita bread from the bakery. Long lines surrounded the bakeries, as every family wanted to have fresh hot pita bread for the meal at the end of the daily fast.

Ahmed would often take Zaynab with him. The smell of the bakery brought saliva to Zaynab's mouth. She enjoyed standing next to her father and watching everyone converse as they waited in line.

Once Zaynab saw one man cut the line, and she pulled on her father's sleeve, "Babo, that man is going straight to the counter without waiting in line!"

Ahmed smiled, "Don't worry Zenzen. Woory

about behaving yourself. People who don't do what is right have luck run away from them."

Indeed, Zaynab, who watched carefully, saw how the man was scolded by the people at the front of the line, and then forced to the end. Eventually he was so upset that he left.

Zaynab also saw people trying to cut the line in more sophisticated ways. She saw a woman come and speak to a lady who stood in the line. When people told her, "Lady, go to the back of the line!" she exclaimed angrily, "I'm not here to buy pita. Can't a person say hello to her friend?"

But Zaynab noticed how the woman stayed in the line until her friend bought some pita for herself and for the woman as well! This upset Zaynab very much. "Babo! This woman cut in line! She pretended!"

Ahmed smiled. "Zenzen, some things you will need to leave to Allah."

Zaynab did not like this answer.

A few days into the month of Ramadan, Zaynab went with her father to a special meeting of the Muslim store owners in the center of town. Her father explained to her that the meeting about street cleanliness.

When they arrived, Zaynab realised she was the only girl. In fact, there were no children there.

When her father was asked why his daughter could not stay home with her mother, he shrugged and smiled, saying nothing.

Zaynab tried to follow everything said in the

meeting, but she did not understand most of it. What she did understand was that her father spoke once, upset about something, saying to the other men, "We cannot leave things as they are! If we do, it will only get worse!"

Zaynab soon fell asleep on the carpet in the corner of the room. When the meeting ended, her father carried her home in his arms. When they arrived home and Ahmed tucked her in bed, Zaynab called "Babo!"

"What is it, Zenzen?" Ahmed whispered, trying not to wake little Abdul up.

"Babo, why can't you leave things to Allah?"

Ahmed did not understand. "Which kind of things?"

Zaynab's eyes shone in the darkness, "You said, 'We cannot leave things as they are! If we do, the situation will only get worse!' You said that, Babo! Why can't you leave things to Allah?"

Ahmed laughed quietly.

Zaynab did not understand what was funny.

Ahmed stroked his daughter's head. "I guess, some things you need to leave to Allah, Zenzen, and some things you need to…" he searched for words, "help Allah bring about."

Zaynab did not say anything. This was a new idea. She wanted to think about it thoroughly, but she soon fell asleep.

CHAPTER 4

When Zaynab was nearly nine years old, her mother gave birth to another baby. This time it was a girl. Zaynab loved baby Nadia very much. She also loved that Abdul was speaking a lot and could play with her in front of the house in the evenings.

As Ramadan approached again, Zaynab's teachers spoke about the holiday in school. At home, Zaynab announced, "This year I'm going to fast like a grown up!"

Aisha laughed. "You are still a child, baby."

"I'm not a child and I'm not a baby!"

Ahmed looked at Zaynab with his loving eyes. "Children are not allowed to fast, Zenzen."

Zaynab pouted her lips and crossed her arms on her chest, "I'm not a child! I'm going to fast with all the adults!"

Ahmed smiled.

When the first day of Ramadan began, Zaynab did not eat nor drink in school or at home. When her father returned home from work early in order to go to the afternoon prayer at the mosque, Zaynab insisted on going with him.

"Zenzen, are you sure you want to come?"

Zaynab, who had been to the mosque several times before with her father, insisted.

Aisha stayed home, nursing baby Nadia. Abdul also stayed with them. But Zaynab accompanied her father.

As they approached the mosque, Zaynab noticed there were many people outside. "Babo," she whispered, "why are there so many people here?"

Ahmed smiled, "It's Ramadan, Zenzen. People know the angels are coming down from the heavens."

Zaynab's eyes grew larger. She wanted to see the angels too.

They entered, took their shoes off, and Zaynab followed her father to the prayer lines. They bowed on the carpet and joined the prayer. Soon two men joined the line behind them. One of them looked at Zaynab and seemed unpleased. He whispered to Ahmed, "She should be in the women's section!"

Ahmed whispered back, "She's still a child."

Zaynab looked away.

The man whispered, "No, she should be in the women's section!"

Ahmed was upset, "I need to be with her. So, you are sending me, too, to the women's section?!"

The men in front of them hushed them.

Zaynab prayed with her father, bowing down, standing, then repeating. In her heart she also prayed that the man would say nothing else.

Later, when they walked back home, Zaynab said, "Babo, I have an idea!"

"What is it, Zaynab?"

"When we go to prayers this evening, I could take my head covering off, so that they won't notice I am a girl!"

Ahmed laughed, "You are a girl, you should be proud of it and wear your head covering with pride!"

"But Babo, I don't want to be separated from you!"

"Don't worry, you won't."

Zaynab trusted her father.

Before the evening prayer, Zaynab began to feel a little dizzy from not having eaten all day, but she did not tell her mother, knowing Aisha would force her to eat.

As sunset came Zaynab headed with her father back to the mosque. Again, someone said to her father: "Girls should be in the women's section with their mother!"

Ahmed wanted to retort, but said nothing.

After the evening prayer people lingered in the

mosque. Ahmed spoke to some of his friends, who were surprised to hear that Zaynab was fasting. One of them joked, "Ahmed, you are raising a little clergywoman!"

Ahmed stroked Zaynab's head and said, "If I had half her wit, I would have become the President of Yugoslavia!"

Then they heard a cannon blast from afar, indicating the end of prayers. Zaynab was a little startled at first, but then she saw everyone shaking hands and greeting each other while heading to a table in the center of the reception hall in the mosque. On the table there were cups of water and a huge pile of dates. Her father brought her a cup of water, and she drank with great pleasure. Then Ahmed took two dates for her and they quickly walked home.

At home, Aisha waited for them with a big meal. Aunt Surayda was also there with her husband. They brought fresh pita bread they had bought at the bakery.

They prayed for the food and eagerly began eating. Zaynab devoured the food.

Aunt Surayda laughed, "Zaynab, you were starving!"

Zaynab gulped the food and smiled.

Aisha was displeased with Zaynab, "Zaynab! You need to eat properly. Don't let the cheese spill that way!"

Ahmed, chewing, showed Zaynab how to take the piece of pita bread and dip it in the melted cheese, and bring it quickly to the mouth without spilling it.

Zaynab tried, but some spilled. The adults laughed.

Soon Abdul fell asleep on the sofa. Ahmed looked at him and then at Zaynab lovingly. He turned to Aisha, "I need someone to go with Zaynab to the women's section during prayer."

Zaynab called, "But Babo!"

Aisha shook her head, "I told you she was too old to come with you."

Surayda said, "My neighbor, Wafaa, is very religious. She goes to each of the five prayers, even in the early morning. I can ask her."

Ahmed nodded, "Thank you."

Zaynab cried, "But Babo! I want to pray with you!"

Ahmed patted Zaynab on the head, "Don't worry, Zenzen. All will be fine."

In the morning, before sunrise, Ahmed woke Zaynab. She was drowsy, "Babo...?"

"Shhh..." Ahmed quieted her, pointing at sleeping Abdul and Nadia. He whispered to her, "Let's eat quickly, Zenzen."

They ate in the small kitchen. It was still dark outside.

They then left the house. It was cold. Zaynab had never been out so early. They walked in a different direction, passing by the old clock tower. "Babo, where are we going?"

"To a new mosque, Zenzen."

"But I like our mosque!"

Ahmed smiled, "You will never know if a new mosque is better, Zenzen, unless you try!"

Zaynab contemplated his words.

When they arrived at the new mosque, Ahmed asked around, and a young woman called Wafaa came to meet him. Zaynab looked at her eyes and thought she was very beautiful. Wafaa complemented Zaynab's beautiful head covering. Then she told Zaynab, "I will show you the women's section and if you want, you can stay with me there, or if you don't, you can go with your father. Is that alright with you?"

Zaynab nodded.

She followed Wafaa to the women's section in the small mosque. A few dozen women were in the room, praying. Wafaa joined the row of women and bent down on the carpet. Zaynab did so as well.

While praying, Wafaa kept an eye on Zaynab as the eight-year-old closed her eyes, raised her hands up to her ears and invoked the name of God. She then placed her right hand over her navel. She prayed quietly and bent down.

Wafaa saw how Zaynab, her eyes still closed, waited for the other women to bow down before joining them in the exact moment. Finally, Zaynab turned her head to the right and mumbled, "May the peace, mercy, and blessings of God be with you", and then turned to her left and repeated the blessing.

When Zaynab opened her eyes she was surprised

to see not only Wafaa looking at her, but also four women—no, six—standing near.

She gulped and looked down in embarrassment. But the women cheered. "Wafaa, who is she?!"

"She's the daughter of my friend Surayda's sister, Aisha. Her father brought her."

One of the women knelt down and looked at Zaynab, "You pray with your eyes closed! Like the grown ups!"

Zaynab nodded and looked down at the carpet.

Wafaa put her hand on Zaynab's shoulder, "How do you know, Zaynab, when to lean down and when to rise back up, without looking?"

"I…" Zaynab mumbled, "I, feel the others, I hear…."

Wafaa shook her head and looked at the other women with a smile.

One of the women asked, "How old are you?"

"Eight and a half, but I'm turning nine next month."

Wafaa looked at the ladies, "Let's not bombard her with questions!"

One of the women said to Zaynab, "Do come again for the midday prayer!"

Wafaa laughed, "She will be in school!"

The woman persisted, "Then at least for the sunset prayer, break the fast with us!"

Ahmed stood at the entrance to the women's

section and coughed, looking down.

Zaynab shouted, "Babo!" and jumped up from the carpet to hug him.

That afternoon, before sunset, Zaynab asked her father if they could go to the smaller mosque. He hesitated, as his own friends were all in the larger mosque near the old city square. He looked at Zaynab.

"Babo, please!"

He laughed.

They went to the smaller mosque near the old clock tower. Wafaa spotted them in the entrance and called, "Zaynab!"

Zaynab joined Wafaa and prayed in the women's section. After the prayer, Wafaa took Zaynab to an old lady who was sitting on a chair, surrounded by a few women. "This woman is called Hakima," Wafaa whispered, "She's very wise. I'd like you to meet her."

Hakima's face was wrinkled. She looked at Zaynab and squinted. "Young girl, oh my, you are very wise."

Zaynab looked down, but old Hakima brought her finger to Zaynab's chin and raised it. "Don't ever look down. You hear me?"

Zaynab nodded.

"Your name is Zaynab, I understand."

"Yes, Ma'am."

"Zaynab, like Zaynab the daughter of the Prophet."

"Yes, Ma'am."

"But also like Zaynab the daughter of Ali, the great heroine."

Zaynab did not know what to say. She had never heard of that other Zaynab.

Hakima continued, searching Zaynab's eyes, "Or are you like Zaynab Fawwaz, the Muslim writer and poet? I have her book at home."

Zaynab looked down, but Hakima raised her chin again with her finger. She stared at Zaynab's eyes. "You are a wise girl. An old soul. You have one brother and one sister, correct?"

Zaynab nodded.

"And you are a fighter of justice, correct?"

Zaynab turned to look at Wafaa, a little scared of the old woman staring into her eyes.

Hakima continued, her eyes now closed, "You are a wise girl, Zaynab. And courageous. One day the whole world will hear of your—"

At that moment the cannon was fired in the distance, and all the women cheered. Wafaa took Zaynab away from old Hakima and whispered, "I hope she did not scare you. She is clairvoyant."

Zaynab did not know this word. But she did not have time to think about it, as Wafaa handed her a date. The taste of it was sweet. She felt at home.

On the last day of Ramadan, Ahmed took Zaynab and Abdul for a long walk with a bag of sandwiches Aisha had made for them, and they climbed one of the hills surrounding the city. From there they saw the whole of Sarajevo, as if they were giants.

They were not the only ones to climb up the hill. Many families came, wanting to watch the cannon being lit for the last time. Everyone gathered at the top of the hill as a man put a large bullet into the cannon.

Zaynab was scared, but her father assured her that this was only a firework bullet, and that she should not be worried. Then the man lit the thread at the end of the cannon with a wooden stick and Ahmed signaled to Zaynab and Abdul to cover their ears. They did.

The cannon fired.

Everyone cheered. Abdul jumped up and down excitedly. Zaynab was ecstatic. Then they sat on the hill as darkness took over the city and lights turned on everywhere. They ate and then descended the mountain.

The following day Aisha woke Zaynab early.

Zaynab was drowsy, "Mama... Is it time for prayer?"

"No," Aisha scolded her. "It's time to help your mama in the kitchen!"

Zaynab woke up slowly. She began praying. Aisha came to her, "No time for praying. We need to cook."

Zaynab finished her prayer fast, skipping the recitation, and got off the carpet.

In the kitchen, Aisha was stressed. Zaynab looked at her, "Mama, aren't we eating at Nana's house?"

Aisha ignored the question. "Watch me as I roll these rollmops. I want you to do the same."

Zaynab followed the instructions. Her mother prepared kebabs and mixed soup on the stove.

When Zaynab finished rolling the rollmops, her mother took a large pot off the stove, and replaced it with another. She took the first pot and placed it on the table. There was a huge hot cabbage inside. "Watch me, Zaynab!" Aisha said, pulling out a hot cabbage leaf. She placed it on the cutting board, put some of the paste she had mixed earlier, made of chopped onion, rice and tomatoes, and slowly rolled the cabbage leaf. "You need to first make sure that the sides are folded on top of the paste, you see?"

Zaynab nodded.

It was an hour later, after Zaynab had helped with a myriad of dishes, that her mother answered her question. "Nana is old and cannot make enough food for all the children and grandchildren; you understand, Zaynab?"

Zaynab nodded.

"Now go and shower quickly, I'm going to wake up your brother and sister. We all need to be ready for the prayer in front of the mosque."

"Mama! You are going to come to the prayer with us?"

"What did you think - that I wouldl miss the prayer of Eid?"

When Zaynab got out of the shower her mother gave her a new white dress.

"Mama!" Zaynab cried with excitement, "Thank you!" She hurried to kiss her mother on her hand, and her mother kissed her back on the forehead, whispering, "May Allah keep you safe and well."

Abdul, too, received a new suit, and even little Nadia received a new white dress.

Their father finished getting ready and sat happily in the living room. Then they all waited for Aisha to come out of the bedroom. She looked stunning, with a matching dress and head covering with golden lace. Ahmed exclaimed, "Like the day I married you, Aisha!"

Zaynab jumped around excitedly. Ahmed took several small rugs under his arm for the prayer. Aisha adjusted her head covering, looked in the mirror, and then took Nadia in her arms. "Quick! We don't want to be late!"

The streets were filled with people dressed in their finest clothes. Everything felt very festive. Ahmed greeted some of the people walking. He held hands with Abdul and Zaynab. They passed by a house and saw a man calling from the yard, "Happy Eid, Mr. Sadik!"

Ahmed stopped, "Happy Easter, Mr. Miloshovic!"

A few seconds later Zaynab looked up to her father, "Babo, why did you say 'Happy Easter' and not 'Happy Eid'?"

"Mr. Miloshovic is a Christian, a Serb, Zenzen."

"Oh," Zaynab responded, "like the man who bought the mahogany table from you, Mr. Hrvatin?"

Aisha scolded them, "If you keep talking so much we will be late!"

Ahmed lifted Abdul into his arms and walked faster. Zaynab ran behind him.

"Mr. Hrvatin," Ahmed said to her, "is not a Serb. He is a Croat."

"But you said he was a Christian!"

"He is a Roman Catholic, like all Croats. But the Serbs are Eastern Orthodox Christians, Zenzen."

Ahmed looked at Zaynab's confused face, "It doesn't matter, Zenzen. They are all just people."

"But, Babo, isn't Allah going to punish them for not coming to celebrate Eid?"

Ahmed smiled, "Well, why did Allah create them in the first place, then?"

Zaynab did not know what to answer.

They arrived at the old bazaar of the city, and

Zaynab gasped as she saw the multitudes of people. Her father smiled and shook some hands; Zaynab was proud of her father being so well-known.

Her mother took two of the rugs from under Ahmed's arm and grabbed Zaynab's hands as they walked toward the back of the square. "Let's go, the prayer is beginning soon!"

In the large square outside the mosque, people with their own carpets fillded the entire space all the way to the bazaar. Zaynab wanted to join her father and Abdul, along with all the other men at the front, but she knew better than to argue with her mother, who joined the last row of women at the back. Aisha held Nadia in her arms while Zaynab spread out two small rugs.

They took their shoes off, and stood there. Then, when they heard the loud voice of the imam calling for prayer, Aisha put Nadia down. She clung to her ankles, but Aisha closed her eyes and began praying.

Zaynab always took the prayers very seriously. But now she only half-closed her eyes, and watched her mother curiously. She had only seen her mother pray a few times in her life, when she was younger, in other Eids. It moved her to see that her mother indeed knew the prayer, bent down, stood up, and recited with everyone else.

Also, the magnitude of the crowds distracted her. When people bent down on their knees, she felt she could hear their clothes touching the carpets. There were more people than she had ever seen in her life. A sea of people.

She felt that Allah must be really pleased to see them all, especially her mother. When baby Nadia began crying for her mother to pick her up, Zaynab took her in her arms instead, not wanting to disturb her mother. There, with Nadia in her arms, Zaynab prayed the prayer of the Eid, which was a little longer than the regular prayers as it repeated the whole prayer cycle twice.

Then, the imam of the great mosque gave a speech. Though he stood far away from them, his voice touched everyone. Zaynab saw how he opened his mouth and pronounced each word. She tried to listen to his speech. Some she understood, about modesty and love, but most of it she did not.

Finally the imam led the people through a short recitation and concluded the prayer. Immediately everyone, as if by a signal, began moving quickly. Aisha picked Nadia up and Zaynab quickly folded the carpets. The women around them exclaimed, "Happy Eid! Happy Eid!" Zaynab ran after her mother through the crowds until they saw Ahmed. They joined him and they all began walking to Nana's house. It seemed like the whole city was in the streets, everyone walking quickly to their Eid meal.

Zaynab began salivating, thinking of all of the great food. As they approached their grandmother's house, Ahmed prepared to go and bring the food from their own home. Aisha glared at him. "Be careful with the tray of cabbage rolls; it needs to stay on top. The pot with the soup should be at the bottom. And be quick! And don't spill anything! Do you want me to come with you?"

Ahmed laughed, "I will be fine; go inside. I'll be right back."

Their grandmother greeted them with much affection. She too was dressed beautifully. "Nana," Zaynab said, "you look like a queen!"

Nana enjoyed the compliment, and made Zaynab repeat it several times that afternoon for everyone to hear. After each repetition, Nana kissed Zaynab on the cheeks. Zaynab did not like that much because Nana grabbed her face firmly with both her hands when she kissed her, and it hurt.

But the girl did not concentrate on Nana, nor on the other cousins and aunts who were there. Her entire attention was devoted to the food. The food was incredible. They began with a soup and broth, then a stew. Then her father arrived, sweating, saying, "Aisha, do you want to kill me?!"

Aisha mumbled, "I will kill you if you spilled anything!"

Ahmed kissed all the uncles and cousins. Aisha brought pie made with grilled meat and vegetables and cabbage rolls to the table. She announced to everyone, "Zaynab helped me with the food. She made the cabbage rolls herself."

Everyone talked as they ate. Zaynab took a little of everything, and was already getting full, but tried not to miss any of the many dishes her Nana and aunts made.

The grandmother ate a cabbage roll. "Zaynab, you are a cook!"

Zaynab smiled proudly.

Aisha, Surayda and the other aunts cleared the table, and Aisha opened her eyes widely at Zaynab, motioning for her to help clearing the dishes. Nana wanted to help too, but all the aunts scolded her, "Sit down Mama!"

After they piled the mountains of dishes in the kitchen, they brought out the desserts. It was the most colorful assortment of sweets. Zaynab tasted every one of the cakes, cookies, and pastries. Her favorite was the sweet pastry made of layers of filo, filled with chopped nuts and held together with honey. She ate three of them. Nana looked at her, "You like the Baklava, Zaynab?"

Zaynab nodded, her mouth full. Everyone laughed.

Zaynab also ate a lot of the sweet apple filled with walnuts. There were also many kinds of halva, some made of sesame paste and some from flour and sugar. Everything was delicious.

Then they all started getting lethargic. Aisha went to the kitchen with the aunts. Zaynab came too, but Aisha told her, "It's alright. Go and lay down in the living room." Aisha turned to her sisters, "Did you know Zaynab fasted this Ramadan?"

"Really?" said the three aunts. "But aren't you only nine, Zaynab?"

Zaynab smiled and nodded proudly. She went to the living room, where everyone was lying on the sofas and on pillows on the carpet. She found a place near her father and cuddled up next to him.

When Zaynab awoke, it was already afternoon. Her mother made three kettles of tea and brought out a tray of sweets. The smell of mint was strong. Zaynab hurried to take some baklava from the tray and cherished the taste.

Everyone around her began waking up. Aisha was tired, and looked at Zaynab, "Could you take your cousins and siblings to sweet-swapping?"

Zaynab jumped, "Yes!"

Each year, she and the other children followed her mother as Aisha knocked on the doors of neighbors. But now Zaynab felt she was the adult. That's what it meant if her mother asked her to take all the children herself. Zaynab hurried to gathered Abdul and all the cousins around her. She took one plate of sweet halva and nuts, and marched out the house, followed by the dozen cousins. They knocked on the neighbor's door. An old woman opened up and they all screamed, "Happy Eid!"

The lady covered her ears with her hands, and all the children burst into laughter. She looked at the plate. "Oh, look at these yummy sweets. Just one moment."

The lady took the plate from Zaynab and walked inside. All the children waited in excitement.

The lady then returned with their plate, now loaded with baklava. Zaynab cheered, "Baklava!"

By the time they returned home, screaming with glee, the plate was empty.

Zaynab's aunt scolded them smilingly. "Leave some for us adults too!" She gave them another small plate with sweets. "Off you go!"

Within an hour they had swapped ten plates with the nearby neighbors, and they were cheerful and happy. It was then that Zaynab noticed her mother and the other women sitting in the corner. The children were playing out on the street, but Zaynab wanted to be inside. She got nearer and saw her aunt Surayda painting aunt Malikah's hand with traditional henna flower paint. She drew flowers and ornamental lines. Zaynab watched with fascination, then turned to her mother. "Mama, can I have my hands painted too?"

Aisha smiled and glanced at the other women. They all had a knowing smile on their faces.

Zaynab persisted, now turning to her aunt, "Aunt Surayda, please!"

The woman smiled. "When you become a woman, Zaynab, you can have your hands painted."

Zaynab let out a long sigh. "I don't want to wait until my *wedding!*"

Her aunts laughed and looked at each other. Aunt Surayda said, "Becoming a woman has nothing to do with getting married. You'll see, in due time."

The following day Zaynab and her siblings went to visit their grandmother again, to meet and play with all the cousins. On the way there her parents argued.

Her father said, "She is too young for this."

Her mother retorted, "She is perfectly capable. She fasted this year. I've seen younger children coming."

Her father sighed. "You can ask her."

When they arrived at Nana's, Aisha took Zaynab aside. "Zaynab, you are a big girl now. We adults are going to the cemetery to celebrate the Day of the Martyrs with the deceased. Do you want to come?"

Zaynab looked past her mother to her father in the corner of the living room, sulking. She nodded. Her mother said to Ahmed, "See, I told you!"

Zaynab waited excitedly while the other children played outside. The aunts and uncles all hugged Nana, and left in a long procession. Zaynab followed them, holding her father's hand.

When they arrived in the cemetery, she saw many people outside. There was a small market outside with flower stands.

The uncles went away for a moment and bought bouquets of flowers.

Zaynab had only been to the cemetery once, with her mother and aunts. But she remembered it being deserted, with only graves and her own family. But now it was full of people, including teenagers and a few children.

The uncles divided the flowers amongst the family, even to Zaynab. Then aunt Surayda began leading the procession into the cemetery. They walked together past many graves until they reached one and huddled around it. Zaynab remembered that grave: her mother had once taken her there and said, "We shall visit grandpa."

Now everyone began moving their lips in prayer. Zaynab tried to mimic the prayer, but she did not know which prayer was being recited. She was alarmed to watch her mother begin to cry, falling on the grave and screaming, "Babo, Babo!"

Zaynab's aunts joined her too. The uncles stood there silently, and Zaynab felt like she was expected to join the women. She had not known her late grandfather and she was extremely uncomfortable to see her mother crying like that. Her mother never cried.

Zaynab looked around, and saw other people doing the same. Even men. This was unique. She had never seen so many sad people.

Then her mother got up. She wiped her tears and smiled at Zaynab. It was odd, because she seemed happy. They all laid flowers on the grave, and walked away slowly. They stopped by another grave, of aunt Zeida, who Zaynab remembered somewhat, but she had died several years before. The ritual repeated itself. After her mother and her aunts cried and all laid flowers they continued to another grave.

They visited graves the whole morning. Then they left the cemetery. Zaynab was relieved. They bought some food and ate near the cemetery before it was time for prayer. Her father went aside to pray with a group of men on a carpeted area near the cemetery gate. Zaynab's uncles did not pray, but stood aside and talked. Zaynab wanted to pray, but was embarrassed to. She stood near her mother and aunts.

After the prayer, and much to Zaynab's dismay, they returned to the cemetery. This time they all went into separate directions, and Zaynab followed her mother and father. They spoke quietly among themselves. They got near one of the graves, and her mother whispered, "Good, her family has already put flowers here."

Zaynab's father looked sad.

Aisha touched the tombstone. "She was so young…."

Zaynab's eyes suddenly filled with tears. Now, with the uncles and aunts away, she whispered, "Mama, who are you talking about?"

Aisha looked at Ahmed, and he nodded. She took a deep breath. "My friend Beba. She was so young. She had three little children…." She began crying. Zaynab tried to console her. "Mama, don't be sad."

She did not want her mother to cry so much.

They then stood by the grave, and put five golden lilies on the large pile of flowers already there.

They continued to other graves, some of people her mother knew, some of people her father knew. It was tiring.

Then they waited outside the cemetery for all the aunts and uncles to return. Zaynab noticed how even the men's eyes were puffy and red.

Many people were out on the streets. They walked on the bridge and crossed the river. A few minutes later they arrived at a newly built cemetery; Zaynab was unhappy to discover they were going into it as well. She did not want to show it, though, and told herself she was taken with all the adults because she was now one of them and she should behave accordingly.

They walked amongst the graves, her father shaking hands with some people who recognized him from the shop. This time her aunt Surayda and her uncle walked with them through the paths, pointing at some graves. She heard her aunt telling her mother, "Here lies Abu-Zaidin, the clockmaker."

Her mother whispered, "His poor wife."

Her aunt nodded. They placed flowers there.

After passing more graves, they went to the end of the cemetery. There she saw many people standing, including her uncles. There was no grave there, but just a big monument with an unbelievable amount of flowers.

Her father stepped forward, placed some flowers on the monument, and bent down and shook his head. It looked as if he was praying. Then he began sobbing.

Zaynab grabbed her mother's hand. "Mama, who lies here?"

Her mother whispered, "It's the grave of the anonymous soldier."

"Anonymous?"

Her mother whispered, "Soldiers who have died in the Great War, but we're unsure where. And other soldiers who were found but unidentified."

Zaynab gulped.

When they finally excited the cemetery in the late afternoon Zaynab was so happy to leave. They returned to Nana's house. Zaynab was exhausted. She looked at the other cousins as they told her of all the games they had played and how Abdul hid inside the barrel and could not climb out until everyone pulled him.

They went home in the evening. Zaynab was tired, but also excited. The following day they were going to go on a day trip to the sea. She had only seen the sea once. And Abdul and Nadia had never been there.

The following day they woke up early, when it was still dark. Zaynab helped her mother prepare food for the train ride and the picnic. They left the house as the sun was rising while Nadia still slept on her mother's shoulders.

They walked across the bridge over the river, and approached the train station, which was already crowded. Many families were planning to spend the last day of Eid outside the city.

As they boarded the train, Zaynab felt very excited, but tried to look indifferent. Abdul, however, jumped around and kept gasping at everything. They sat in a small booth facing each other. As the train left the station, Zaynab looked through the window at the changing views, the familiar buildings of Sarajevo passing as the train quickly exited the city. She saw the five hills surrounding the city. She recognized the hill they were passing and exclaimed to Abdul, "This is where we saw the cannon being blown!" She lifted Abdul onto the seat so that he could see.

They also saw the Sarajevo river gushing beside the tracks. It was very exciting. A few minutes later Ahmed said, "Here is where the Sarajevo River meets with the larger Bosna river."

They tried to eye it through the window, but they only saw trees. Ahmed smiled, "Do you know, children, where the Bosna river ends?"

They did not. Ahmed looked at Zaynab, "Come on, Zenzen. Where are we now headed?"

"Oh, to the sea, Babo!"

"Right!"

Zaynab looked through the window for the next hour. Then they all got off the train along with everyone else, and Zaynab held Abdul's hand as they excitedly jumped onto the platform. While they waited for another train Zaynab asked, "Where are we now, Babo?"

"We are in Konic," Ahmed said. "We will take the train to Mostar, and then another to the sea."

"Why can't they just take us to the sea directly, Babo?"

Her father seemed amused. "So that you could get on so many trains, not just one!"

The parents held the children's hands firmly as the new train approached the platform. Abdul cheered. They boarded the train.

The train rode quickly through the valley. Abdul and Zaynab looked fascinated at the views, while Nadia slept on their mother's lap. Then they suddenly saw on the horizon a huge mountain and gasped.

Ahmed pointed to it. "The Prenj Mountains."

The mountains touched the clouds, and Zaynab noticed the mountain top was white. "Babo, do they still have snow there?"

"I think they have snow there all year long."

"What? Even in the summer?"

"Even in the summer."

The train made its way through a narrow valley in between the mountain peaks. Zaynab and Abdul were glued to the window.

Then the landscape changed, opening into large plains filled with trees. Soon after, the train entered Mostar. They got off, and waited on the platform for another train. The platform was filled with families and it was very noisy. Their mother looked distressed.

Then they boarded a train that seemed smaller and older, as the seats were a little torn. It was very noisy but the train ride was not long. The train stopped at a small train station. They got off and followed the throngs of people out the station and through the small streets of a little village. The smell in the air was different.

Then they saw it.

Zaynab gasped.

Ahmed laughed. "What? Zenzen, you don't

remember the sea?"

Aisha looked at Ahmed. "How do you expect her to remember! She was only four years old."

Abdul jumped. "The sea, I see the sea!" He pulled forward, but Ahmed held his hand firmly. They kept walking, the sea growing larger before them. Zaynab murmured. "It's so... blue!"

The beach was flooded with picnicking families. Ahmed and Aisha set their picnic blanket down between two families, and Abdul kept pulling on his father, wanting to run into the water. Aisha said to Ahmed, "You go with Zaynab and Abdul. I will come with Nadia later."

Abdul and Zaynab ran to the shoreline, Ahmed following behind, laughing. But when they got near the water, they stopped. It was scary! Abdul ran back to his father. Zaynab laughed, but she too was a little apprehensive about the vast pool of water.

Ahmed took off his sandals, folded up his pants, and walked in slowly, holding Abdul's hand. He wanted to help him into the water, but Abdul clung to him, "No!"

Zaynab saw other girls in the water around them, still wearing their head coverings. She took her sandals off, raised her skirt in her hands, and dipped into the water. "It's cold!"

"You'll get used to it," Ahmed smiled. "What do you say, Zenzen?"

"It's terrific, Babo!"

After several minutes and some pleading from his

father, Abdul was willing to dip his toes in the water as well. Once he did, he could not stop giggling, and soon started kicking and splashing water at his sister. His father rebuked him. "You can run together if you want, but do not fight."

Zaynab and Abdul ran on the shore, splashing in the shallow water, laughing, and when their father was not looking pushing one another.

Then Aisha called them to eat. Nadia was playing in the sand. They ate hurriedly, wanting to go back to the water.

After they ran back, Ahmed took Nadia in his arms, and Aisha, too, joined them in the water. She waded almost to her waist. Zaynab looked at her father. "Babo, can I join her?"

"Of course, Zenzen!"

Zaynab walked deeper, her whole dress in the water. It was so exciting. The sun was hot and the water was cold. She saw her mother crying.

"Mama! Are you sad?" Zaynab asked.

Her mother shook her head and said nothing.

"Mama! Don't cry!"

Aisha smiled. "These are happy tears, baby." Then she reprimanded Zaynab. "Don't touch your eyes. The water is salty and it will burn your eyes!"

On their way back in the late afternoon, they stopped in Mostar.

They walked through the small streets and the bazaar. Zaynab was surprised to see her father shaking some people's hands and talking to them. He spoke to one old man for several minutes, and then introduced Aisha and the children to him.

After they left the old man, Zaynab held her father's hand. "How do you know that man, Babo?"

"Oh I used to come to Mostar a lot when I was younger."

"Really?"

"Yes. I used to buy and sell old furniture, Zenzen. I would travel to Konic, to Mostar. I once even went to Venice."

"That's in Italy, right Babo?"

Ahmed laughed. "Yes, very good, Zenzen!"

They walked through the bazaar filled with carpets and fabrics. "Babo, is Italy pretty?"

"Very pretty," Ahmed said. "But our Yugoslavia is the most beautiful country in the world."

They exited the bazaar and found themselves in a small plaza. Aisha was nervous. "Don't we need to start heading back?"

"I just want the children to see the old bridge, and then we'll head back to the train station."

They walked along a small crowded street, and Zaynab felt proud of her father for knowing where to lead them. As they found themselves climbing a steep street crowded with people, Zaynab saw the river below and suddenly realized they were on a huge bridge.

"Wow!" she gasped. "Abdul! We are on a bridge!"

Abdul could not see the sea as the stone parapet was too high, so Ahmed lifted him up to glance at the gushing water beneath them.

Once they reached the top of the bridge, they began descending down toward a small alley on the other side. "Babo," Zaynab said, "why isn't this bridge flat like our bridges?"

Ahmed smiled. "You ask good questions, Zenzen. This is a very old bridge."

Abdul asked, "Older than you, Babo?"

Ahmed laughed. "It is *very* old, more than 300 years old, children. Much older than me!"

Aisha shook her head. "Now your father will tell you all about it."

Ahmed looked at her, "Of course I will. Listen, children, you see that tower there, and that tower there?" He pointed at the two towers on both sides of the bridge. The children nodded. Ahmed whispered, "They were built to protect the city from attacks."

Abdul jumped. "From pirates?"

Ahmed laughed. "No, from enemies of the Turks."

The children nodded although neither of them knew who the Turks or their enemies were. Ahmed continued, "But it was very difficult to build. It took them nine years!"

Zaynab gasped, "That's my age!"

Ahmed nodded. "Imagine your whole life building a bridge!"

Aisha gave him an impatient look. Ahmed nodded and said, "Now we'll cross back and head to the train station." They began ascending the old bridge again while Ahmed kept speaking. "It was said, children, that there was no such man-made bridge in the world. They called it a rainbow in the sky."

Zaynab looked at the river from the ledge. The bridge was so tall. "The bridge never fell, right Babo?"

Ahmed whispered. "Never! And it never will, perhaps... except for..." he suddenly grabbed Zaynab, "now!"

Zaynab giggled. Aisha muttered, "Ahmed! Watch out, will you!"

They descended the bridge, passed through the bazaar, and walked down the old streets. Zaynab noticed that there were many women not wearing head coverings.

As they waited for the train heading to Konic, Zaynab whispered to her father, "Babo, I did not see many believers in the streets."

Ahmed smiled. "Oh, there are. The city has many Croats, but there is a small Muslim community here too."

Zaynab looked disappointed. "I thought Mostar

was ours!"

Ahmed smiled. "It is ours, Zenzen. It is Yugoslavia's. It's all ours."

Zaynab thought about his words as the train arrived. They boarded it, and Abdul fought to be seated near the window. Zaynab let him, but he soon fell asleep. The train made its way through the narrow valley near the Prenj Mountains. They switched trains in Konic, and by the time they arrived back in Sarajevo it was dark.

CHAPTER 5

Zaynab missed her city. She liked it more. She had to admit to herself, though, as they crossed the bridge over the river walking home, that it was not as tall and beautiful as the bridge in Mostar. ^b

The following year Zaynab started her last year in elementary school. She liked the girls in her class, and her teachers as well. She did not know that the most meaningful lessons would arrive soon, but not in school.

One Friday, Zaynab's aunt Surayda and uncle Muamar were visiting. During the traditional Friday evening meal Surayda said, "Zaynab, do you know who asks about you all the time?"

Zaynab looked up from her plate. "No, who?"

"My friend Wafaa. Do you remember her?"

Zaynab nodded. She remembered Wafaa taking her to the women's section in the small mosque. She liked Wafaa.

"Well," aunt Surayda said and looked at Aisha, "Wafaa speaks all the time of the 'bright Zaynab' and of the 'smart Zaynab,' and wants her to come to a study group in the mosque."

Aisha shook her head disapprovingly. "It will distract her from her schoolwork."

Zaynab looked disappointed.

Aisha spoke sharply. "Next year you are going to a junior high school. It won't be as easy there as it is in your little school. You need to study." She got up from the table.

"But Mama!" Zaynab said.

Ahmed said nothing.

Aisha muttered on her way to the kitchen, "We want you children to get a better education than we did. So no arguing!"

Zaynab looked at her aunt, who smiled sadly at her. Zaynab then looked at her father. Ahmed blinked his eyes at her reassuringly.

At night, when everyone was sleeping, Zaynab heard her parents arguing in their bedroom. Ahmed whispered, "But why don't we try it?"

"I don't want her to turn into one of those religious old spinsters, saying Allah this and Allah that!"

Ahmed sighed.

Zaynab closed her eyes tightly, praying, "Please, God. Make her let me go!"

She was not sure what a "study group" was. But it sounded like something for grown ups. It sounded so interesting.

She heard her father's voice. "Aisha, you say you want a good education for her, but she comes back from school and babysits Abdul and Nadia. She can benefit from—"

"But they will brainwash her there, I tell you!" Aisha whispered. " She is already very easily influenced!"

Ahmed was quiet again.

Zaynab bit her lip.

Ahmed said, "Then go with her and see for yourself what it is all about."

"I don't need to go to the mosque!"

"But what if it invigorates her, and helps her in her schoolwork?"

"They will brainwash her, I tell you!"

Ahmed paused for a long moment. "Alright. You decide. You are her mother. You know what's best for her."

Zaynab folded her hands together, thinking, "No, Babo, please make her say 'Yes!'"

Suddenly she heard her father's voice again. "What if we just let her try. If at any point you want to pull her out, I will be the first one to agree. You know what is right for her, you are her mother."

Zaynab heard nothing else.

The following week Ahmed returned home early one day. He looked at Aisha, and the two of them went to speak in the bedroom. A few minutes later Aisha came out, fully dressed. "Zaynab, put your coat on."

Zaynab put on her coat and shoes quickly and placed her head covering on. "Where are we going, Mama?"

"I will tell you later."

Outside, her mother walked quickly. Zaynab followed her. After a few minutes Aisha spoke. "We are going to see what this study group is all about."

Zaynab jumped excitedly. "Oh, Mama! I promise you won't regret—"

"I already do."

In the mosque, Wafaa was happy to see Zaynab. She hugged her, which Zaynab found a little odd. None of the adults she knew ever hugged her. Wafaa turned to Aisha. "Thank you for bringing her. Will you join our study group as well?"

"No! I am too busy with the household. And Zaynab is very busy with her schoolwork. Who is behind this group?"

"You mean, the teacher?"

Aisha nodded.

Wafaa smiled. "It's our dear old Hakima."

"I want to see this Hakima."

"But the class is now beginning, can you wait until—"

"I'm either going to meet her now, or the two of us are going home."

Wafaa tried to smile, obviously surprised, and hurried to the room across the entrance hall. Zaynab looked down at the floor. She hated when her mother behaved this way. And to kind Wafaa!

Wafaa returned escorting old Hakima walking with a cane. Zaynab saw several women inside.

Hakima walked slowly toward them. She did not look at Zaynab. She bowed her head gently before Aisha and said, "Mrs. Sadik, thank you for coming."

"I want to know what this… group is about."

Hakima nodded, but said nothing. She looked at Aisha's face, and then looked at Wafaa. "Mrs. Sadik and I shall speak in private."

Wafaa nodded and put her arm around Zaynab. "Come."

Zaynab followed Wafaa, worriedly looking behind at her mother.

In the room the women greeted her. Zaynab kept glancing through the door. Wafaa invited her to sit, and she reluctantly did so, fearing a scene outside. Inside the room there were a dozen ladies, as well as one teenager. Most of the women were much older; some very old. The women asked Zaynab some questions, but she was not listening. Instead she watched her mother outside in the entrance hall.

Hakima's head moved as she spoke quietly to Aisha. She put her hand on Aisha's. Zaynab noticed her mother asking short questions and shaking her head. They spoke for several minutes.

Inside the room the women began conversing among themselves.

Finally Zaynab saw Hakima walking slowly toward the room. "Zaynab, your mother wants to see you."

Zaynab got up quickly, heavy hearted, realizing that Hakima had failed. She walked, disappointed, to her mother.

"Zaynab, today I will let you stay. But—"

"Really Mama? Really?"

"Yes. Wafaa will take you home, all the way to our door. But I want you to memorize everything that is said here and tell me all about it later this evening, word for word, you hear me?"

Zaynab nodded excitedly.

"Good." Aisha said and quickly left the mosque.

Zaynab made her way back to the room in disbelief. She feared her mother would turn around and take her back. But she did not.

Once she walked into the room, Wafaa closed the door behind her and locked it.

This was a little strange for Zaynab, but it was nothing in comparison to what happened next. All the women, including Hakima, took their head coverings off.

Zaynab had never seen women who were not her family without their head coverings. It was not modest. She could not understand how they could do it, showing not only their eyes, but their entire faces to complete strangers.

Wafaa murmured to her, "Zaynab, you can take your head covering off. We are like a family here."

Zaynab gulped, and looked at the other teenager, who she had never seen before, sitting without her head covering.

Hakima said, "She can do whatever she wants. Leave her alone, ladies. Now, where were we? Khadijah, you were reading about Fatima Al-Fihri. Read again, from the beginning."

One of the women held a gigantic-looking book in her hand and read, "Fatima Al-Fihri was the daughter of a wealthy merchant, and had been educated in several languages. Her family had immigrated from Tunisia to Morocco. Al-Fihri was known for helping the poor in her city. Later in her life, in 859 A.D. Al-Fihri opened her university—"

Hakima interjected, "The oldest university in the world, now over a thousand years old! Go on, Khadijah."

Khadijah continued. "The University in Morocco served as an inspiration for new universities to open elsewhere in the world, such as the second oldest university, University of Bologna in Italy, or the University of Oxford, England, founded two centuries later. Fatima Al-Fihri meticulously collected books for the library of the university, often corresponding with many scholars around the world, buying precious manuscripts—"

Hakima interrupted again, "So when the Christians tell you that they have brought education and enlightenment to the world, don't forget that a Muslim woman opened the first university while Christians were still in the dark Middle Ages." She looked at Khadijah. "Go on."

Khadijah continued reading, "The library contained thousands of manuscripts, and is considered the oldest continuously operating library in the world, with over 4,000 books and manuscripts. Fatima al-Fihri herself attended the university, and her diploma, carved on a wooden plank, is hung in the library today."

Khadijah closed the large book.

Hakima said, "Well done. Now we shall continue with Sara."

The heavy book passed between the women and stopped at the hands of a beautiful lady. She held the book and said, "I don't need to read. I've memorize it."

Hakima sat up in her seat. "Well done, Sara."

Sara nodded, and looked at the group. "Hakima gave me the task of reading about Rabia Al-Adawiyya. I must say I was so impressed by this woman who lived even before the time of Fatima Al-Hiri," she said and looked at Khadija, who nodded back approvingly.

"Rabia," Sara continued, "was born in Iraq in 717

A.D. to 1a poor family. She was orphaned at a young age and was eventually… sold into slavery."

The women tut-tutted. Zaynab looked at their reactions carefully. She was still shocked to see so many women's actual faces.

Sara continued. "She was sold into slavery, but kept praying and speaking to Allah. One day the slave owner witnessed her bowing in prayer, surrounded by a bright light. He realized that Rabia was a saint. Fearing the consequences of enslaving a saint, he granted her freedom. Rabia went on to become a Sufi poet and, according to some, the most important early one."

Sara took a breath and continued. "An interesting legend about her recounts how one day she was walking through the streets carrying a pot of fire in one hand and a bucket of water in the other. When she was asked what she was doing, she said, 'I want to put out the fires of Hell with the water, and burn down the rewards of Paradise with the fire. The thoughts of Hell and Heaven block the way to God. I do not want to worship from fear of punishment or the promise of reward, but simply for the love of God.'"

Sara nodded to mark she had finished.

The women clapped and said, "Well done."

Hakima, however, was more reserved. "Well done, Sara. You have memorized well. But you could have also added a poem of hers to share with us."

Sara looked down.

"Sara, I am only saying this to further help you develop. Had another woman here memorized the passage, I would have applauded her. But you can do better than that."

Sara nodded. "You are right, Hakima. I did think of bringing a poem, but I was scared that my presentation would be too long."

Hakima smiled. "Never be afraid of being too long or too thorough." She looked around the room. "We must not make ourselves smaller out of fear that our power will intimidate others. Had Rabia thought that, she never would have written her poems. Do you understand?"

The women nodded.

Zaynab stared at them, fascinated.

Hakima looked at Wafaa. "Go to the library and bring us the collection of Early Sufi Poetry; you know which one I talk about? The one with the white binding?"

Wafaa placed her head covering on, and rushed outside.

Hakima cleared her throat. "In the meantime, I believe I remember one of Rabia's short poems. It is called 'My Love.' We know of course who her love was."

Zaynab looked around the room as the women nodded.

Hakima closed her eyes. "'My Love! My joy. My hunger. My shelter! My friend. My food for the journey. My journey's end.'"

She wet her lips. "'You are my breath. My hope. My companion. My craving. My abundant wealth. Without You I would never have wandered across these endless terrains. You have poured so much grace into my cup. You have done me so many favors, given me so many gifts—I look everywhere for Your love—and then, suddenly, I am one with You.'"

Her voice trembled. "'O Captain of my Heart! O radiant eye of yearning in my breast! I will never be apart from You as long as I live! Be satisfied with me, my love! That is all I need!'"

She opened her eyes. The women clapped. Zaynab joined them too. She was riveted. She had never heard such a thing before.

Wafaa entered the room with a book in her hand, hurrying to lock the door behind her. She handed the book to Hakima.

"Thank you, Wafaa. I am afraid we only have time for one more poem. Sara, would you?"

Sara nodded, and the book passed to her. She opened it, looked through the index, and then turned to the right page.

Hakima smiled. "Choose well!"

Sara nodded and took a moment. "I think I'll read this. The poem is called, 'My Peace.'"

Hakima seemed pleased. "Well chosen! Remember, ladies, that Rabia was an ascetic who lived a reclusive life."

The women nodded. Hakima motioned for Sara to

begin.

"'My peace, O my brothers and sisters! My peace is my solitude!

> And my Beloved is with me always,
>
> I can find no substitute for His love,
>
> He is my temple, towards Him my sail is set;
>
> O Healer of souls!
>
> The striving after union with Thee has healed my soul,
>
> You are the source of my life,
>
> And from Thee cometh my bliss.
>
> I have separated myself from all created beings,
>
> My only desire is for union with Thee.'"

Sara finished reading, and everyone clapped.

Hakima smiled. "Thank you, Sara. Now we have a better sense of Rabia, the Muslim Sufi mystic, who walked this earth a thousand years ago."

Hakima looked around the room. Zaynab felt Hakima's eyes fall on her and pierce into her soul. She looked down.

"Now ladies, for next week. Who would like to present?"

Everyone raised their hands. Zaynab looked around the room, surprised. Apart from her and Hakima, all the women raised their hands eagerly, including the teenage girl.

Hakima smiled and looked around the room slowly. She then closed her eyes and said, "Lubna."

One of the younger women reached for her notebook excitedly.

Hakima spoke, her eyes closed. "You shall present the life of Nusaybah bint Ka'ab, the courageous woman who taught our Prophet, peace be unto him, a valuable lesson."

Lubna wrote it down and nodded eagerly.

Hakima paused, pursing her lips. Still with her eyes closed she said, "Hannah."

One of the older women nodded and opened her notebook.

"You shall lecture about Sultan Raziyya. She was the Emperor of Delhi in the thirteenth century. A fascinating woman, who refused to be addressed as Sultana because it meant 'wife of a sultan' and answered only when people addressed her as 'Sultan.' You shall present her life and her struggles. The two of you can be assisted by Zaynab, but also rely on other sources."

Zaynab looked at Wafaa in panic. Wafaa smiled back and whispered. "She is talking about a book written by Zaynab Fawwaz."

Zaynab let out a sigh of relief.

Hakima opened her eyes and smiled at everyone, "Good work, Khadijah, good work, Sara!"

Wafaa exclaimed, "Good work, everyone!"

The women began getting up from their seats and

adjusting their head coverings. Some began talking and chatting. Wafaa put her coat on and looked at Zaynab, "Shall we? I will walk you home."

Zaynab nodded. She looked at the room. She would have liked for the meeting to continue. It felt short. She followed Wafaa outside, feeling Hakima's interrogative eyes on her back as she left the room.

She and Wafaa exited the mosque into the cold night. Wafaa said, "You live not far away from your aunt, Surayda, right?"

Zaynab nodded. "At the tobacco factory street."

"You know the way?" Wafaa asked.

Zaynab nodded.

The streets were mostly empty. They walked quickly, passing by the old clock tower. Zaynab thought of her mother.

Wafaa looked at her. "So, what did you think, Zaynab?"

Zaynab smiled sheepishly.

"Did you like it?"

Zaynab nodded.

"Good. It was so nice to have you there. Do you want to come back? I don't want to put pressure on you or anything, but we would be very glad if—"

"Yes, I want to!"

Wafaa seemed very pleased. "You will see, Hakima can seem a little… scary, at first, but she has a good heart, and she can be funny, too. And we learn so much! I wait for it all week. The girls are like my second family."

Zaynab wanted to ask if Wafaa went there every week. And whether it cost money. And whether Wafaa and Hakima were friends. And was it okay for her to join the group even though she was much younger than the others?

But she said nothing.

Finally they arrived at Zaynab's house. Ahmed opened the door. Wafaa smiled at him. "Your daughter, Mr. Sadik, was very polite and cordial! It was our pleasure to have her!"

Ahmed smiled and patted Zaynab's head. "Sounds like our Zaynab!"

Aisha hurried from the kitchen. "Here you are! What took you so long!" She looked at Wafaa and said, "You always finish so late?!"

Wafaa tried smiling. "Mrs. Sadik, we would be very glad to see Zaynab again—"

"Well, we'll see about that. Good night!"

Zaynab wanted to thank Wafaa, but her mother closed the door in the woman's face.

"Come," Aisha said and went to the kitchen. Ahmed followed them.

"Tell me," Aisha said in the kitchen, "what did they discuss?"

Zaynab told her mother of the Moroccan princess who founded the first university and library, and of the Iraqi woman who was a poet. "She wrote beautifully, Mama!"

Aisha looked at her. "And what did they say about the Prophet, and Islam, and Islamic law?"

Zaynab shrugged her shoulders. "They didn't say anything, Mama!"

Aisha grabbed her hand. "I want you to tell me everything!"

Ahmed, who until now had stood quietly near the entrance to the kitchen, said, "Aisha, leave her alone!"

Aisha looked at him. "You must be tired, Ahmed."

A long silence followed, after which Ahmed walked away to the bedroom.

Aisha sat down near the small table and looked at Zaynab. "Well?"

"Mama," Zaynab murmured, "I cannot recall anything like that. They spoke of these two women, and read two poems, and then Hakima, the teacher, assigned two of the members to speak of two other women in the next class."

Aisha searched her daughter's eyes. "They did not read the Qur'an?"

"No."

"And pray?"

"No, Mama. I swear."

Aisha looked in disbelief. "They didn't say that women should be veiling themselves even at home or near their brothers and uncles?"

Zaynab shook her head. She thought about saying

the women did not veil themselves at all during the meeting. But she knew it would sound strange.

Aisha continued. "How about the importance of Qur'anic law being above the State?"

Zaynab did not understand what her mother was talking about.

"Did they swear you to any secrecy? Did they say anything about non-Muslims being non-believers?"

Zaynab kept shaking her head.

"How about the importance of returning to the days of the Prophet?"

Zaynab exclaimed, "Mama! I swear!"

Aisha sighed and looked at her daughter. "You see, Zaynab," she spoke slowly, "the reason I am asking is that I don't want you to get a... warped understanding of our faith."

Zaynab looked at her mother in confusion.

Aisha leaned back in her chair. "I read our Holy Book. It may seem to you that I am not... observant, but I believe our God never would tell us to put our faith above things like family. Many people who claim they are Muslims only imitate Christianity and the crusaders, you see?"

Zaynab nodded, though she did not quite understand her mother.

Aisha took a deep breath in. "Good. Now go to sleep."

"Mama, can I go next Wednesday?"

"We'll see about that. Now don't tire me."

Zaynab bowed her head and kissed her mother's hand. "Good night, Mama."

The following week Zaynab made sure to show her mother her completed homework every day.

When Wednesday finally came, Zaynab said, "Mama, can I go to the study group this evening?"

Aisha sighed. "Have you completed all your homework?"

Zaynab showed her homework to her mother, filled meticulously in her notebook.

Aisha shook her head. "But how will you get there? Your father works late today. He told me this morning he'd be installing a bed in some client's house. I cannot leave Abdul and Nadia to go with you."

"Mama!" Zaynab pleaded, realizing she had not planned well.

"I'm sorry, Zaynab. Perhaps next week."

Zaynab cried, but her mother shooed her away. "Now don't upset me, Zaynab!"

Zaynab thought of running to Aunt Surayda's home, and asking her to take her, but it was already getting dark outside. She ran to the children's room and fell on her bed, thinking of all the women, unveiled, in that warm room. She thought of the two women Hakima said they'd be discussing. She remembered the names. She wanted so badly to learn about them. She wanted so much to be a part of that strange group.

As if God had seen her weeping, a knock rapped at the door. Zaynab jumped and ran to the door, "Babo! Babo!"

Aisha came from the kitchen and opened the door.

Wafaa stood there, smiling. "Good evening, Mrs. Sadik!"

Aisha sighed and shook her head disapprovingly. Zaynab jumped around the door. "Mama, please. I have completed all my homework!"

Aisha squinted and spoke to Zaynab without taking her eyes off of Wafaa. "Alright. You can go tonight. But walk straight there and straight back, you hear me?"

Zaynab nodded.

Wafaa bowed her head. "I will bring her back safely, Mrs. Sadik!"

Zaynab ran to put her head covering on, her coat and her boots. "Thank you, Mama!"

Abdul came to the door. "I want to go too!"

Aisha glared at him. "Oh, leave me alone Abdul!"

Zaynab smiled at Wafaa as they left the house, hearing the door close behind them. She waited until they were far enough from the house and said, "Thank you for coming to take me, Wafaa!"

Wafaa smiled, "The pleasure is all mine."

CHAPTER 6

As the weeks passed, Zaynab greatly anticipated each meeting at the mosque. Wednesdays became her favorite day. She excelled in school, fearing that any bad grade would lead her mother to forbid her from going to Hakima's study group.

At the second meeting, she felt more comfortable.

At the third meeting, she took her veil down, feeling a little exposed in front of these women.

At the fourth meeting, she allowed herself to laugh at one of Hakima's jokes.

But it took her a whole year before she dared to raise her hand. And the consequences led her to the most unnerving week of her life.

Zaynab always feared raising her hand in the study group. Old Hakima seemed as if she could pierce the ladies with her eyes, and then hit them with her words of wisdom, coming in short, poignant sentences.

Hakima once said to a shy woman called Amina: "If you look down when you speak, you do not only insult the God who made you, but you also insult us."

Amina looked down and mumbled, "Why?"

"Because," Hakima said loudly, "if you look down, it means that you think that I, and the others, are beneath you, at the level of the floor! You regard us like the cockroaches and ants, crawling on the floor!"

"But I didn't—"

"Well that's how it feels Amina!"

Another time Hakima said, "The way you read this poem, Wafaa, is bringing shame unto the great poet!"

Zaynab was alarmed to see the cheerful Wafaa begin to stammer. "I'm, I'm, I'm so sorry…."

"That's exactly the problem!" Hakima said, "Now stand up and read it properly, so that the poet can finally smile in her grave!"

Zaynab often thought Hakima was too harsh and scary. But she also noticed how her comments made the women more confident. After Wafaa read the poem, standing, articulating and not rushing through the words, everyone applauded her.

She wondered why everyone always volunteered to read, including the young Jasmine, who was fifteen years old and the only other teenager in the group.

Zaynab was not happy when Jasmine was chosen to present the following week. She knew very well what it meant for her.

Jasmine presented the story of Lubna of Cordoba, who became the palace secretary of two sultans in the tenth century and excelled in mathematics and sciences. When Jasmine finished, Hakima complimented her eloquence. She even said, "Ladies, as we can see, we can all learn from the younger generation here."

Zaynab felt everyone's eyes on her.

She tried to tell herself that she was too young. She was only eleven years old. Surely Hakima would understand her reluctance!

She also had to focus on school, she told herself. Junior high school was much harder than elementary school. She found mathematics challenging. Bosnian, Serbian and Literature were also very demanding, as was Arabic, with its odd shaped letters. She sometimes found herself doing homework late into the evening. Hakima must understand the importance of her schooling and not expect her to present.

During that last year her mother began working, helping an affluent old lady in the community with cooking and household chores. She was gone each afternoon for three hours, sometimes more, and it was Zaynab's responsibility to see that Abdul was doing his homework and improving his reading and writing. Nadia was now three years old and there was plenty of work to care for the two while trying to find time to do her own homework. Surely, she hoped, Hakima would understand...?

But each week she attended the study group, she sensed pressure building. She felt expectation weigh on her. All the women raised their hands in each meeting, as if it was sacrilegious not to. And Zaynab's hand, placed on her lap, burned with the desire to rise as well.

For several weeks, Zaynab thought of quitting the group. This, at times, felt better than the pressure of speaking in front of the whole group. It felt better than presuming she could teach these older ladies. It felt better to think of resigning than to imagine that she had something valuable to share.

The weight of Hakima's expectation was a heavy burden to carry. Leaving the group could put an end to that terrible feeling and ease the immense pressure she felt while attending the meetings.

It was not that the meetings were not exhilarating. But ever since Jasmine presented to the group, Zaynab felt an immense pressure. She no longer enjoyed the study group. She knew that everyone was looking at her, disapproving of her. She knew that Hakima was thinking badly of her, scolding her in her head. This explained why Hakima only rarely looked at her, as if intentionally ignoring her.

Zaynab began thinking of leisurely spending Wednesday evenings at home, listening to the radio with her father or helping her mother in the kitchen. The anticipation of knowing that soon she'd have to be in that room, without her veil, with the women's eyes penetrating her, demanding her to raise her hand like all the others knotted her stomach

One day, as they were walking home, Wafaa said to her, "Is everything alright, Zaynab?"

Zaynab nodded.

They walked quietly. Wafaa tried again. "You seemed very preoccupied this evening. Are you still enjoying the group?"

Zaynab bit her lip. She wanted to explain her feelings to Wafaa. About the fear that crept up her body, making her legs feel heavy any time she felt Hakima looking her way. She wanted to say she was simply not read to present in front of the group.

But she said nothing.

When they finally arrived at her house, Zaynab was relieved.

She wanted her mother to forbid her from going. But her mother seemed more content that Zaynab attended the group. She liked it when Zaynab told her about forgotten princes and poets and sultans and mathematicians, women who left their mark on humanity and were now included in books.

Aisha also liked seeing her daughter grow more confident, speak more eloquently, use proper language. She wanted to attribute it to Zaynab's new school, but in her heart she knew that something good was happening in the small mosque near the old clock tower.

Zaynab knew her redemption was not going to come from her mother. Nor was it to come from her father.

Finally, she resolved she would leave the group.

Coming to the decision was hard, but one that made her feel more at ease. Now that the decision was made, she began contemplating she should show the women—especially Hakima—that she was not a fool. And that she was smart. And that she was not leaving out of cowardice, but due to a purely mature decision.

A new sense of resolution washed over her. Armed with this new sense of clarity, when the time came at the end of the weekly session for the women to volunteer to present the following week, she too raised her hand.

It was only when her hand was raised that she suddenly realized what she had done. A huge wave of fear washed over her, and she instantly lowered her hand.

Hakima, her eyes closed, said, "First to present will be Layla."

Zaynab let out a silent sigh of relief.

"Layla will present to us Queen Arwa al-Sulayhi of Yemen, who ruled in her own right, for thirty-seven years, until her death at the age of ninety. And Zaynab"— she said and paused for a long moment while all the women smiled at the terrified Zaynab— "will present to us, appropriately enough, the story of Zaynab Fawwaz, the author of our beloved book 'Scattered Pearls of Women in Islam.' She died only fifteen years ago, in 1914, and yet left a great legacy of poetry, journalism, plays and novels."

Zaynab was frozen in her seat.

Wafaa, noticing Zaynab had not written Hakima's instructions, whispered, "Don't worry, I wrote it all down."

Hakima concluded the meeting. "Good work,

Maryam and Lubna."

The women began putting on their head coverings and coats. Zaynab was too nervous to think clearly. She slowly put her head covering on, her heart throbbing fast. What had she done?! Why did she raise her hand?

Wafaa grinned at her. Some of the women shook Zaynab's hand. It was an odd gesture, and the touch of their hands was strange. "Congratulations, Zaynab!"

"Zaynab, you will do fine!"

"What an honor to present Zaynab Fawwaz herself!"

Zaynab tried smiling, and mumbled a few thank-yous.

The room cleared, and only Zaynab, Wafaa, Hakima and Layla stayed. Layla sat down near Hakima, who said to her; "Queen Arwa al-Sulayhi. There is much material written about her. I want you to go to the library and conduct thorough research. If it is only based on Fawwaz's book, it will greatly disappoint me."

Layla nodded, "But could I borrow the book, to begin my research?"

Hakima shook her head. "You can find it in the library. My copy will go to Zaynab."

Layla seemed disappointed, but quickly nodded and got up. She thanked Hakima, said goodbye and left.

Hakima looked at Zaynab. "Come and sit here."

Zaynab did so obediently, not daring to look at Hakima. Wafaa sat down as well.

Hakima looked at Wafaa. "No need, Wafaa, thank you."

Wafaa looked surprised. "But I thought I could help—"

"I will personally guide Zaynab," Hakima said.

Wafaa nodded and left the room, lingering near the open door.

Hakima looked at Zaynab, "You are a very brilliant young woman, Zaynab. I have seen it in your eyes."

Zaynab did not move. She looked down.

"I have seen you whenever a poem is read. You are alert and present, even if you do not speak." She pointed at the heavy book, "This is yours for the week. It has a short introduction about Zaynab Fawwaz and her motives for writing the book. Unfortunately it is insufficient for a presentation. After you read it, come to my house, and we will find more materials together."

Zaynab nodded.

Hakima handed her the book. Zaynab had never held such a heavy book in her life. She bowed her head and left the room.

Wafaa looked at her excitedly as they left the mosque. Zaynab wondered whether Hakima stayed there or if not, how she returned home. But she said nothing. She then realized she did not know where Hakima lived. She looked at Wafaa, who was in the middle of a long speech about how exciting this was, and how Zaynab must not be intimidated, and how, in fact, this would make Zaynab feel more comfortable—

"Wafaa, I do not know where Hakima lives."

Wafaa looked at her, "Lives?"

"She told me to come and visit her after I finish reading the introduction."

"She did? To her house?"

Zaynab nodded.

"Well," Wafaa said, "she lives not far away from the market, a few minutes from her. I know the building but I've never been inside. I can take you to her."

"What's this book?" Aisha asked when Zaynab entered the house.

"It is a book by Zaynab Fawwaz."

"Who?"

Zaynab tried to explain, but Aisha grabbed the book and placed it on the kitchen table. She looked at it, flipping through the pages. She looked puzzled.

"Mama, it is about women."

"But I see here also names of women who are not Muslim. Catherine the Great? It says here she was an Orthodox Christian!"

She kept flipping through the pages, "Esther Moyal, a Jewish journalist in Cairo?"

She looked at Zaynab.

"Mama, we learn about all kinds of women. I told you."

Aisha raised her eyebrows. "How come you were given this book?"

Zaynab sighed. "I need to give a presentation about the author."

"A 'presentation?' Aren't you too young?"

Zaynab shrugged.

Aisha got up from the table and mumbled to herself, "That Hakima of yours; she's something else...."

Zaynab spent the following two days reading the introduction to the book. She sat in the kitchen well into the evening, trying to understand. Many words were foreign to her.

"Mama, what is 'colonial?'" and "Mama, what is 'suffragette?'" or "Mama! What is 'emancipation?'"

Her mother knew some of the words, but some she did not. And neither did her father.

What frustrated Zaynab the most was that through the whole introduction, Zaynab Fawwaz did not tell much about herself. She wrote:

> "While history presented many examples of

talented women who could compete with the greatest male scholars and the best of poets, I could not find even one Arabic book dedicated to them. Thus I have embarked upon the writing of this book, for the sake of my fellow sisters."

But still, this did not say anything about who Zaynab Fawwaz *was*. Hakima always stressed that the women in the group must explain such things as family circumstances, social background, etc.

Zaynab felt she had no information about that.

Could she have misunderstood Hakima?

The book covered the lives of 456 women, offering a couple of pages for each figure. Zaynab flipped through the pages longing to find one titled "Zaynab Fawwaz" that would finally tell her what her background was, and what she did apart from writing this heavy book.

But there was nothing.

Zaynab felt helpless.

Luckily, over the weekend, Aunt Surayda told Zaynab that Wafaa wanted to come on Monday afternoon to take her to Hakima's house.

Aisha was not pleased, but she relented.

On Monday afternoon, Zaynab and Wafaa walked the cold Sarajevo streets without speaking. Zaynab held the heavy book tightly in her arms.

They arrived at a three-story apartment building. They looked at the names, then climbed to the second floor and rang the bell.

They heard the sound of three locks opening. Hakima was not surprised to see them. "Finally," she murmured as she gestured for the two of them to enter.

By the looks of the apartment, Zaynab thought that they must have entered some kind of library. All the walls were covered with bookshelves from floor to ceiling. The apartment was dark; the curtains shut.

Hakima told them to sit down, and slowly made her way to the kitchen leaning on her can. Zaynab wondered how she was able to climb the stairs each day.

Wafaa walked hesitantly toward the kitchen, and Zaynab was left to stare at the books nearly threatening to devour the apartment. Had Hakima read all these books?

"The tea is ready in the kitchen. You can each take a cup." Hakima made her way out of the kitchen carrying a cup that rattled as she walked slowly to the small dining table in the living room. Wafaa offered to assist her, but Hakima said, "No! This I can do myself. You bring your own cup."

Wafaa brought her cup and Zaynab hurried to bring hers. She could still not take her eyes off of the many books. In her own house, there were only three books, two copies of the Qur'an and the spoken tradition of the Hadith.

They sipped their tea silently.

Zaynab did not know what to say, so she waited for Hakima to speak, but Hakima only looked at Zaynab's face, which made Zaynab very uncomfortable.

Finally Wafaa spoke, "Such a beautiful apartment you have."

Hakima said nothing, and let out a long sigh.

Zaynab finished her tea and stared at her cup.

Wafaa tried smiling at Hakima. She then tried smiling at Zaynab. Zaynab grimaced and looked at her feet.

And so they sat there for a long time.

Wafaa cleared her throat. "Shall we?"

Zaynab looked hopefully at Wafaa and then at Hakima. Hakima looked back at her. Zaynab quickly lowered her gaze.

Hakima said nothing. She took a deep breath and exhaled slowly.

And so they sat there for some half an hour.

It was only when Zaynab noticed a pile of books opened on the coffee table in the corner of the room, that she gained the courage to say, "The book, the Zaynab Fawwaz book... It does not say much about Zaynab Fawwaz herself."

Hakima's clouded face seemed to clear at once, and a smile revealing a hidden golden tooth filled her face. "Does it not?"

Wafaa looked at Zaynab encouragingly.

"It does not," Zaynab said, "it only speaks of *why* she wrote it, but it does not speak of who she *was.*"

Hakima smiled again. "It is a riddle, isn't it?"

Zaynab shrugged.

Hakima smiled and looked away. "I have been thinking about it for a long time myself. Could she not have written, among the many biographies, about herself as well?"

Zaynab shook her head. "I searched through the whole book," she said proudly, "she did not!"

Hakima smiled. "Well, ever since I put my hand on this book thirty years ago, I have tried to find out more about Zaynab's career. She wrote two novels and a play, and many articles in newspapers. But we do not know much about her personal life. All I have found is there." She pointed at the coffee table, and stood up.

Wafaa hurried to help but Hakima waved for her to sit down.

Hakima carried a brown book back to the table, her hand rattling. She looked at Zaynab, "How good is your Arabic?"

Zaynab said proudly, "Very good, I already know all the letters."

Wafaa smiled.

Hakima said, "But reading, writing…?"

Zaynab said, "We just began this year."

"You must learn Arabic well, you hear me, Zaynab? For a Muslim, Arabic is what Latin is for a Christian, you see?"

Zaynab nodded.

"Bosnian and Serbian will only take you so far," Hakima said, "but if you want to enjoy the tradition of over two millennia of poetry, biographies, plays, anything—you will have to learn Arabic well, for all genres."

Zaynab hesitated, "What is genres?"

"Genre is a field of writing. All biographies are in the *genre* of biographies. All plays are in the *genre* of plays. You understand?"

Zaynab nodded.

Hakima looked at her. "So if I told you that Zaynab Fawwaz wrote across genres, what could you understand from that?"

Zaynab looked at Wafaa, smiling encouragingly at her, and then at Hakima, "It means that Zaynab Fawwaz wrote not only biographies or poetry, but both?"

"Exactly," Hakima said. "But her beginnings were not promising." She opened one of her books, in Arabic, and translated as she read, "Fawwaz was taken into the local ruling household of Ali Bek... as a maid or assistant of his consort."

Zaynab interrupted her, "What's a consort?"

Hakima smiled, "Good, asking questions is a gift from God. Make sure to ask as many questions as you can, yes?"

Zaynab nodded.

"A consort is the wife or the companion of a ruler." She continued translating, "...a maid or assistant of his consort, Fatimah—"

Zaynab interjected, "Where was this?"

Hakima smiled, "Good question."

Wafaa seemed happy, enjoying the compliments Zaynab was receiving.

Hakima closed her eyes. "It was in southern Lebanon, where Ali Bek was the ruler for the second half of the nineteenth century."

Zaynab nodded.

Hakima continued translating, "...Fatima Al-Khalil was not only a literate woman—"

Zaynab felt guilty for interrupting, but asked, "Literate?"

Hakima smiled, "Knowing how to read and write."

Zaynab nodded, "Oh."

Hakima continued, "...but was also a poet."

"Wait," Zaynab said.

Wafaa whispered to her, "No need to disturb Hakima on every word."

Hakima turned to Wafaa. "One more comment and you will be asked to leave, Wafaa. Zaynab is doing very well."

Wafaa looked down, her cheeks burning.

Hakima looked at Zaynab, prompting her to speak.

Zaynab murmured, "I thought, I know the name, Fatima Al-Kahlil, I... saw it in the book."

Hakima grinned, her golden tooth showing again, "Brilliant, Zaynab! Indeed, Zaynab Fawwaz included

Fatima Al-Khalil in her book as one of the women who left her mark on humanity. Good of you to notice."

Zaynab could not help but smile.

Hakima looked at the book and continued translating. "Fatima Al-Khalil recognized… the potential of her illiterate maid Zaynab… and taught her the rudiments of reading and writing."

Zaynab murmured, "'*Potential*' and '*rudiments*'?"

Hakima smiled, "Potential is the yet-to-be-uncovered possibility of a person. You have a great potential. And rudiments is the basics of things."

Zaynab nodded.

Hakima continued. "The relationship that developed between the old Fatima and her maid Zaynab is unclear. The only thing one can deduce is that Fatima must have made a great impression on her maid, who years later would include a short biography about her first tutor in her book *Scattered Pearls*…."

After a few hours, when it had grown dark outside, Wafaa and Zaynab left Hakima's apartment. Wafaa nearly danced in the street, "She likes you, Zaynab!"

Zaynab looked at Wafaa, "She does?"

"Of course! I've been studying with her for nearly a decade, and she had never, *ever*, invited me to her house! And spoke to me that way, complimenting…!

You are a very lucky girl!"

The following week Zaynab gave a presentation that won great applause. Hakima looked at her and said, "Well done, Zaynab. You presented eloquently, you spoke with relative confidence, and you have done justice to Zaynab Fawwaz's legacy."

Zaynab felt immensely proud. She had experienced pride before in her life. She liked it when she received A's in school, or when her mother commented to the aunts and uncles that she had helped with the food. She liked it when her father complimented her cleaning at the shop, or when Nana mentioned how kind she was to her young brother and sister. But never had Zaynab felt as proud as when Hakima looked at her and nodded in approval at the end of her presentation. She felt invincible. As if she could conquer the world.

CHAPTER 7

One day Zaynab did not come to the study group.

Hakima looked at Wafaa worriedly as the woman entered the class in the mosque on her own. "Where is she?"

Wafaa said, "She… she is not feeling well."

Hakima was worried. Zaynab, now nearly thirteen years old, was one of her favorite students in the study group. "Not feeling well?" She closed her eyes. "Oh. I see." She shook her head.

Wafaa said, "Her mother said she must have eaten something bad. She has not left her bed for two days."

Hakima shook her head. "Ignorant people."

Wafaa was taken aback by the comment.

Hakima nodded to herself, "Our meeting today will have to be shorter."

At the end of the study group's meeting Hakima took her cane and said to Wafaa, "Take me to her house."

Wafaa was startled, "But Hakima! It is late! And... coming unannounced?"

"Enough of that!" Hakima said, "The poor girl needs us!"

"But it is far away—"

"We shall take a carriage."

"But at this hour I don't think—"

"You will find some near the bazaar. Now stop wasting our precious time. I'll wait for you here. Go!"

A few minutes later Wafaa returned in a hackney carriage, the horse disturbing the silence of the quiet street. Hakima stood outside leaning on her cane.

She climbed up, her face twisting with pain.

The driver asked, "Where to?"

Wafaa said, "The Tobacco Factory Street."

They made their way past the old clock tower, through the small streets of the old city, past the cinema, the cathedral, and the post office, toward the poorer neighborhoods. The carriage turned quickly into the street leading to the Tobacco factory.

Wafaa shouted, "Here, stop here!"

The carriage driver stopped the horse. Hakima took some bills from a small purse hidden in her dress. Wafaa saw Hakima hand the driver more than needed. Hakima said, "Come back exactly in one hour."

The driver nodded and took the money.

Wafaa helped Hakima out the carriage. They walked to the door of the small house. Wafaa knocked on it quietly. There was no response. Hakima hit the door loudly, shouting, "Open up! Open up!"

The light in the living room was on. Ahmed opened the door and looked at the women with concern. "Wafaa, is everything okay?"

Hakima said, "We came to see Zaynab."

At that moment Aisha came to the door, "What on earth is happening here?"

Wafaa lowered her gaze. Hakima said, "Mrs. Sadik! We came to see your daughter!"

Aisha tried to be cordial, "Zaynab does not feel well, I have told Wafaa—"

"Which is why we are here!"

"But—"

Hakima looked at Ahmed, "Would you allow us some privacy, Mr. Sadik?"

Ahmed looked at Aisha, bewildered, and then at Hakima's burning glare. He bowed his head and went down the hall to the bedroom.

Hakima looked at Aisha and then at the street. "This place is unfit for our conversation."

Aisha pouted her lips and allowed the women into the small living room, closing the door behind them.

Hakima hurried to grab both of Aisha's hands, "Congratulations, Mrs. Sadik! Your daughter must have received the gift of womanhood!"

Wafaa reddened. Aisha whispered, "My daughter?! But Zaynab is only—"

"Zaynab is nearly thirteen years old, Mrs. Sadik! I am quite confident of what I sense. Let us ask her if you doubt."

Aisha looked stunned. For the first time in many years she was speechless. She tried to gain her composure. "I doubt that she—"

"Have you spoken to her about this?"

Aisha shrugged searching for words.

Hakima tut-tutted, closed her eyes and whispered, "You were her age too, twelve... but you had your older sister to assist you! And that, too," she opened her eyes, "with much agony on your part!"

Aisha's mouth opened widely. How did Hakima know?

"Now," Hakima said, "if you'd excuse me, I need to see her. Where is she?"

Aisha, shocked, led Hakima through the corridor. She stopped by the children's room curtain. She whispered, "Zaynab?"

"Yes, Mama?" Zaynab's voice came from over the curtain.

"You have a... *guest*."

Hakima waited no more and pushed the curtain.

The light from the hallway shown on Zaynab's face, laying in her bed, as well as a young boy lying wide awake on the other, and a toddler sleeping in a small bed on the corner. Zaynab murmured, "Hakima! I'm so sorry for missing—"

Hakima turned and looked at Aisha, "The boy!"

Aisha took a moment, nodded, and then whispered, "Abdul, come!"

Abdul whined, "But I want to—"

Aisha gained back her senses, "Come now I say!"

Abdul came out of his bed, Aisha grabbing him by the arm into the parent's bedroom. "Ahmed! Keep the boy!"

Abdul, sensing something interesting was happening, tried to run back to his bedroom, but his father grabbed him, "No... this is a... time for the ladies."

Hakima sat down on Abdul's bed, holding her cane and looking at the pale Zaynab. She smiled a large smile at the girl and spoke dignifiedly, "Zaynab Sadik, I congratulate you upon leaving the gates of childhood and entering the kingdom of womanhood."

Aisha, standing near the curtain, glanced at Zaynab's face.

Zaynab mumbled, "How... what... how..."

Aisha excused herself, "I... have to..."

Hakima looked at the terrified mother. "We need a Qur'an, as well as a collection of the spoken traditions of the Hadith."

Aisha obediently nodded and quickly exited the room.

Hakima looked at Zaynab. "You must not understand what is happening to you."

Zaynab looked at Hakima, trying not to cry. She bit her lip.

Hakima whispered, "This moment is a sacred moment, one of great importance, a blessing from Allah. Now ask me, 'How do you know that, Hakima?'"

Zaynab, on the verge of tears, mumbled, "How do you know that, Hakima?"

Aisha returned with the two books and handed them to Hakima, "Forgive me, but I need to attend to Wafaa...." She quickly left the room.

Zaynab murmured, "Is Wafaa here too?"

Hakima nodded, "You want her to come into the room?"

Zaynab shook her head 'no.'

"Very well," Hakima said. "Where is the light switch here?"

Zaynab pointed near the door. Hakima stood up slowly and turned the light on. Nadia turned around in her bed and cuddled in the blanket, undisturbed.

Hakima, standing, looked at Zaynab, "Let me sit next to you."

Zaynab moved, half sitting up. Hakima sat next to

her and sighed. She opened the book of the spoken tradition and flipped through the pages. "Here, read this."

Zaynab nodded. She read, "'Aisha, the wife of the Prophet—'"

"Peace be onto him."

Zaynab nodded and repeated, "Peace be onto him, 'said, 'We set out with the sole intention of performing the mandatory pilgrimage, and when we neared Mecca, I got my menses.'"

Zaynab stopped reading, her mouth opening widely.

Hakima pointed at the book, "Keep reading!"

Zaynab nodded, "'...Then, Allah's Apostle saw me weeping and came to me. He said 'What has happened? Have you got your menses?' I replied, 'Yes.' He said, 'This is a thing which Allah has ordained for all the daughters of Adam.'"

"Indeed," Hakima said, pleased. "Now ask me any questions you have."

Zaynab was speechless.

They sat there for a long moment. Hakima sighed and shook her head, "When I was your age, my mother prepared me for this blessing. But nowadays women do not know the old ways anymore."

Zaynab looked at her.

Hakima sighed again, "Have you said your prayers today?"

Zaynab felt guilty, "I slept through the prayer

time...."

"Of course you did. Your body requires rest. Over time you will see it will become easier. But, you should know that you are not required to pray now."

"But," Zaynab hesitated, "prayer is the second pillar of every Muslim—"

"Yes, but you have just read, that the Prophet himself, peace be onto him, explained that this was God ordained, correct?"

Zaynab nodded.

Hakima took back the book and flipped through its pages, "Here, read this."

Zaynab read, "'The Prophet—'"

"Peace be onto him."

"Peace be onto him, 'said to me, 'Give up the prayer when your menses begin. Once it is finished, take a bath to wash—'" Zaynab stopped reading, astonished.

Hakima looked at Zaynab, nodding with a smile. "Keep reading."

Zaynab looked back at the book, "'...when it has finished, take a bath to wash the blood off your body and begin praying again.'"

Zaynab looked at Hakima, amazed. If only Hakima knew the thoughts that Zaynab had in her mind these past two days. Was she sick? Was she dying? Had she commited some terrible sin and this blood was her punishment?

Hakima smiled. "This blood is a gift, Zaynab, signaling you are now a woman. It will visit you every moon, until you are old; then it will go away," she sighed, "When you are an old lady like me."

Zaynab nodded. She had so many questions.

"Ask, ask, my dear."

Zaynab bit her tongue.

Hakima sighed again, "Ask! Our proverb teaches us: He who asks a question is a fool for a moment, yet he who does not ask remains a fool for a lifetime. Ask. Ask!"

Zaynab thought of a proper question to ask. "Girls do not have to pray while…?"

Hakima nodded.

"But what if I want to?"

Hakima sighed. "You can speak to God, but the ritual of prayer is not required."

Zaynab nodded, and then asked, "But does this not create… injustice or… inequality with men?"

Hakima smiled. She took the Qur'an on her lap and opened it, flipping through the pages. "This is what Allah promised, 'I will not allow the deeds of any one of you to be lost, whether you are male or female, you are both the same to me.'"

Zaynab nodded slowly.

"You understand, Zaynab? Allah said that no deed of yours would be lost. And Allah has given you the gift of womanhood. He would not leave you nor forsake you, you understand?"

"But," Zaynab pressed, "am I not *allowed* to pray?"

Hakima sighed a long sigh. "My dear girl, you are asking difficult questions. The Qur'an only says you are not allowed to do one thing, and that is come in touch with a man."

"I cannot touch my brother?" Zaynab exclaimed.

Hakima smiled, "You can touch your brother. Aisha touched the Prophet, peace be onto him, while she was in menses. Of course you can touch," she grabbed the other book and flipped through it quickly. "Here, read this."

Zaynab looked at the short quote Hakima's finger pointed at. She read, "'Aisha was recorded saying: 'While in menses, I used to comb the hair of Allah's Apostle.'"

Hakima nodded, "Of course you can touch, the term I used is not 'touch' but 'come in touch,' meaning," she hesitated and sighed, "as in knowing a person, such as in 'Take the bride to her new home during the night.'"

Zaynab blushed, "Oh."

Hakima looked at Zaynab's face. "This is the only thing that the Qur'an forbids, as it may cause harm to your body. But, the spoken tradition," she pointed at the book in Zaynab's hands, "has many more prohibitions."

Zaynab looked at Hakima, who ceased speaking.

Zaynab pressed. "Prohibitions?"

Hakima seemed reluctant to speak of it.

"Remember, child, that our religion was given to the people of the desert, with all of their existing traditions… A woman in her menses, like you my dear, was not allowed to enter shrines, nor fast, nor pray… and some of these have made their way into our tradition. But what I want you to understand is that our holy book," she placed her hand on the Qur'an, "says none of that."

Zaynab nodded. She wanted to ask more questions, but Hakima seemed preoccupied. "Zaynab, your mother will buy you a menstrual apron or pads, for you to use until the blood slows down. What are you using now?"

Zaynab closed her eyes and whispered, "A towel."

Hakima shook her head. "Poor girl, were you afraid?"

Zaynab, her eyes still closed, nodded, tears appearing in her eyes.

Hakima kissed her on the forehead. "It is the blessing of Allah. You are congratulated. If you have more questions do ask your mother."

"Wait, how long does this…?"

"Several days. It shall pass. Does your belly hurt?"

"No, but my back really hurts."

Hakima nodded, "It shall pass too. When you are feeling better, you can go to school, and of course, come to our classes. I will ask Wafaa to inform you of all that we studied today," her eyes shone as she got up and leaned on her cane, taking the books with her, "we spoke about the great African princess, Nana

Asma'u, who spoke seven languages and was also a poet and a teacher. She founded one of the first schools in Africa. A wise woman…."

Zaynab smiled. She did not want Hakima to go.

Hakima turned the light off and recited a quiet prayer, looking at Zaynab and turning toward Nadia as well, "'O Allah, there is nothing easy except what You make easy. It is You who can make even pain easy to bare.'"

Hakima walked slowly to the living room. Aisha and Wafaa quickly stood up. Aisha took the books from Hakima and murmured, "Thank you, Hakima."

Hakima sighed and nodded knowingly. She looked at Wafaa. She then turned to Aisha, "Get her the needed menstrual apron or pads or whatever is used. I have not had mine in years."

"I will."

"And speak to her." Hakima's eyes glared. "The famous Sufyan from Mecca said, 'The first step in knowledge is to *listen to it*, then to *preserve* it, to put it into *practice* and then to spread it!' Spread it, Mrs. Sadik! Fear not of speaking of what is the gift of Allah."

Aisha nodded and gulped.

Hakima and Wafaa exited the house slowly. The carriage was waiting there. Hakima whispered to Wafaa, "Rejoice, Wafaa, tonight we have done the work of God."

Wafaa grinned and helped Hakima into the carriage, leaving the dark street with one girl a little less frightened than before.

CHAPTER 8

That year, at the end of Ramadan, Zaynab sat with her aunts and mother, and had her hands painted with henna.

Aunt Surayda applied henna paste on Zaynab and the girl felt special, not running around and playing with the younger children, but spending time with the grown-up women.

The henna paste felt a little cold. And it smelled like grass after the rain. Zaynab stared with fascination as Surayda squeezed the paste from the cloth and onto a thin brush and drew a swirling, intricate line from Zaynab's pointing finger all the way to the back of her hand. Zaynab gasped as Surayda drew a large flower right at the center. The flower had many petals, and it's leaves stretched to Zaynab's wrist. "Oh it's gorgeous, Auntie!"

Surayda smiled. "I'm doing yours with love. Not every day a woman gets her first henna."

Then Surayda proceeded to the others. The sensation on Zaynab's hand grew more uncomfortable each minute as the mud began to dry and crack. "Are you sure, Auntie, that the mud should feel so dry?"

Surayda nodded, but then gave Zaynab a bowl with a white liquid, "Put some of this on."

"What is it?"

Her mother answered. "A mix of lemon and sugar."

Surayda smiled, "So that your life will be sweet like sugar."

Aunt Latifah smirked. "Even if your life is lemon-sour!"

Everyone laughed. Though she did not understand their laughter, Zaynab joined as well.

Three days later, when Eid ended, the henna on Zaynab's hand was much darker. She felt proud going to school with her hand like that.

The painted hands gave Zaynab much attention in class. During the break, the girls gathered around Zaynab and examined the design.

One girl called Maryam clung to her. "Zaynab, can I come to you next Eid and have my hands painted too?"

Zaynab smiled. "I will ask my mother."

A girl called Basila added, "Too bad it is only acceptable to do henna during Eid."

"No it's not," Maryam jumped, "also when you get married!"

The girls laughed, "Why, Maryam, are you planning on getting married soon?"

Maryam blushed, "Not at all!"

Zaynab used to spend time with her siblings at home in the afternoons. But her mother insisted that Zaynab concentrate and keep up with her school work. And so, twice a week Nana would visit and spend time with Abdul and Nadia, while Zaynab went to the library to study.

Oftentimes, however, Zaynab would prefer going to her father's shop to study instead. There, she would sit at the back of the shop, near one of the old antique writing tables, and feel like a princess in her study. She thought of poets and writers, all of whom she learned about in her favorite Wednesday study group at the mosque.

Her father enjoyed her company, and often they would speak of world events. Zaynab liked how her father never treated her as if she was too young to understand anything. He would patiently talk to her about politics, business, the Qur'an and the spoken tradition, and many other affairs.

One day as she was studying at the back of the store, a peculiar young man with a black hat entered in a cheerful mood. He brought with him candies and called to the back of the store, "Mr. Sadik! Where are you?"

Ahmed got up and went outside, "My good friend Mr. Kabilio!"

"Please," the man insisted, "call me Joseph! We are like family!"

"Well, you call me Ahmed then!" Ahmed noticed the bag with candies in Joseph's hands. "What are the candies for? Has your wife already given birth?"

"No, she is due in two months, but we have a holiday today!"

"Wait, don't tell me! A holiday... Can it be your Hanukkah? No, it's too early in the year!"

Joseph smiled. "No, it's not Hanukkah."

"But your new year has already been celebrated, no?"

"Indeed. This is not a calendar holiday, but a Sarajevo holiday for our community!"

"What is it then?"

"Today is the fourth of *Marheshvan*, the eighth month in our calendar. A day like today, over a century ago, there was a historic act of benevolence."

"Wait," Ahmed interjected, "I want my daughter to listen as well. Zaynab!"

Zaynab stood up and walked, hesitatingly, to the front of the shop, adjusting her head covering.

Joseph looked at her and noticed her large, dark eyes. "What pretty eyes! Is this your daughter?"

"She is! My greatest pride."

Joseph tipped his hat, "Pleasure to meet you, young Miss Sadik."

Zaynab smiled and bowed her head gently.

Joseph noticed the books at the back of the store. "I see you are studying! That is very important!"

Zaynab smiled again and kept her head lowered. She knew Hakima would not approve, but she felt overwhelmed by the man's attention.

Ahmed clapped his hands together. "Well, tell us about this holiday of yours!"

"Today, over a hundred years ago, in 1818 I believe... Wait, in your calendar," he calculated, "in the Muslim calendar it would be the year 1233."

"Joseph, aren't you quick!"

Joseph bowed his hat. "Well, in that year, the ruler of Sarajevo, Rushdi-pasha—"

Ahmed interjected, thinking of the name the people of Sarajevo have given to that brutal ruler. "You mean the Butcher!"

"Exactly. The Butcher! Rushdi-pasha decided to ask the Jewish community for 500 sacks of silver coins, an unthinkable sum! And he took as a ransom the great rabbi and ten other Jewish men and locked them at the old citadel. He announced that if the 500 sacks of silver were not paid within two days, the rabbi and the ten men would be beheaded!"

Joseph paused in suspense, enjoying the look in Ahmed and Zaynab's eyes. "Well, the Muslims of Sarajevo could not agree to this and, understanding that the Butcher Rushdi-pasha would not back off from the execution, they decided to act!"

He cleared his throat and murmured, "And so on the morning of the fourth of the month of Marheshvan, three thousand men gathered from all sects of the Muslim community, and together they attacked the citadel, liberating the rabbi and the ten men!"

"I did not know that!" Ahmed said.

Joseph looked at him, pleased. "And this is why we celebrate this holiday today! Here are candies for the two of you!"

Ahmed and Zaynab took a piece of candy each and thanked him.

After Joseph left the shop Zaynab whispered, "Babo, he was a funny man."

Ahmed looked at his daughter, "Maybe. But don't be mistaken, Zenzen. He may seem strange, but he is very successful, a hard worker. He has a small factory of pipes and drainage and the like. He employs quite a few people."

Zaynab nodded as she ate her candy. Then, hurriedly, she went back to her desk. She had much more reading to do for school.

CHAPTER 9

It was in the fall of 1934 that Ahmed returned home in the evening with a white face.

He told Aisha to put the children to bed, even though it was too early.

Zaynab, now 16, stood near the curtain of the children's room, listening as her father whispered to her mother, "They murdered the King."

Zaynab was alarmed. The King? Murdered?

Ahmed turned on the radio. Zaynab strained her ears.

"Recent news from Belgrade. Our beloved King, Alexander I of Yugoslavia, was shot by an assassin while in a state visit to France. The King will be brought for a burial tomorrow in Belgrad. Prince Paul will be crowned. The government calls all people of Yugoslavia to fret not...."

Ahmed turned the radio down. He looked at Aisha, "It is a bad sign. I hope it was not a Serb who killed him."

"Why not?" Aisha looked at him worriedly.

"Because the last time a Serb killed a king, the Great War started."

The following day it was published that the King was assassinated by a member of the Croatian Revolutionary Movement who fought for the independence of the territories dominated by Croats. They wanted an independent Croatian state.

Zaynab did not understand why Croats would want autonomy from the greater Yugoslavia, their wonderful country. But when her father tried to explain it to her, she only halfheartedly listened. She was too busy thinking about the new cinema opening in Sarajevo, which promised to show Turkish films. She watched two Turkish films with her aunt, Surayda, at the *Pearl* Theatre near the great mosque, and she absolutely loved them. She especially liked Muhsin Ertugrul, an actor with thick eyebrows and strong chin. Her favorite film told the story of the Turkish independence war, in which Muhsin Ertugrul played along with the first Muslim Turkish actress to appear on screen, Neyyire Neyir.

Zaynab was jealous of her. She was even more jealous when her aunt told her that the handsome Muhsin Ertugrul had become engaged to Neyyire Neyir. "Isn't it fabulous, Zaynab?"

Zaynab wanted to cry. She hoped Muhsin Ertugrul would be her own husband.

At school, Maryam and Basila, two of Zaynab's

best friends, had already gotten married, and big farewell parties were celebrated before their weddings. Zaynab knew that her parents would never allow her to marry and leave school. Countless times, when her father saw her by her books, he would praise her and ask, "Zenzen, do you remember what the famous Imam from Basra said?"

"Yes, Babo, 'Seeking knowledge at a young age is like engraving on a stone.'"

Her father's face lit up each time she recited such phrases of wisdom.

Yet, as the years progressed, knowledge was the *last* thing Zaynab sought. She often thought of Maryam and Basila, who already spent each night in the arms of their husbands.

She wanted to be embraced in the arms of a young man. Better yet, in the arms of the famous Muhsin Ertugrul.

School was boring. Zaynab studied a lot, but saw no use for it. At nearly 17, she felt like an old spinster.

She had heard through her aunt Surayda, that there were several men interested in her. But her parents said nothing of it.

Once, when Zaynab went with Surayda to the cinema, her aunt told her, "Your father is very special. He is not interested in the bride price. Though the money can help your parents, he wants you to finish school. You should be very proud of your progressive parents. I was married when I was sixteen."

"But do you know, Auntie, who exactly is interested?"

"Oh, many fine men," Surayda laughed, "do not worry. Do not wish to hasten Allah's pace."

"But," Zaynab murmured, glad she could confide in someone, "how would I know if the one who comes is the right husband for me?"

Aunt Surayda smiled all-knowingly. "Do like the old proverb: Slap each suitor! The one who slaps you back, from him you should run away! But the one who turns around and leaves, after him you should chase!"

Aunt Surayda laughed heartily, obviously amused by her comment, "I should have done it to Muamar when I first met him!"

Zaynab was not amused. For her it was a grave issue. She knew of miserable women who had married the wrong men. She remembered her Nana saying once, before she passed away, "The most important decision you'll ever make in your life, Zaynab, is whom to marry."

When Zaynab tried to talk about it with her mother, Aisha dismissed her, "It's too early Zaynab, leave me alone!"

Zaynab dared not speak about it with her father. She understood that kind of talk would disappoint him. She knew that look in his eyes.

CHAPTER 10

One day, during her last year at school, Zaynab was studying at the small desk in the living room, when Abdul, now 14 years old, came to her and whispered, "Ziyyad has asked me if you are beautiful."

Zaynab's eyes widened. She looked at Abdul. His eyes twinkled. She lowered her voice, not wanting her mother to hear from the kitchen. "Ziyyad? The grocer's son?"

Abdul nodded.

"What did you tell him?"

Abdul smirked, enjoying the suspense.

"Oh stop it!" Zaynab exclaimed and threw her pen at him. "Tell me already!"

They both heard their mother's steps shuffling in the kitchen. Then came her recent signature cough. Aisha peered from the kitchen. "Abdul! Let your sister study!"

Zaynab interrupted. "Oh Mama, it's fine, he is...

he is… helping me!"

Aisha looked at her daughter suspiciously. Then she heard the boiling pot in the kitchen and hurried back.

Abdul leaned toward his sister and whispered, "I told him you are the most beautiful girl in Sarajevo!"

Zaynab's frown turned into a grin. "Aw! You did?"

Abdul nodded.

Zaynab thought for a moment. "But that's a shallow question! A man should choose his wife not according to her looks, but according to her brains."

Abdul shrugged and headed to the children's room. Zaynab wanted to ask him more about Ziyyad, but she didn't have the courage to.

When Ziyyad married Malika, another young girl from Zaynab's class, she was distraught. It was not that she even liked Ziyyad. On the contrary, she felt his eyes were always searching impolitely, his gaze penetrating through her veil. She did not like his stare. And yet, when he suddenly married Malika, Zaynab was beside herself.

She was so upset she could barely eat or speak.

Her father noted her silence at the dinner table. "Zenzen, how is school?"

Zaynab nodded. Her eyes were fixed on her plate. She did not eat much.

Abdul smirked, as if about to say something. Zaynab turned to him and glared, her already-large eyes becoming even larger. Abdul lowered his gaze.

Nine-year-old Nadia, unaware of her older sibling's affairs, said, "Babo, today we studied the independence of Turkey!"

Ahmed turned to his younger daughter, "You did?"

Nadia nodded proudly and reverted her attention to the food.

Ahmed turned to Zaynab. "Perhaps Zaynab can tell you of that movie about Turkish Independence. What was the name of that actor you liked?"

Zaynab murmured. "Muhsin Ertugrul."

"Right! What a talented actor."

Abdul smirked. "But Zaynab doesn't like him anymore since he got married!"

Zaynab elbowed Abdul.

Aisha banged on the table. "Zaynab! I don't want to see my daughter acting like a—"

"Sorry, Mama."

Aisha, agitated, began coughing. Ahmed hurried to give her water. When the cough subsided, Ahmed looked at Zaynab. She averted her eyes, not wanting to meet her father's.

One evening Ahmed came to Zaynab, who was

studying into the evening on her desk in the living room. "Let us go for a walk, Zenzen, just you and I, like the good old days."

"Babo, it's freezing outside."

"But it's not snowing yet." He seemed lost in thought and then said, "Remember how you used to love the first snow?"

"I don't like it anymore."

Ahmed sighed. What had happened to his beloved, bubbly and joyful daughter? These days she was always sour.

Zaynab saw the disappointed look in her father's eyes. He looked so sad. She took a deep breath. "I guess I can dress warmly."

"That's my girl!"

A few minutes later they were walking passed the tobacco factory and heading toward the main street. Sarajevo had grown. A streetcar ran on the main road. They walked quietly.

Ahmed wanted to initiate a conversation. He saw his daughter's eyes. She was so tall. A woman now.

He thought of what to say. "How is school, Zenzen?" He immediately regretted the question.

Zaynab mumbled, "Fine."

They walked quietly. Their breaths made hazy clouds around their mouths.

Zaynab wanted to speak. But she did not want to disappoint her father. He seemed so preoccupied recently. It has also been a while since she had visited the store.

"Zenzen... Your mother and I have been to the doctor."

"The doctor?"

"Yes. Because of her cough."

"Oh," Zaynab said, her head attacked with a multitude of questions at once. "When? What did he...? Why did you not—"

"I did not want to bother you, with exams coming up. But...."

Zaynab could see her father closing his eyes tightly. "Babo?"

"She is not well, your mother."

"Not well?" Zaynab asked, immediately thinking her question was dumb.

Ahmed exhaled. He wanted to say more. He wanted to tell his eldest daughter about the look on the doctor's face as he used the stethoscope and mumbled, "High." He had asked Aisha if she had pain in her joints, and she nodded. That look in the doctor's eyes haunted Ahmed ever since.

"Babo, tell me! It is not serious, is it?" Her mother, she knew, was the healthiest of all. She was never sick, never ever.

"The doctor recommended for her to rest."

They continued walking. Ahmed did not want to burden her with more information. He did not want to scare her. He did not want to scare himself either. Aisha was strong. She has always been so strong.

"I will help more around the house, Babo. I will help more with cooking and cleaning. Mama should rest."

Something in his daughter's words choked Ahmed. He swallowed and mumbled, "Thank you, Zenzen. But do not neglect your schoolwork."

Zaynab did not realize how much her mother aged. At age 42, Aisha Sadik looked 60. Her husband, who was eight years her senior, looked younger than his wife.

Zaynab tended to the house chores. Aisha protested vehemently, each protest resulting in another surge of coughing. "Not like that, Zaynab! Stir it slowly, allow the texture to build, not as if you were running somewhere!"

"Yes, Mama."

The silence in between their short sentences was thick and pregnant with all that they could not say.

"Gentle, Zaynab! Be gentle with the filo dough. Wrap the three layers tightly, but gently, no, not like that. Here, like that!"

Several times Zaynab nearly burst into tears. There was a reason she had neglected the kitchen all these years; her mother was a tyrant.

Aisha could not stand the hastiness in which her daughter was working. "Zaynab Sadik! What you put in the oven is what you take out of it!"

Zaynab did not seem to listen.

"If you make it like this," Aisha threw her hands around, "then this is what you'll eat."

Eventually, after yet another rebuke by her mother, and after two weeks of tyranny, Zaynab couldn't take it anymore. Her chin quivering, she ran out of the kitchen, "Do it yourself then, alright, Mama?"

Aisha was stunned at her daughter's reaction.

Despite the stress, Zaynab helped more around the house. She changed the sheets, cleaned, and did the laundry. At least her mother was not watching her as she worked.

Zaynab also decided to skip several afternoon classes at school, saying to her mother that lessons were cancelled.

"It doesn't matter, Zaynab, you should have stayed in the school's library to study."

Zaynab said nothing, but instead went to the children's room and began cleaning. A few minutes later Aisha called, "Zaynab!"

Zaynab came, "What is it?"

Aisha corrected her, "'What is it, *Mama*,' or 'What

is it, *Ma'am*!'. Do not forget your manners, Zaynab."

"What is it, Ma'am?" Zaynab said, only noticing a second after she pronounced it how her choice of *Ma'am* over *Mama* hurt her mother.

"I need help pulling the tray out of the oven, it's hot and—"

Zaynab hurried to take the towel and pulled out the tray of chicken burek. It smelled delicious.

Her mother sat down with a sigh, murmuring. "I would have done it myself, but yesterday my chest just—I was pulling the tray and—everything dropped on the floor...."

"Oh, Mama," Zaynab said as she sat down.

"Don't pity me! I'm fine, I'm... fine. Just fine."

Zaynab nodded. She looked away. Then she felt her mother staring at her.

"You are a beautiful young woman, Zaynab."

Zaynab's eyes widened as she looked at her mother.

"Yes, Zaynab. Your eyes are a little big, and your chin is wide like your father's, but you are not homely."

Zaynab looked down. Her mother really knew how to ruin a compliment.

Aisha tapped her fingers on the table. "There is this man." She sighed. "He is older than you...."

Zaynab's heart began pounding. She looked at her mother, waiting for her to continue.

"Bring me a glass of water."

Zaynab poured from the pitcher. The water was cold. "Here, I'll heat some water for tea."

Aisha looked at Zaynab as she placed the kettle on the stove. "You'll be a good wife after all."

Zaynab smiled, glad that she had her back to her mother.

Aisha said nothing. Zaynab began organizing the kitchen, wiping the already clean counter, moving jars of pickles and jam, doing anythin not to look at her mother at that moment.

Aisha sighed. "His name is Mustafa. Mustafa Hardaga."

"How much older is he?"

"Stop hastening me!" Aisha shouted.

Zaynab bit her lip so hard that she tasted the familiar metallic tang of blood.

Her mother said nothing for a long moment.

The water boiled. Zaynab poured a cup of tea. She placed it on a small plate and gave it to her mother. It had no sugar, and a lot of lemon, like her mother liked it.

Zaynab leaned against the counter and watched as Aisha smelled the tea and brought her hand closer to the hot cup. She recited the *Bismillah* prayer slower than usual and took a long sip.

Zaynab nearly exploded at her mother's calmness. Did she not know what this subject meant to her?

Here her mother was, about to discuss the most important decision of her daughter's life, and instead she sipped her tea as slow as ever, as if deliberately.

Zaynab tried not to breathe, not to do anything to make her mother divert the subject.

"Don't lean against the counter."

Zaynab pulled away from the counter and began wiping it again.

"I want you, Zaynab, to be a good wife. And I want you to have a good man. A good husband."

Aisha rubbed her eyes. It seemed as if only yesterday Zaynab was crawling around the house, barefoot, playing on the kitchen floor.

"There were many suitors who approached your father. I rejected them all—"

"Mama, why did you not—"

"Let me speak!" Aisha said, banging her fist on the table. Some tea spilled from the teacup.

"Because," Aisha continued, "none of them was fit for my daughter!"

Zaynab looked down.

"Sit, don't stand like that."

Zaynab sat down, still not looking at her mother.

"Mr. Hardaga comes from a respectable family. Wealthy. They have properties in the center of town, near the cinema. They are good Muslims. They helped build the mosque in the new quarter. Mustafa is the youngest of the two brothers. His older brother, Izet, is already married."

Zaynab said nothing, her mind racing. Did she know this Mustafa? Last Eid, at city square, there were so many men. She stared, looking, searching, imagining, wishing to find the one. Her mother scolded her then, "Stop staring, Zaynab!"

Now Aisha remained silent. Zaynab played with her fingers, and then caught her mother looking at her fidgeting hands. She immediately put them on her lap, poised.

"Mustafa is 32 years old. He is said to be wise. A good man. I'd like for you to meet him."

Zaynab said nothing. 32 sounded so old. She was only 18.

"Your father was 30 when we married," Aisha said, as if reading her daughter's thoughts. "Mustafa's father, Mr. Hardaga, spoke with your father a week ago—"

Zaynab wanted to shout. A week ago?

"What?" Aisha looked at her daughter. "Yes, a week ago. I don't want to give the impression we're in any hurry."

Zaynab nodded.

"If you would like, I will arrange for a meeting. Should I?"

Zaynab nodded.

"Well, that is that. Now, put a towel over these bureks, I don't want them to get cold."

A week later the Sadik family house looked completely different. Abdul helped his father carry some of the finest furniture over from the store. Antique cabinets and cupboards, an Edwardian mahogany display cabinet, a tall chiffonier and two large divans along with a Victorian carved rosewood center table. A curtain was hung in front of the kitchen door to block the view of the run-down cabinets.

The main problem was the mahogany display cabinet, which had four shelves and three glass doors, with much room for elegant vases, which the Sadik family simply did not own.

A cry was made quickly to the extended family, and cousins, nieces and nephews walked the snowy streets of Sarajevo with their finest vases and china, knocking on the Sadik family's door only to be brushed away a moment later by nervous Aisha, after having taken the precious porcelain from them.

In the morning of the special afternoon meeting, Ahmed looked around the house. "Now I feel like a king!"

But Aisha was not in the mood for jokes.

Aunt Surayda, in the children's room, was putting eyeliner on Zaynab. 15 year-old Abdul was not allowed into the room, though he had tried to enter. 13-year-old Nadia stood near the curtain, blocking Abdul's way.

Zaynab was nervous.

Aunt Surayda smiled. "Don't worry. Just don't say much. Smile and it will all be alright."

"But he won't be able to see my smile through my veil!"

"Oh no, when you smile your eyes smile as well. Smile the whole time," Surayda said as she finished applying the eyeliner, "smile until it hurts. Good. I think we're done."

Nadia handed Zaynab the small mirror. Zaynab gasped, "My eyes! They look huge!"

Aunt Surayda shook her head. "No, they don't."

Nadia looked at her older sister's eyes; Zaynab had often complained about them being too large.

Zaynab cried, "Nadia, aren't they too big like this?"

Nadia hesitated. Aunt Surayda glared at her, warning her to say nothing. Zaynab caught that look, "Oh, no! They look huge, oh Auntie, take it off, take it off please!"

Aunt Surayda shook her head disapprovingly. "It's a strong paste, it won't come off that easily."

Zaynab began crying.

Aisha passed in the corridor, pushing Abdul, "Go away! Stop standing in my way! Girls," she said as she peered into the room, "are you ready?"

Seeing her daughter crying, Aisha muttered, "What is it now?!"

Zaynab gulped, wiping her tears.

Aunt Surayda whispered. "She thinks the eyeliner makes her eyes look too big—"

"Well, it was a silly idea, Surayda, making her look like some cheap actress! When she wakes up next to him in the morning she's not going to wear this thing on her eyes, will she?"

Aunt Surayda murmured, "I just wanted to help—"

"Well, you're not helping are you? Take it off. And Zaynab, wipe your tears already!"

Aisha mumbled as she left the room, "I have to do everything alone in this house!"

Zaynab looked at her aunt. "I'm sorry, I didn't mean to…."

"It's fine. Here, let's take it off with some hot water and alcohol."

Half an hour later the Hardaga family came. Ahmed opened the door and Aisha, standing behind him, nearly fainted. She expected the parents of the suitor and perhaps a sibling. Instead, there was a throng of 15 people standing at the door. How rude of them not to have announced it in advance. "Welcome!" Aisha exclaimed, "How glad that you came, all of you!"

She quickly glared at Aunt Surayda and whispered, "We need more food. And chairs from the neighbors!"

Zaynab was waiting in the room to be called for. She heard a lot of noise from the living room, chairs being dragged, and hurried steps to the kitchen. What was going on?

She sat there, quietly, trying to understand. No one was waiting with her. She paced around the room nervously. Her eyes lay on the Qur'an, her favorite book, and she opened it looking for encouragement. The words blurred before her:

"O mankind! Your Lord has created you from a single soul. From it He created your spouse and through her He populated the land with many men and women. Be aware of the One by whose name you swear, and show veneration for the wombs that bore you."

The words startled her. She had read this passage before, as she had read all the Qur'an countless times. She could always find words of inspiration hidden behind a seemingly simple phrase.

"Show veneration for the wombs that bore you."

Her thoughts turned to her mother. Her mother, her stubborn, stern, disciplinary mother.

"Zaynab," she heard her mother's voice as she opened the curtain to the room, "We are ready for you."

Zaynab stood up. Her mother looked at her. Zaynab adjusted her head covering. She put on a big smile.

"No," Aisha whispered as she looked at Zaynab, "do not smile. Be poised, calm and disinterested. You could not care less."

Zaynab took her smile off and nodded.

"Good, now walk slowly, and only speak when you are addressed."

Zaynab nodded, feeling her heart beating fast.

The suitor's mother seemed aloof and somewhat disgusted by the little house. As she spoke in praise of her son, her chin nearly hit the ceiling. Zaynab noticed how her own mother was also playing the chin game, her chin raised way above where it would be comfortable.

Zaynab sat in between her parents. On the opposite divan sat the groom, who was surprisingly handsome. He fashioned thick eyebrows, and a neat, trimmed mustache. He was tall. Zaynab measured him up, and looked at his hands.

"I asked you a question," Mrs. Hardaga said to Zaynab.

Zaynab heart stopped beating. She looked at Mrs. Hardaga in terror, seeing the look of disdain on her face.

Silence followed. Aisha interjected, "Well, repeat that question then, Mrs. Hardaga! I too did not notice your speech turn into a question."

Mrs. Hardaga snorted. "I said," she said slowly, "that we will not accept anything but a proper, pristine Muslim wife. Mustafa has many possible matches from families who are well known in the community. We are only interested in a truly fine and noble Muslim bride."

Zaynab cleared her throat and quoted, "'Remember your Lord with humility and in private without boasting of it and do not be among the heedless.'"

A murmur passed through the room. Ahmed patted Zaynab's knee with pride and looked at Mr. Hardaga. "You see, Mr. Hardaga, all I told you is true!"

Mrs. Hardaga was far from impressed, "Every girl can memorize a phrase from the Qur'an. Where is this verse taken from?"

Zaynab did not miss a beat. "Surah Al-A'raf 7:205, I believe, Madam."

Mrs. Hardaga frowned, her eyes narrowing through her veil. She turned to her husband. "Is that correct?"

Mr. Hardaga shrugged, "I think."

Mrs. Hardaga said, "Recite the opening Sura please."

Zaynab shook her head in disbelief and looked at her mother and then at Mrs. Hardaga, "Surely, you could ask of a greater task, not the seven-line chapter we recite daily!"

Mrs. Hardaga's eyes widened.

Zaynab smiled. "As the food here is laid on the table, allow me to recite the fifth Surah."

Mustafa smiled. The fifth Surah of the Qur'an was known by its other name, "The Surah of the Table Spread with Food."

Zaynab began reciting. The room became quiet. Mrs. Hardaga pouted her lips under her veil. Mr. Hardaga's eyebrows were slightly raised. Mustafa's grandmother, who sat behind them, nodded her head approvingly. Mustafa's brother and his wife looked at each other, surprised.

Zaynab went on. "'...And whoever slays a person it would be as if he slew mankind entirely. And whoever saves a life, it would be as if he saved the life of mankind entirely.'"

Mrs. Hardaga moved uncomfortably in her seat. "That will be enough."

Zaynab nodded and became silent.

Mustafa tapped on his mother's lap. It was ever so gentle, no one noticed it but Zaynab, who followed her suitor's hand attentively.

Mrs. Hardaga cleared her throat and said. "Well, let's leave the children to speak in private."

Aisha stood up at once, and signaled for Ahmed to stand as well. She approached a chair at the back of the room and sat down next to Nadia, who looked at her mother. Aisha whispered, "Bring coffee, and all the sweets we have."

Mustafa stood up. Everyone looked at him. He sat down near Zaynab.

Mrs. Hardaga turned her chair around halfway, as if to give privacy to the couple. She kept glancing over, though, as did everyone else in the room, while speaking quietly to each other.

Zaynab stared forward, ignoring Mustafa.

The room grew louder as sweets were brought and conversations developed between Ahmed and Mr. Hardaga about the state of real estate in Sarajevo and the recent German annexation of Austria.

Mustafa looked at Zaynab. She still did not look at him. He whispered, "Well… This is an odd situation for both of us."

Zaynab nodded slightly. She still stared at the room in front of her. She saw Nadia and Aunt Surayda come from the kitchen and offer coffee to everyone.

Mustafa chuckled, "That recitation of yours was rather impressive. You are quite a scholar, it seems!"

A small smile broke on Zaynab's face.

Mustafa did not notice the smile in her eyes, and felt rather nervous. Her eyes were beautiful. Deep, dramatic brown eyes.

He cleared his throat. "I might not be as scholastic as you. My knowledge of the scriptures is rather limited, I must admit."

Zaynab, still not looking at him, murmured, "It is in the application of the scriptures that a man is measured, not in the recitation of them."

Mustafa smiled. He liked her. Could she really be only 18 years old? She spoke more eloquently than the older women he had met thus far.

He moved in his seat uncomfortably. "I understand you are in your last year of school?"

Zaynab nodded gently. She noticed Mrs. Hardaga's glance at them. Her mother, too, kept her eyes on them.

"And…" Mustafa began, not knowing what exactly to say. He saw his older brother, Izet, looking at him.

Mustafa tried to gain his confidence. In the many previous arranged meetings with potential brides he was always so sure of himself. Yet something about this wide-eyed girl unnerved him.

Mustafa's brother glared at him, motioning with his hand, "Speak, speak!"

Mustafa took a deep breath and said, "I am not sure what to say, Zaynab."

Zaynab, still looking away, glanced at him without moving her head. She wished to see his face. He was a good man, she felt. Though he was much older than her, she could see the child in him. He reminded her of Abdul.

Mustafa hesitated. "I would be a good husband for you."

Zaynab could not stop herself from turning to look at him.

At that very moment they heard a clap from the end of the room. Aisha stood up. "Well, thank you all for your visit!"

Everyone startled, looking at Aisha. Mrs. Hardaga glanced at her son, who looked stunned. Their conversation had been too short. "Mrs. Sadik, surely we could give the children a few more minutes, could we not?"

"We must not forget, Mrs. Hardaga," Aisha pronounced with a large feigned smile that could be heard in her tone of voice, "that our little Zaynab is still a student, and she has school tomorrow. Surely," she said, repeating the same tone of Mrs. Hardaga, "we would not want our meeting here to intervene with her schoolwork, would we?"

Mrs. Hardaga stood up. "Of course not." She nodded to Mustafa, who quickly stood up. Everyone did so as well. Ahmed looked at his wife, amused.

A train of people emerged by the door as the men shook Ahmed's hand and the women kissed Aisha goodbye. The kisses between Mrs. Hardaga and Aisha were particularly swift.

Finally, when everyone left, Aunt Surayda looked disapprovingly at Aisha. "Why did you have to call it off so soon?"

"Because," Aisha muttered, "Zaynab was drooling all over him!"

"I was not!" Zaynab protested and stood up.

Aisha looked at Abdul and Ahmed, "Go take the extra chairs back to the neighbors."

Abdul protested, "But they said we could return them tomorrow!"

Ahmed took two chairs under his arms. "Abdul, let's not argue with your mother."

As soon as Ahmed and Abdul exited, Aisha turned to Zaynab. "Don't you ever, ever, stare at a man's eyes like that, you hear me?"

"Aisha," Aunt Surayda cried, "she did not stare!"

"Surayda," Aisha said calmly. She needed not say anything else. Aunt Surayda left and joined Nadia in the kitchen.

Aisha looked at her daughter. "You heard me?"

"Yes, Mama."

"And what a long recitation!"

"I'm sorry, Mama."

"No, that was excellent. You showed them."

Zaynab's eyes widened as she glanced at her mother. But Aisha had already turned, taking a tray with half-drunk coffee cups to the kitchen.

CHAPTER 11

The end-of-school exams were easy for Zaynab. What was not easy was to see the quick deterioration of her mother's health; Aisha complained of headaches and chest pain, and had alarmingly low appetite. She found it hard to walk around.

Zaynab's suitor, Mustafa, came to visit the family, escorted by his brother, several times, and with each visit brought chocolates and flowers.

Izet tried to occupy Zaynab's parents to allow for some privacy of conversation for his younger brother and Zaynab.

Mustafa was infatuated after that first meeting, and kept repeating to Izet and his wife, Bahriya, "And she recited the whole chapter! The entire chapter!"

It was not exactly the recitation which impressed him, yet it was hard to explain what did. Was it the young girl's eyes? Or was it her voice, so sure of herself, so dignified?

Meeting Zaynab again in her home, Mustafa was

gracious. Izet conversed loudly, trying to probe Aisha to speak to him and Ahmed.

Mustafa murmured to Zaynab, "Thank you for being willing to see me again."

Zaynab nodded.

Mustafa could not stop thinking that she was more remote than last time. She didn't even glance at him. The house, too, looked bare and different. Had he just been mesmerized the first time? Was it all his imagination?

Again, in her presence, he found himself dumbfounded.

Zaynab noticed Izet speaking loudly with large hand movements. She also noticed her mother's constant watch over her.

She bit her lip. This was so strange, so odd. Still not looking at her suitor, she asked, "Why did you come?"

Mustafa seemed baffled by the question. "Why did I come? Well, because... I guess... I am interested...."

Silence followed. Ahmed was politely listening to Izet's stories while Aisha kept her eyes on Zaynab.

Zaynab sighed, "I am not the typical Sarajevo girl."

"That is good," Mustafa answered promptly, "because I'm not the typical Sarajevo man."

"How so?"

Mustafa swallowed, searching for a quick answer, "I... like to help people... I... have many friends... I am very responsible—"

"And that is not typical?"

Mustafa tucked his hands under his thighs, trying to gain his footing. "I would be a good husband, Zaynab."

Zaynab turned her head slightly toward him. "Will you?"

"Oh most definitely. I am very respectful. I am progressive! I am kind."

Zaynab hurried to quote a Qur'anic phrase her mother often repeated, "'Indeed Allah does not love the proud and boastful ones.'"

Mustafa was taken aback by the quote, frustrated. This was beginning to become strenuous.

Zaynab asked quietly, "What books do you like reading?"

"Books? Well, I read, of course, the Holy Book, and... the collection of the spoken Hadith, and... the newspapers."

"I see," Zaynab said coldly.

"Listen, Zaynab," Mustafa said loudly.

By the look of the faces looking at him he realized he had spoken too loudly. He apologized with his hand and his head bowed toward Ahmed. Izet hurried to say, "As I was saying, the properties on Kings Street have gone down in value, and it has only to do with the new market on Kupernica street...."

Mustafa whispered to Zaynab, "I am a good man.

I may not be as well-educated as you, and no, I cannot quote a whole chapter from the Qur'an…" he searched for words. He wanted to take her hand and hold it in his. "I am a good man. Yes, I know it is not humble to praise oneself, but you can ask around. I am God-fearing. I have waited for long, not wishing to take just any bride who did not…."

He searched for words again. Why was it so difficult to speak to her?

Zaynab nodded, "'A bride who did not…?'"

"Who did not seem right for me. I… I will take good care of you."

Zaynab's heart was beating fast. She thought of the many times her mother had told her, "With such a stubborn mind, Zaynab, no man would want to marry you!"

She spoke quietly, "You should know I have a very independent, stubborn mind."

"That is exactly what I like about you! You have an independent mind."

"You do not know me."

"But I want to know you!"

Aisha, seated near Ahmed, began standing.

Mustafa quickly whispered to Zaynab, "Don't say 'yes' to anyone else. I will come again soon."

Zaynab smiled. She was glad he could not see her face.

Mustafa stood up and bowed his head, "Mrs. Sadik, Mr. Sadik, thank you for your hospitality."

CHAPTER 12

Aisha did not like her daughter's response.

"But Mama, I like him!"

"'Like!'" Aisha exclaimed, "You know nothing of him. He may be an impostor!"

"But Babo said he heard good things about him. That he is a good man! Babo's friend rents his property and has a factory there. He praised Mustafa!"

"That's business! What do you expect, that he would badmouth his landlord?"

Zaynab did not know what to say anymore.

"Zaynab, you don't just say 'yes' to the first man coming to court you! I am… I am surprised at your attitude."

"But Mama, I have a feeling, a good feeling—"

"Enough of that!" Aisha mumbled. "We shall arrange for other meetings. You must see some other men before you come to a decision."

Hakima was upset.

Zaynab was surprised. First her mother, and then Hakima? What was happening? She expected all the women around her to push her into the marriage, not hold her back from it!

Hakima looked disappointed. "Why do you want to lose yourself and become the property of a man you do not even know?"

Zaynab was at a loss for words. The small apartment that once had held so much magic, now seemed suffocating. The books towering the walls seemed to threaten to fall and to swallow the tiny old woman.

"Answer me, Zaynab! Why would you do such a foolish thing?!"

Zaynab had expected to win Hakima's blessing. She had met Mustafa five times already, which was more than customary. And she had met three other men, all of whom were utterly boring and dull.

Mustafa seemed special. He was kind, genuinely kind. He was shy, which evoked in Zaynab a sense of motherly affection, yet he was also confident enough to declare to her that he'd take good care of her. And he was honest about his shortcomings. Yes, he was not a scholar, but he was a good man with a sound mind. All the people her father had asked about him told of Mustafa's good character, his honoring of his word, and his benevolence.

He seemed ideal to Zaynab. Why could she not convey that to her favorite teacher, her guide and councelor?

Zaynab began saying, "He is kind, and he is a good man—"

"How do you know that?!" Hakima burst in anger. She seemed unhinged by the visit.

"Everyone says so!" Zaynab cried.

"You never know, Zaynab! One may seem like a sheep on the outside, but behind closed doors may behave like a wolf!"

"Hakima!" Zaynab cried, "Don't you trust my judgment?"

Silence followed. Hakima did not dare look at Zaynab. Here was her favorite student—her best student—the most promising of all the women who have ever been to her group—the one who for nearly a decade she had poured her love, patience, and wisdom into. And now Zaynab was going to throw it all away.

The silence hurt Zaynab. "I came to ask for your blessing," she murmured.

Hakima sighed. She turned away from Zaynab, facing the book-filled wall. Zaynab could not see the tears emerging in the old lady's eyes.

Zaynab stood up, hurt and disappointed.

"Go," Hakima whispered, raising her hand toward Zaynab while still not looking at her. "And may Allah"—Hakima's voice broke— "grant you blessings and descend His blessings on both of you and keep you united."

"Oh Hakima!" Zaynab said, her eyes filling with tears, "Thank you!"

"Now go! Go! Leave me alone!"

When the door closed, the agony that Hakima felt was unbearable. She sat there for an hour, unable to move.

The wedding was scheduled for the end of the summer. Ahmed did not want to wait any longer. Aisha's health was failing rapidly. They had gone to several doctors, including an old lady who practiced the ancient ways and gave Aisha a special paste to put on her chest, but Aisha's situation only worsened.

Zaynab was busy with the preparations for the wedding. To her dismay, the closer the wedding day, the less certainty she had about the marriage. Perhaps Hakima was right? What *did* she know about Mustafa? Was she lured by his family's wealth? Was she just desperate to get married? Was she making a dire mistake?

A day before the wedding, Zaynab's aunts, cousins, and friends gathered at her house for the henna ceremony. Abdul and Ahmed left the house for the night to give the women full privacy. Aisha, pale as ever, presided the ceremony, whispering and coughing as aunt Surayda and aunt Latifah applied the henna paste on Zaynab's hands.

The drawings were exquisite. Patterns of flowers, leaves and petals swirled around each finger, each palm, and onto the forearm, nearly reaching the elbows.

All the while Zaynab's friends from school chanted bridal songs about the happiness of the newly-wed.

After her hands were painted, gentle decorations of foliage and tendrils were painted on her feet. Her white feet looked as if she wore a brown lace of ancient queens. Zaynab wanted to enjoy it all—the henna, the singing, the blessings, the attention—but in the back of her mind she wondered whether she was making a mistake.

After everyone left, Aisha called her daughter into her room. Ahmed and Abdul were still away, and Nadia had left to help aunt Surayda with the last cooking preparations for the following day.

Zaynab walked into her parent's room sheepishly.

"Zaynab," Aisha said, her voice hoarse, her face contorting with pain. "Tomorrow is a big day for you."

Zaynab nodded.

Aisha bit her lip, "I am worried."

Zaynab smiled and sat near her mother. "Do not worry, Mama. The wedding will be fine, everything is arranged—"

"I am not worried about the wedding." Aisha took a deep, hoarse breath. "I am concerned about... after the wedding."

Zaynab suddenly understood. Her face froze.

"Young men today…." Aisha said, "Who knows…? I only hope that your husband will be like your father. Gentle. Caring."

Zaynab's face remained unmoving.

"Zaynab, I spoke to your aunt, and she told me not to ask you. But I must. This shall be your first time, daughter of mine?"

Zaynab gulped and stared at the floor.

"Because if it is not, we need to be prepared. He will look for the blood; you understand? We must—"

"Yes, Mama. It will be my first time."

Aisha nodded. "I thought so."

She stretched her hand and caressed her daughter's hair. Zaynab was so young. What did she know? Aisha wished to impart her with all of her knowledge; all the pains, the joys and suffering of childbearing, of the intimacy with her husband, of running the household, of raising children. All of a sudden Aisha felt a strong sense of inadequacy, as if she had not done enough. As if she had not prepared her firstborn for all that was to come.

Tears rolled down Aisha's cheeks. Zaynab put her hands on her mother's as she, too, got teary eyed. Aisha looked at the decorated henna hands and smiled. "Remember how you used to want, as a child, for your hands to be painted as well?"

Zaynab laughed and cried, nodding.

"You are a good girl, Zaynab. You always were.

Your husband has chosen well."

Zaynab pursed her lips, tears dropping on the linens.

"Now," Aisha said, sniffled, and closed her eyes, "tomorrow night you shall not sleep here anymore. When you leave this house, when you walk out of my door, don't let anybody else raise you—you hear me? Remember, you've been raised."

Zaynab nodded, sobbing quietly.

"You've been raised. You know right from wrong."

Aisha paused and closed her eyes. What must she not forget to say? The enormity of the situation dawned on her. She sighed and looked at her daughter, her eyes filled with tears, her beautiful face. She remembered seeing those large, frightening eyes, when she was born, in this very room, so many years before. It all seemed to have passed so quickly. Where had all the years gone?

"Oh Zaynab… Walk proudly to his house. Be courageous, but not foolhardy. And remember," she paused and raised her daughter's chin with her hand until Zaynab looked at her straight in the eyes, "You can always come home. Remember that, no matter what they tell you or what you may tell yourself. I will try to be here for you always and if not here—"

Aisha began crying. Shallow and hoarse sounds came from her throat as she sobbed.

Zaynab squeezed her mother's hand tightly.

Aisha cleared her throat. "If not here, Zaynab,

then in the other world. I will be there for you."

"No Mama, you are not going anywhere."

Aisha took a deep breath and said nothing.

A moment later Aisha wiped her eyes. "Now go. You need to rest."

Zaynab lingered next to her for a long moment. But Aisha patted her. "Now now, you need to rest."

Zaynab stood up, and as she was about to exit her mother's bedroom Aisha called, "Oh, and make sure he says the prayer!"

"The prayer?"

"Make sure Mustafa goes on the floor, and recites the premarital prayer! You want Allah to be with you."

CHAPTER 13

The groom's procession filled the streets with singing and laughter. Mustafa led the way, followed by his brother Izet, his father, cousins and friends. All the while everyone would come to shake his hand or give a hug that always finished with a strong tap on the shoulder or the back. The men made their way through the city streets, from his parent's house in the wealthy center of Sarajevo, to the far away Tabaco Factory Street.

Meanwhile, inside the house, nervous, dressed up in a bright white dress, with a beautiful white head covering, was Zaynab, surrounded by her sister, mother, aunts and friends.

Nadia jumped at the sounds in the distance, "It's them! I can hear them! They're coming, he is coming!"

Zaynab's hand fondled her dress. The lavish lace texture met her searching fingers. Her heart was pounding fast.

The women reached to the window. Indeed, a

moment later, the noise grew louder. Aisha hurried to see if Ahmed was waiting outside. He was.

Sweating in the midsummer sun, Mustafa's brother lifted him up on his shoulders, while loud clapping and out-of-tune songs surrounded them in a havoc. Nearby neighbors stood on their doorsteps to watch the celebration. Men shook hands and congratulated old Mr. Hardaga, saying, "Finally your younger son has found his bride! Congratulations!" Mustafa, sitting up high, waved at the excited neighbors. Some did not know him, and wanted to have a look at the groom who was to take Zaynab.

As they approached the house, Izet let Mustafa down. The procession quieted. Dozens of men looked toward the small house. Ahmed was waiting outside, dressed up in a new fine suit, with Abdul on his side.

Mr. Hardaga, followed by Mustafa, walked toward Ahmed. The moment Mr. Hardaga and Mr. Sadik shook hands everyone cheered.

Mustafa looked nervous. Ahmed shook his hand and gave him a reassuring look. Ahmed then proceeded to shake the hands of many of the close family members, some of whom had visited the house four months before for the matchmaking meeting.

Ahmed reached for the door, and, on the prior request of Aisha, called, "We ask only for family members to enter for the Nikkah ceremony. Please, only family! We'll meet all of you later at the celebration, but for the Nikkah, only family, please!"

This did not help much, as within seconds the front door was surrounded by dozens of shoes and sandals as people tried to make their way inside to witness the ceremony.

Zaynab was already seated on a pillow. Mustafa came and sat opposite her. Between them a large chair was ready for the old imam. Everyone waited in relative silence, whispering to one another. Zaynab looked at Mustafa, who smiled shyly. They were both very nervous.

The old imam came with his wife a few minutes later, and as he entered the small Sadik family house, everyone stood up in silence. He greeted the people quietly and nodded at the familiar faces, shaking the hands of some of the elders. He walked slowly to the chair prepared for him, nodded and began reciting the prayers.

After he was done he said quietly, his voice not as strong as it used to be, "We have the honor of witnessing today a holy communion between a husband and wife. Our good book says, 'He created for you mates from among yourselves, that you may dwell in tranquility with them, and He has put love and mercy between your hearts…'"

People nodded in agreement. So did Zaynab and Mustafa.

The imam seemed thoughtful. "Does anyone here know where this phrase was taken from?"

Silence followed. One elder at the back said, "From the Qur'an."

"Of course it's from the Qur'an," the imam

scolded him, "Certainly not from the newspaper!"

People laughed. But the Imam frowned, "Don't any of you know where this verse is from?"

Zaynab murmured from under her veil, "The thirtieth Surah."

The imam's eyebrows rose, and he looked at Zaynab's eyes. "Very well." He then he looked at Mustafa and smiled, "You are marrying a sheikha!"

Some giggles passed through the room. Mustafa nodded nervously.

The imam continued, "What does it mean, when the verse says, 'That you may dwell in tranquility with them,' and Allah has put 'love and mercy between your hearts?'"

Silence followed. The Imam continued. "It means that today this couple," he said and pointed at Zaynab and Mustafa, "is to be joined in a bond of love and mercy, so that they can be a testimony to the power of Allah. The stronger the respect and the mercy they show to one another, the stronger is their devotion to Allah."

The elders in the room nodded.

The imam closed his eyes, "For does not our good book say, 'The wives are as a garment to the husbands, and...'"

Everyone completed the famous verse, "...And the husbands are as a garment to the wives!"

The imam looked surprised and smiled, "So we are not that ignorant after all."

People laughed. The imam was in a good mood. "In order to perform the ceremony I need to have the consent of all sides." He turned to Mr. Hardaga, who sat with his fine clothes on a chair behind Mustafa, "Mr. Hardaga, are you, on behalf of your son Mustafa, requesting the hand of this woman?"

Mr. Hardaga nodded and cleared his throat, "I am!"

People cheered. Zaynab smiled under her veil. Tears collected in her eyes.

The imam looked at Mustafa, "Mustafa, is your father acting on your behalf?"

Mustafa nodded.

The imam turned to Ahmed, sitting proudly behind Zaynab. "Mr. Sadik, do you, on behalf of your daughter Zaynab, agree to give your daughter's hand in marriage to this man?"

Ahmed nodded, his lips quivering. Silence followed as Ahmed looked at Zaynab. "I do!"

Cheers followed.

The imam nodded slowly and smiled all-knowingly at Ahmed. He then turned to Zaynab, "And is your father acting on your behalf?"

Zaynab nodded, bowing her head slowly.

"Then," the imam continued and reached his hand to his wife, who stood at the corridor, "according to the power I was given by the ancient Islamic law, I invite you to sign the Nikkah."

His wife handed him a scroll. He placed it on the

stool in front of him and looked at Mustafa, "Recite the first Surah."

Mustafa recited the first Surah.

The imam gave him the pen and pointed at the place to sign. Mustafa signed.

The imam whispered, "Qabul?"

Mustafa shouted, "Qabul! Qabul! Qabul! I accept! I accept! I accept!"

Everyone applauded. People shook each other's hands in congratulations.

The imam signaled with his finger for Zaynab to come closer. She reached for the table.

"Recite the first Surah."

Zaynab recited the first Surah. The imam gave her the pen and pointed for her to sign by her name. She signed and exclaimed, "Qabul! Qabul! Qabul! I accept, I accept, I accept!"

Applause followed. The imam's wife, two dates in her hands, hurried and put one straight into Mustafa's mouth, and then went to Zaynab, who raised her veil slightly for the Imam's wife to push a whole date into her mouth. Tears collected in Zaynab's eyes. So many times she had witnessed this moment in the weddings of friends, cousins and aunts; now she herself was eating the date.

The imam made both fathers sign the Nikkah and said, "Where is the Walima celebration to be held?"

Mr. Hardaga announced, "The Walima celebration will be held in our home."

"Very well," the imam said, "Now I shall spend some time with the groom alone for the consultation. Only married men can stay."

People began leaving. Zaynab got up and hugged her mother, then her sister and her aunt, but the imam's wife came and interrupted, "That you can do at the Walima, Zaynab, now come with me to the room."

She pulled on Zaynab's arm and drew her to the corridor. The living room soon emptied out, apart from a few men who stayed.

The imam's wife closed the curtain in the children's room, and had Zaynab sit on the bed. She sat next to her and cleared her throat, obviously feeling great importance in her role.

In the living room, the imam spoke quietly, nearly whispering. "Mustafa, you are now a married man."

"Zaynab," the imam's wife whispered, "you are now married. There are things a married woman must know."

"Mustafa," the imam asked in the living room, "after the Walima you shall wash up, come to the room tender and peaceful. Recite two full prayer cycles. Is that clear?"

"Zaynab," the imam's wife whispered at the children's room, "you will wash up and put ointments, oil, whatever you wish. You must come pure and pristine. You recite the first Surah and then wait for your husband on the bed."

"Then, Mustafa, you approach your bride," the imam continued, "put your hand on her forelock and pray, 'O Allah, I ask you for her good and the good of what you have given her, and I seek refuge from her unkindness and the unkindness you have given her.'"

"Your husband, Zaynab," the imam's wife continued, "will put his hand on your forehead, and recite a short prayer. Then, he will take off your veil. Allow him to do as he pleases."

"You must be gentle with her," the imam whispered, his eyes glaring at Mustafa. "Give her a candy, like our Prophet, peace be onto him, gave his wife, and then offer a cup of milk to her mouth. You understand?"

"Do as he pleases, Zaynab," the imam's wife looked straight into the girl's eyes. "Prepare in advance a towel next to you. Did not the Prophet's wife herself say, 'If a woman is intelligent, she should have a rag with her. When her husband has intercourse with her, she gives it to him to wipe himself off and then she wipes herself off, then they can pray in their clothing as long as no fluid has come upon it.' Do like the good Prophet's wife, always remain clean and have him be clean as well."

The imam lowered his voice, "You are aware, Mustafa, that you are never to go to a woman who is not your wife? The Messenger of Allah, peace be upon him, said, 'If one of you is attracted to another woman and something occurs in his heart, he should proceed to his own wife and have intercourse with her as that will repel what is in his soul.' You understand?"

"When you have your menses, Zaynab, you shall not lie with your husband. You shall wait until you are completely clean. Then, do as the good Prophet said, 'Take some cotton with musk on it and purify yourself with it.'"

"Mustafa, what happens between you and your wife in bed is no one's business. The Prophet, peace be upon him, said clearly that 'Among the people with the evillest position with Allah is the man who satisfies himself with his wife and then spreads his private relations in public.' The act of consummation is for you, for her, and for Allah, not for anyone else. Is that clear?"

"Always, Zaynab, keep yourself beautified and pleasant for your husband. The Prophet's wife said, 'If a woman does not beautify herself for her husband, she will not be important to him.' To remain important to your husband you must always, Zaynab, be clean, beautiful, pleasant to look at for your husband and for Allah looking down upon you."

"When you travel, Mustafa, and you finally return home, never surprise your wife. Always let her know in advance when you are to come, so that she can get ready for you. Has not the Messenger of Allah, peace be upon him, forbidden that a man returns unexpectedly at night to his wife, finding something that will 'arouse his suspicion concerning the wife or coming across some of her faults?'"

The imam's wife put her hand on Zaynab's knee. "I have said much. When you do not know what to do, come to consult with me. But it is all very simple. Have affection for your husband in your heart, and he will have affection for you. Be his garment and he will be your garment. You will be a very happy wife."

The imam took a deep breath. "Any questions, Mustafa?"

Mustafa, pale as a ghost, shook his head slowly. The men who had sat around him in the room quietly, now murmured, "May Allah be with you! May Allah be with you, young man!"

Zaynab nodded at the imam's wife, who patted her hand. She got up slowly and Zaynab hurried to stand up, trying to smile and conceal her utter mortification. As the imam's wife came to the curtain and pushed it open, the aunts who stood past the curtain were startled. Aunt Surayda, aunt Latifah and the others smiled apologetically. The imam's wife shook her head, "She will be fine. Allah will be with her."

Night finally came. Zaynab washed herself well in the bath of the Hardaga family. The night had been exhausting. In the past she had always envied the bride for sitting in the elevated "queen chair" next to the groom, while all the visitors paid their respects to them. She envied being at the center of attention, being the reason for the celebration.

And yet, the evening had proved exhausting. After the Walima reception she danced among all the women in the partitioned area, and she was kissed and hugged, somewhat forcefully, by many elder women, most of whom she did not even know.

Now, applying the oils she received from aunt Surayda, Zaynab sat on the small stool in the bathroom, anxious, worried and frightened.

The wedding was a success. Even her mother, who had rarely smiled since her sickness, spent the evening beaming. No one could even guess that she was severely sick.

Zaynab's thoughts turned to her father. It was when the Nikkah and the consultation ended and Zaynab had to follow her husband for the Walima ceremony and leave her house, that Ahmed suddenly broke into tears, hugged Zaynab, and sobbed profusely in her embrace. Then they had stood outside the house and waited for the four-horse carriage.

Now, applying the oil between her fingers to smoothly rub each one, Zaynab's thoughts were drawn back to that moment of separation from her parents. Her mother was poised, blessing Zaynab with a raised chin, royal and dignified. Her father, however, sobbed like a boy. "My Zenzen," he hollered, "my Zaynab, my pride…."

Thinking back on it Zaynab began feeling tears in her eyes. "No," she whispered to herself. She would not cry, not now. Not before her husband saw her for the first time.

She looked in the mirror and took a deep breath. She put on her head covering for what may be the last time she would wear it around her husband.

Her husband. That word shook her to her core. Was she ready? Was Hakima right? She felt Hakima's absence from the wedding. She had gone to Jasmine's wedding two years earlier. Why couldn't she come to Zaynab's?

The thought hurt her. She clenched her jaw, smiled widely and looked at her reflection. She adjusted the head covering, looking at her large eyes. She hoped Mustafa would not find them excessively large in comparison to her face.

She took a deep breath and recited the first Surah; then she added her own short prayer.

She took another breath and exhaled slowly. She had been in the bathroom for too long already, she knew.

Her hand reached out to the door handle.

Mustafa was nervous, but tried to hide it. He smiled at Zaynab as she entered the room. She smiled back. Much was left unsaid in that silence.

Mustafa asked what Zaynab thought about the wedding. Her response was short. He asked another question. Her response was short again. He offered her some sweets. She could not look or imagine eating more sweets, after being cajoled to taste from everything that the many neighbors and relatives have prepared. "No, thank you, Mustafa."

Disappointed, Mustafa said nothing.

Zaynab sat down on the bed.

Mustafa gulped.

His heart beat fast. He kneeled down on the carpet and performed two quick prayer cycles.

He then rose, came to the bed and sat down at some distance from Zaynab. The silence was thick.

He reached his hand to her forehead and gently laid it. It was the end of August and extremely hot. His hand was sweaty. He mumbled the prayer, his hand on her forehead.

Zaynab took his hand and helped him take off her head covering.

He gasped. She was so beautiful.

PART TWO

CHAPTER 14

A week after the wedding, on August 31, 1939, Aisha Sadik, aged 42, died in her sleep. Her last words to Zaynab were, "Take care of your father."

The following day Germany invaded Poland.

The war wasn't felt in Sarajevo in the beginning. The radio did broadcast alot about the Nazi forces entering Poland, but Zaynab was so taken with the death of her mother that she did not even care. She spent the three days of the traditional *Hidaad* mourning along with her father, brother and sister in her old house, and when the mourning was over, she returned to live with Mustafa. Mustafa's brother, Izet, his wife Bahriya, and their newborn boy, Kemal, shared the same house. It was a two-story house in the center of town, and Zaynab felt like a queen. If it wasn't for her mother's death and her concern for her father and her sibling's wellbeing, one might have said that Zaynab Hardaga was happy.

Soon after the wedding Zaynab discovered she was pregnant.

She already knew the name she would like to give the baby if it was a girl.

Winter came. News about the war in central Europe did not bother the people in Sarajevo.

When Zaynab was in her seventh month of pregnancy the newspapers announced that Germany invaded Denmark and Norway; spring had just arrived and everyone was simply glad that the snow had disappeared.

Ahmed, who came to visit his pregnant daughter and his son-in-law, seemed distressed. He tried smiling at them, as well as at Izet and Bahriya, but he could not. He also did not eat much, even though Zaynab prepared his favorite dishes that her mother used to make.

"Babo," she spoke quietly, "why are you so quiet?"

Ahmed sighed. He looked much older, as if the combination of his wife's death along with the breaking war was all too much for his hopeful soul. He said nothing, and Zaynab put her hand on his.

Mustafa tried to cheer the atmosphere up. "Babo," he said, "don't you fret. The war is in northern Europe. That's far away."

Ahmed mumbled, quoting the Quran, "'The sky is far away. But God is near. We are closer to Him than His jugular vein…'" He shook his head. "And now we are closer to that Führer than we think."

Izet leaned forward, "The Jew who is renting the factory space from us, Joseph, do you know him? Well he—"

"Fool," Mustafa scolded his brother, "Babo knows him well."

"I'm sorry," Izet said, "well, he says that now that Churchill was made Prime Minister of Britain, the war could end this summer!"

Ahmed smiled bitterly, "You all are too young. This is what they said about the Great War too."

Silence followed.

Bahriya turned to Zaynab. "With the help of God your birth will be easy, and Allah will bless you with many children."

Everyone followed with "Amen," but the atmosphere at the dinner table was sour.

The news kept getting worse. The Nazis invaded France, Belgium, Luxembourg and the Netherlands. The Soviet Union seemed to be responding slowly. The United States declared its neutrality.

Belgium surrendered to the Nazis. So did Norway. Italy joined the Nazis and declared war on Britain and France.

On June 14, as the Nazis entered Paris, a cry was heard in the house of the Hardaga family. A little baby was born. The name given to the brown-eyed baby girl was Aisha.

Ahmed enjoyed his granddaughter. He would often close the furniture store early to spend a few hours at his daughter's house before the evening. These hours brought him the most joy during those dark days, when the newspaper's headlines became more depressing. He would play with little Aisha and chant to her his favorite Qur'anic verses.

Zaynab was glad to see her father soften. She also enjoyed the commotion in her house. Nadia and Abdul came to visit daily. While it was exhausting for Zaynab to host everyone with proper food and sweets, her sister-in-law took over. Bahriya made plenty of food, as she spent most of the day in the family's kitchen upstairs.

Ahmed would stay as late as was appropriate. Only at eight in the evening he would leave with Nadia and Abdul and head to their own house in the less affluent area of town.

One evening, as the three of them left Zaynab's home, Ahmed heard a sound from the factory building next to the Hardaga house. Given the late hour, he became alert and walked over. Nadia and Abdul waited for their father on the street. Ahmed peered in, "Hello? Who is here?"

A man came to the door, "Why, Mr. Ahmed! What a pleasant surprise!"

"Joseph! I was afraid someone was burglarizing your factory! What are you doing here so late?" Ahmed then caught himself being impolite, "and how is your wife and your son and daughter?"

Joseph smiled, "Fine, fine," he noticed the

teenagers outside, "Why don't you come in and have some tea?"

Abdul squirmed, uninterested in his father's boring acquaintances. Nadia looked at her older brother, but Ahmed's his glare brought them straight to the door as he whispered, "Hospitality is charity!"

Abdul mumbled, "I need no charity."

Ahmed's face showed disappointment at his son's behavior.

"Come, come," said Joseph to Abdul and Nadia, "is this your first time in my factory?"

The two nodded.

"Well, here we make these things," he said and laid his hand on a tall pile of metal pipes, "for water to go through." He gestured to Abdul. "Knock on it."

Abdul politely knocked on one of the metal pipes.

Joseph smiled, "Strong, isn't it? The strongest in Sarajevo!"

Ahmed smiled and complimented Joseph, "They say the best in the whole of Yugoslavia!"

Joseph shook his head. "Maybe number two. In Mostar there is a bigger factory, but they have been in business since the era of wooden pipes!"

Joseph invited them to follow him as he proudly showed them the three large halls of production. "During the day we have 35 workers here!" He looked at Abdul, "Perhaps you can join us one day? You can earn a good income."

Abdul's attitude changed at once. "Yes, sir, that would be splendid!"

Joseph laughed. "Call me Joseph."

Nadia, tired, glanced at her father. Ahmed saw her and said, "Well, so good to see you, Joseph, but we were on our way home."

"Well let me drive you there, then."

Ahmed shook his head politely. "We can take the street car." But Nadia's eager nod was not missed on Joseph, who said, "Here, let me take you, I was on my way home anyway."

"But you live near the Synagogue," Ahmed protested, "Really, there is no—"

Abdul smiled and whispered to his father, "'Hospitality is charity.'"

Ahmed shook his head disapprovingly as he exclaimed to Joseph, "My own children are rebelling against me!"

Joseph smiled, turned the lights off in the factory, rolled the heavy metal door and shut the large lock. They followed him to his Ford pickup truck.

Nadia was excited to sit by the window. Ahmed thanked Joseph.

"Oh it's nothing, Ahmed. Now, tell me, how is the furniture business?"

Ahmed nodded and said, "Good, thank God." He did not want to say that whenever political uncertainty broke, the first thing to suffer was the furniture industry. He knew it was much better to work in industries that supplied the Yugoslav army. He looked at Joseph as he drove by the old clock tower. "How is the factory doing?"

"Oh, very well, we have a lot of orders from the army."

Ahmed's face turned sour. The thought of the war spoiled the good mood he was in after seeing his granddaughter.

Joseph glanced at him, "What do you think?"

"Of what?"

"Of what's going on."

Ahmed shook his head. "When I was younger, your age, even younger, I had just set up my furniture shop. And one good friend of mine, a Jew also, was leaving Sarajevo. He warned me that business was going to be low, but I was optimistic, like you, like everyone. But he was right."

"What was his name?"

"Mr. Nathan."

"Nathan Kabilio?"

"I don't know his family name… It was years ago…."

"Was he tall? Did he move to America? Had four children?"

Ahmed's eyes widened, "Yes, I think so!"

Nadia and Abdul looked at their father's astonished face.

Joseph smiled as the car turned to their small

street, "Well, what do you know! Nathan is my great uncle! We're all just one big family."

Ahmed smiled and pointed at the house. "Here. Thank you, Joseph."

Joseph stopped the car and Nadia, Abdul and Ahmed got off. Ahmed exclaimed, "God bless you Joseph!"

"He has already blessed me with good friends."

Abdul waved at the car, "Thank you, sir, good night sir!"

The months passed and Zaynab was pregnant again.

Ahmed glowed when he heard the good news. "A second child! What a blessing!"

Mustafa smiled at him. "With the help of God it will be a boy this time!"

Ahmed smiled politely, "As the Prophet, peace be upon him, said, 'Whoever raises daughters shall find his place in heaven.'"

Mustafa smiled back, "What Allah brings we will receive with both hands. But may it be a boy!"

As the summer proceeded it seemed as if the whole continent was burning. Soviets took Lithuania, Latvia and Estonia. In August German bombings filled the British skyline. Italy joined the Germans and invaded

Egypt. Soon Japan joined the Germans and Italians as well.

The Nazis had a superb air force. Each attack began from the air. Only then did their land troops defeat the crumbling local armies. In October German troops invaded Romania. Then their ally, Italy, invaded Greece. Then Hungary. Winter came with more invasions, more displacement, and more death.

CHAPTER 15

It was during a bright afternoon in Sarajevo in the early spring of 1941, a few weeks after baby Salih Hardaga was born, that an alarming sound filled the air of Sarajevo.

Airplanes.

Their sound brought horror to everyone who had been reading the news.

There were many of them, and they were flying low. Salih began crying, the acoustic booms were terrible. Zaynab embraced him and looked through the window.

There she saw them. Grey planes, filling the sky like crows.

Little Aisha began crying too. Zaynab grabbed Aisha's hand, not knowing where to go. Bahriya ran toward them with her son Kemal in her arms. "Let's hide in the bedroom!"

They lay on the bedroom floor.

Then came the bombs.

The ground shook as if an earthquake had hit the city.

Then again. And again. The sickening smell of gunpowder.

Screams. Shouts.

Laying on the floor, with Salih tightly held against her bosom, Zaynab could see the sky through the window. The house shook. The airplanes in the sky were all heading east. Toward the old city.

Half an hour later Mustafa came running into the house to find Zaynab and Bahriya with the children on the floor, his wife reciting Qur'anic verses.

"They're gone!" he shouted, "The planes, they left! You can come out," he said as he reached his hand to his wife. He felt guilty for not having been in the house.

Little Aisha clung to her father's leg, "Babo, babo!"

The sun was setting outside, oblivious to what had just happened. Distant cries and shouting were heard far away.

Zaynab was pale. Mustafa lifted little Aisha and looked at Zaynab and Bahriya. "They left. I ran here as fast as I could."

Zaynab did not say a word. She seemed

speechless. Then she headed to the stairs. "I need to see how my father and my siblings are doing."

"Are you out of your mind?" Mustafa shouted, "You are going nowhere! They might return."

Zaynab seemed stung by his shouting, "I am now the mother of my siblings! I promised my mother that they would want for nothing and neither would my father!"

Mustafa's face paled. He had never heard his wife shouting like that. "I will ask someone to go to their neighborhood and see."

Zaynab nodded.

The medieval city of Sarajevo was stunned. Never in its five centuries had the sky dropped parcels of fire.

Zaynab wanted to go outside. She wanted to go and see what had happened. She wanted to help. The news from the messenger boy that her family was well and safe in their little house on the Tobacco Factory street was reassuring, but her heart was still heavy. The boy explained that the airplanes had bombed the army base, the town hall and the Jewish quarter.

Zaynab prayed for strength. After both Aisha and Salih were sleeping, she sat in the kitchen with Mustafa, Izet and Bahriya. She had no appetite.

They spoke quietly. Izet said, "Within a day or two there will be a new regime here. I bet they'll put up some puppet government, like they did in France."

Mustafa nodded. "They'll choose the Croats."

Izet sighed. "Of course, who else would they choose? Not the Muslims, of course, and they'd never get near the Serbs."

Bahriya looked at her husband. "Why not the Serbs?"

Zaynab murmured, "They are Eastern-Orthodox, Bahriya. They are aligned with the Soviets, who are the enemies of the Nazis."

Izet smiled at Mustafa. "Your wife is versed not only in the Qur'an."

Zaynab walked restlessly to the window. The street was quiet; no one was foolish enough to leave their house. "We need to go out. What about the people whose houses were raided? We need to see about Joseph and Rebecca and their children. We need to help the people at the city hall. Perhaps there are people under the ruins."

Mustafa took a deep breath. "Tomorrow I'll send someone. Now we need to take care of ourselves first."

Zaynab knew better than to challenge her husband in front of his brother and sister-in-law. But at night, in bed, she clung to him and began crying.

Mustafa laid next to her, not knowing what to say or do. That day had been the first day he had heard his wife shouting. And that night was the first night he had seen her cry. She did not cry at their wedding, nor did she cry at her mother's funeral, trying to be strong for her younger brother and sister. She did not even cry while giving birth, twice.

But now she was crying in his arms.

He embraced her, at a loss of words. "Allah will do His will."

Zaynab shook her head, "Allah uses man as his instruments. For His will."

Mustafa took a deep breath. Suddenly he heard a sound. He jumped out of the bed. The factory outside. Someone was meddling with the lock. Mustafa quickly put on his slippers and ran downstairs.

Zaynab got up, her heart beating fast, and ran to the window.

In the darkness outside she could see a few figures. Three figures; one shorter, a child? One of the figures was carrying something. Only when they opened the door to the factory and turned the light on could Zaynab see their illuminated faces and recognize Joseph, his wife Rebecca and their ten-year-old son clinging to his mother's coat, while she was holding her toddler daughter in her arms. What were they doing coming to the factory now?

In a flash it hit her. Their house must have been bombed. She dressed at once, seeing Mustafa through the window running toward them. She put on her head covering and her coat and hurried downstairs.

The door to the house opened just as she descended the stairs. Zaynab could hear Izet and Bahriya moving upstairs as well. She saw her husband at the door, telling Joseph behind him, "Please, please, come in! Please!"

Joseph followed him with his wife. Zaynab had met Rebecca a couple of times, but they had never said much to each other.

Rebecca seemed distraught. She stood at the door, with her daughter in her arms, and holding the hand of her 10-year-old son. The boy looked pale.

Mustafa urged them, "Please, step inside." He turned to Zaynab. "Tea."

"Of course," Zaynab said and began ascending the stairs.

Izet and Bahriya headed down the stairs. Bahriya looked at Zaynab, but Zaynab did not say a word and continued past them to the kitchen.

Downstairs, Joseph shook his head, upset with all the commotion he had caused for his landlords. "Please, really, we will be fine at the factory. Right, Rebecca?"

Rebecca, looking pale, could not pretend that the thought of spending the night at the lofted, dirty factory, without proper beds, held any appeal. The children needed a suitable place to stay. Words could not describe the last few hours, as they heard the airplanes and ran to the woods, hearing the first bombs dropping within seconds. They hid on the hill as the Jewish quarter was bombarded relentlessly. The tall, impressive synagogue was hit. Then, when they finally returned to their home, they found the top floor had collapsed onto the bottom. Their house was destroyed, as was the house of Rebecca's sister. But what stung her the most was to see the tall, grand synagogue in ruins. The thought of it made her cry.

"What is going on?" Izet said as he came down.

"I invited Joseph and his family over," Mustafa said, trying to appear relaxed about it. "I told them it would be our pleasure, right?"

Izet was speechless.

Zaynab hurried downstairs carrying two blankets. It was freezing outside; the children must be cold.

Mustafa looked at Izet, "I told them that our home is theirs, right, Izet?"

Izet nodded, "Yes, yes, of course...." The implications of having a *Jewish* family in *his* home flashed before his eyes. He had heard the Nazi propaganda. He knew what having Jews in his house meant.

Mustafa brought a chair for Rebecca, "Please, feel at home. You are like family to us."

Zaynab smiled at Rebecca and handed her one blanket, giving the other to the boy.

Joseph, touched by the gesture, said, "We will leave first thing in the morning, perhaps some of our family's houses were not—"

"Forget about it," Mustafa said. "You will be here as long you need. You will be like house members." He turned to Zaynab. "Where is the tea?!"

"It's boiling!" Zaynab said and hurried upstairs. She glanced at Bahriya, who looked at her worriedly.

A minute later Zaynab returned with a tray and a teapot. Mustafa looked at her as she descended the stairs. "And Joseph, since you are like a family," he turned to Izet, "our wives shall be without a head covering around you."

Rebecca gasped. "No, there is really no need to—"

Izet spoke, "Yes. My brother is correct." He looked at Bahriya and nodded.

Bahriya's eyes widened. She looked at her husband, then at Mustafa, then at Joseph, who looked down at the floor. Never had she taken her head covering off in front of strangers, let alone a man. Let alone a man who was not a Muslim! She looked at Zaynab.

Zaynab placed the teapot on a stool and looked at Mustafa. He nodded at her. She nodded back and took her head covering off.

Mustafa turned to Joseph. "Our children will sleep with us and you will have their room."

Joseph tried to protest but Mustafa said, "You would have done the same for us, would you not?"

CHAPTER 16

The Jewish community of Sarajevo was distraught. Those who were brave enough to leave their houses in the days following the air raid gathered in front of the ruins of the grand synagogue. The Torah scrolls were buried under the ruined ceiling.

People argued. Could it be that a new government would do here what they were doing in Poland and elsewhere? It was hard to believe. Anti-Semitism was mostly a thing of the mainland, of Europe as a continent, not of Sarajevo, where the majority of the population was Muslim, and therefore Semitic.

It seemed mindboggling to think of demeaning laws against Jews. Elsewhere, yes. Not here. Not in Sarajevo. Sarajevo was a safe haven. Centuries ago Jews fled from Spain to Greece, and from Greece to Sarajevo. It had had a continuous Jewish community for hundreds of years. The city Museum held the ancient Jewish scripture of the *Haggadah* as its most cherished historical artifact—one that made its way all the way from the Spanish inquisition five centuries before.

Could it be that *here,* in *Sarajevo,* the Nazis could do what they were doing elsewhere?

People found it impossible to believe.

The new government declared Sarajevo as a part of "The New Independent Croatia."

The new title made many people laugh. "*Independent* Croatia?" If there was one thing that the new puppet government was *not* that was *independent.* It came to power because of the German army. It was to be a German government wearing Croatian clothes.

The Jewish community quickly began rebuilding the destroyed buildings. Many Muslims living near their Jewish neighbors helped. Serbs, however, quickly fled the city.

The new radio station declared the "New Independent Croatia" as a *purely* Croatian state.

People still laughed. It all sounded like a hoax of unruly youngsters who wished to receive some respect and status.

But laughter soon turned into incredulity as posters were hung around the city announcing that all Jews must wear an armband with the Star of David on it to identify them.

Joseph's factory was recognized by the new government as key due to its supply to the new army, and therefore Joseph was allowed to keep running it.

As the days turned into weeks, the brutality of the Croat soldiers in the streets shocked everyone.

The evening dinner table now had three couples and their children. Food had become more expensive, as much of the crops and food went to support the army.

The radio station broadcasted relentlessly, speaking against the "filthy Serbs and Jews," enemies of the "New Independent Croatia".

The Jewish school was closed by the government. Benjamin, Joseph and Rebecca's son, had to stay home all day along with his young sister Tova.

Zaynab tried to entertain the children as much as she could. She and Rebecca quickly became friends and together sang old Bosnian songs to the children. Bahriya, who was shier than Zaynab, took a liking to the new strange woman, as well as to her friendly husband and their two children.

All along, Joseph, Mustafa and Izet were searching for ways for Joseph's family to leave Sarajevo. Mustafa insisted. "It's not safe for you here."

Joseph agreed, but was reluctant to leave behind his parents-in-law and siblings-in-law with all their children, who were all now sharing a small apartment in one of the few buildings that remained intact in the Jewish quarter.

At dinner Mustafa argued with Joseph and Rebecca. "These people, these Croats, are not God-fearing people—"

Izet interrupted, "But they believe in Jesus, they say they are God-fearing—"

"Izet," Mustafa said, upset about being interrupted, "they burnt the Orthodox church of the Serbs. Now, is that God-fearing?"

Silence ensued. Only the sound of forks meeting the plates could be heard.

Mustafa sighed. "Our good book says, 'We have appointed a law and a practice for every religion or nation. Had God willed, He would have made you all into one single community, but Allah wanted to test you. So compete with each other in doing good!'"

Joseph was impressed, "The Qur'an says that?"

"Oh, yes," Mustafa nodded eagerly, "In the 'Examination' Surah, *Al-Mumtahina.*"

Zaynab murmured, "It's actually in the *Al-Ma'ida.*"

Bahriya couldn't hide her smile.

Mustafa frowned. "Well, wherever it says it, it says it! And these people," he pointed outside toward the cinema building across the street, which was taken by the new government to serve as one of their offices, "they are *not* God fearing!"

Silence followed again.

Rebecca spoke softly, "I have been missing the city so much. Do you think that perhaps you could get me a Muslim garment so we could go out to the market together?"

Zaynab rejoiced, "That is a great idea!"

Mustafa shook his head, "No. It's a bad idea. The other day they found a Serbian woman who stayed in the city dressed as a Muslim. They flogged her on the street."

Zaynab looked at Mustafa, "We'll be careful."

"No," Mustafa said, "if you want to go out, you go out as you are. They'll do nothing to you."

Rebecca shook her head, "But I cannot stand walking with that armband, as if I were a prisoner!"

Mustafa looked at Joseph, "You should wear it with pride. The shame is on them—"

At that moment they heard a knock at the door. Everyone jumped. Joseph's family had not registered their address at the Hardaga's home, and did not go to the Jews and Serbs registration offices opened by the Independent Croatia administration. Being discovered at the Hardaga's home was dangerous for everyone.

Rebecca and Joseph ran to their room to hide behind the closet, as it had been agreed before.

Rebecca shook her head in the small space, looking in the darkness at Joseph, disbelieving the surreal situation they had gotten into.

Soon Zaynab ran into the room, her face covered, "It is fine, it is a friend of Mustafa, you can come out!"

At that moment both Salih and little Tova began crying. Zaynab and Rebecca went to them.

Joseph walked out of the room to find Mustafa and Izet speaking with another Muslim man. He was older than the two brothers and wore a large mustache.

Mustafa noticed Joseph. "Come, Joseph, come sit with us. This is my good friend Suliman."

Joseph shook Suliman's hand and sat down. Mustafa looked at Joseph. "I have asked Suliman to sniff around and see about getting you all papers."

Joseph nodded in appreciation.

Suliman spoke, his voice deep and hoarse. "Even if we get the papers, it will be too dangerous to go like that, the four of them."

Mustafa nodded. "Go on."

"Papers are not enough. At the train station they check everyone on the public register. They take those who are not written on the register straight into the investigation offices across the street."

Izet asked, "Across the street?"

"They've turned the cinema into their secret police headquarters."

"Oh," Izet said.

They were silent for a moment, then Suliman spoke again, "You must be registered on the public register, otherwise it is like heading straight into their hands, and for false papers the punishment is—"

Mustafa interrupted him, noticing Joseph's pale face. "Then what do you suggest, Suliman?"

The man sighed and shook his head.

Joseph said, "We can go through the forest, we can advance toward Mostar, where the Italians are, and—"

Suliman shook his head again, "You won't even make it to Konic; the new army patrols the forests. The decree is that Jews must not leave Sarajevo, unless they are sent to a working camp by the government."

Joseph shook his head, "But we will be careful, I know the forests, I travelled—"

Suliman raised his voice, "With two children? And the winter is coming. In a month you will find yourself covered in snow. It is suicide."

Joseph noticed Rebecca standing at the entrance to the kitchen, listening in the darkness. He spoke to her, "Rebecca, go to bed, I will—"

"But I want to—"

"Go to bed, Rebecca!"

The men remained alone in the kitchen.

Izet got up. "Well, Suliman, you are offering nothing."

Suliman raised his eyebrows, upset, and stared at Izet. Mustafa smiled and said, "Sit, Izet, sit. Now, Suliman, surely you can help us, a great man like you with your connections and acquaintances."

Suliman took a deep breath and kept his gaze at Izet. "There is an option. But it is not a good one, because it is both dangerous and..." he paused, "un-Islamic."

"Un-Islamic?" Mustafa asked.

Suliman nodded. "I know a man, a Croat, but a good Croat, who has a wife and two children, a boy and a girl."

He paused. Joseph, Mustafa and Izet looked at him eagerly.

Suliman looked down, "If your wife could dress as a Catholic, and go with your two children as if they were his, then perhaps he could take them on the trains to Mostar."

Silence followed. Joseph swallowed. This sounded crazy. For Rebecca, Benjamin and little Tova to go with a stranger? What if they got caught? What would become of them?

Mustafa looked at Joseph.

Suliman said, his deep voice breaking, "I'm sorry. I would like to have brought better news."

They decided to wait. As Britain was fighting Germany, there was possibility of a swift victory.

But two weeks later soldiers gathered all the Jewish men of Sarajevo and sent them to a work camp named Jasenovac. No one knew which kind of work they would be asked to do or when they'd return.

Some days later the rumors began spreading. The camp was not designated for work.

Joseph came to Mustafa after having consulted with Rebecca in a long night of many tears. "Mustafa, we'd like you to arrange for that Croat man to take them, if possible."

Mustafa glanced at Joseph. "Are you sure?"

Joseph nodded. He could not bring himself to say anything else.

Rebecca Kabilio, now Maria Novak, climbed onto the train with her husband, Mark Novak, their son Anthony and their little five-year-old daughter Izabel, who looked much younger than her age. The children were instructed not to answer any questions that soldiers might ask them. Benjamin was told to ignore the large cross necklace on his mother's bosom, nor to ask when his father was going to join them. "Soon," was Rebecca's answer to her son's question.

As they boarded the train, Rebecca thought of her early morning farewell to her husband of twelve years. She gave Joseph her earrings and her grandmother's ring to keep. They looked at each other for brief moments, afraid that a longer glance would make them cry. And they did not want to, for the sake of the children.

As Maria Novak left to go downstairs and meet the man who was to take her and her children to Mostar—if all went well—she glanced at Joseph for the last time. Her lips were pouted, her chin raised. No, she would not cry.

Only her hand, when she squeezed Joseph's at the very moment that she began descending the stairs, showed her great distress, fear, and longing to do anything but what she was about to do.

Soldiers passed through the train with their rifles,

checking everyone's IDs.

An older couple with a young boy at the end of the train car were shouted at by a soldier. They were brutally shoved out of the train, and Maria Novak quickly pushed her son's face into her lap to shield him from the beating outside.

She knew these people; they were the Berkowitz family. She had studied in Jewish school with their daughter. That boy was her son.

In the train everyone glanced the other direction.

Joseph Kabilio was a broken man. He did not have his family, nor could he step downstairs or out of the house to go to his factory, which now had a new Croat manager. Joseph was trapped, as if in a cage.

No news came from Mostar.

As winter began, a new transport was organized for the women, children and elderly to leave Sarajevo.

They too were taken to the work camp.

Jasenovac.

Zaynab tried to keep spirits high in the house. Nadia and Abdul came over often, as did Ahmed. He was glad to see Joseph, who was much quieter. He was not the only one, however. Everyone spoke little these days.

The things they had seen and heard in the past half a year, ever since that hateful day of the air raid on their beloved city, were too much to bear. The screams and shouts that came from the building across the street that used to be the center of much joy when it was a cinema. The empty and ruined houses downtown. The closed shops. And worst of all, the stories about Jasenovac.

"It is Ramadan next month," Zaynab said, trying to lift everyone's spirits. "You should stay here, all of you, with us. We can make room for everyone, can't we Mustafa?"

"Of course, of course," Mustafa said, his thoughts elsewhere.

"How is school, Nadia?" Zaynab asked.

Nadia shrugged. Many girls stopped coming to school because of the comments they would hear on the streets from the Croat soldiers. She recognized some of the soldiers. One of them was the son of the flourmill owner, a funny looking boy who was always ridiculed. Now he was wearing uniforms, walking puffed with his long rifle, shouting insulting comments at everyone on the street.

Zaynab turned to Abdul. "And how is school for you?"

"Fine, very interesting. We are studying a lot to prepare for the exams at the end of the year."

Something in his voice sounded odd to Zaynab, but she could not decipher what it was.

Ahmed sensed his daughter's anxiety. "The food is very tasty, Zaynab, Bahriya, thank you."

The two women nodded.

Mustafa nodded as well. "We should be grateful to Allah for the food."

New posters were hung around town: "Sarajevo is Croat-Pure. Any Croat or Muslim who hides a Serb or a Jew will be executed."

The Independent Croatia soldiers meant it. One Muslim family who was caught hiding a Serbian woman was shot. Everyone. Including the children.

Joseph sensed the atmosphere in the house becoming tense. Bahriya was not smiling to him any longer. And the evening meals were quieter than ever.

Every knock on the door frightened Joseph. Through the upstairs window saw soldiers going back and forth on the street, taking people into the old cinema building. Some of the shouting and yelling from torture could be heard into the night.

As Ramadan began, Joseph decided to fast with the family. He longed to hear news from his wife in Mostar, but no news came. He feared the worst.

His thoughts turned all too often to Rebecca. To his children. To his parents-in-law. But he tried to brush those thoughts away the moment they came. He knew that he would go mad. Thinking those thoughts was too hard to bear.

But so was life with the Hardagas.

Zaynab tried to make evening meals that broke the

daily fast as varied and festive as she could, but they only consisted of variations of potatoes and leeks. Other food, like small pieces of meat, became extremely expensive.

Nevertheless, Zaynab kept praying for Ramadan to bring joy and cleansing to the family and to the country.

Ahmed was not in town. He travelled to Konic to help a friend who was closing his furniture store. These were bad days for business.

Abdul was extremely quiet at the dinner table, and when addressed he put on a flippant smile.

Nadia enjoyed living with her older sister, and was hoping she could ask Zaynab if she could stay after Ramadan.

When Ahmed returned to Sarajevo he seemed much older. Though only 57 years old, he looked seventy. He did not want to speak about what happened in Konic.

Two bodies were thrown from the top of the cinema building. They were left there for the day, for people to notice. Joseph glanced at the broken, bloodied bodies from behind the curtain; by the end of Ramadan he knew he had to leave. He was now endangering not only Mustafa and Izet's families, but also Ahmed's children. Three families were risking their lives to keep him hidden.

Mustafa kept searching for ways to buy an ID. He searched for other arrangements to help Joseph get to Mostar or to any other area controlled by the Italians. However, transporting any member of the Jewish community was difficult. Authorities had become wiser and more organized, and no one wanted to cross them.

Joseph, Ahmed and Abdul were sharing a room at night. Ahmed mumbled in the darkness. "Oh Joseph, may Allah keep your family safe. May he cast a shield of protection over your wife, children, everybody."

Joseph was touched by Ahmed's words, but did not know what to say.

Abdul laid staring at the ceiling. His muscles ached from all the training.

"Allah is always most merciful, most loving," Ahmed said.

Joseph remained quiet.

"I was in the train station in Konic a week ago about to come back to Sarajevo, when all of a sudden I saw a Jewish family, dressed in all your traditional clothes, getting off the train from Dubrovnik. I asked the man where were they going. He said Sarajevo."

Joseph turned in bed toward Ahmed.

"Yes," Ahmed continued, "Sarajevo. I told them, 'there are no more Jews in Sarajevo!'" Ahmed sighed. "He was surprised. He told me they had no place to go, because in Dubrovnik the soldiers had taken all the men as well, but they were able to escape."

Ahmed sighed. "But now they are supposed to be safe in Mostar, the grace be to Allah."

Abdul turned to his father's bed. "How did they get there, Babo?"

"I took them to the room I was renting from Abu-Musa and I began asking around for fake IDs. Two days later I found someone who could get me four for the parents and children. We filled them out, I cut the man's hair, got clothes for them, and off they left."

Abdul nodded in the darkness. His father was courageous.

"I wanted to stay in Konic," Ahmed said, "to see if anyone else would come. But people began talking, I guess someone saw me taking them to the room I was renting. But I say, let them talk. Allah will choose what is just."

"Amen," Abdul murmured.

"Amen," Joseph said, inspired by Ahmed's courage.

The following night, Joseph dressed as a Croat, left the house without any ID, documents or money. He gave his wife's jewelry to Mustafa.

"Where will you go?" Mustafa asked.

"I have a friend who can host me, and he says he already got me papers, so I can go to Mostar and search for Rebecca."

Mustafa seemed hurt. Had Joseph arranged all this without telling him?

"Very well," Mustafa said politely, "May Allah bless you."

"Take care, Mustafa," Joseph said. "Take care of your family. I cannot say how much I appreciate—"

"Nonsense, you would have done the same for me. Now, what was the name of your friend? Do you want me to take you to him?"

"No, he'll…" Joseph lied quickly, "he said he'd meet me."

"I'll come with you then—"

"No, I don't want to attract much attention with a Muslim and a Croat walking together at night. He'll wait for me, don't you worry."

Joseph stepped into the cold night. He waved at Mustafa assuredly and turned the corner past the old cinema house. He did not have anywhere to go.

The next morning Abdul was gone as well.

He did not return the following day. Finally, frantic Zaynab found a small note in her brother's handwriting under his blanket.

"I joined the Partisans. Destroy this note."

CHAPTER 17

After months of hiding in the a Mostar woman's house, Rebecca Kabilio and her two children were found; a neighbor had reported them. While Mostar was under Italian rule, the Italians were obliged under their agreement with the Nazis to hand over any Jew or Serb to the government of the New Independent Croatia.

The Italian police officer was clearly not pleased with his job of taking a woman and her two crying children from the small one room apartment. But these were the regulations. The woman should have run and hid in the Prenj mountains with the Partisans. She should have known better than to stay in Mostar.

The woman cried, protested, begged, and fell on her feet clutching the Italian officer's boots. "Please sir, please, my children! Do not take us! I have done nothing wrong! My name is Maria Novak—"

"Lady," the officer said, "your ID is fake. All three of your IDs are fake. I am sorry."

"Sir, please, sir...."

Her cries were unbearable to the officer. The 11-year-old boy looked at him with accusing eyes.

The officer stepped to the door. "I am sorry, but if you refuse to come I will need to declare you as uncooperative, and you will not be taken into detention but straight to jail—"

Rebecca, with a look of contempt on her face, got up, and with a sharp command called Benjamin. "Come." She took crying Tova in her arms. She took her purse, grabbed Benjamin's hand and walked proudly out of the house to the street, following the officer to the police car. The neighbors looked from their windows at the Jewess and her children climbing into the police car.

"You see," the Italian officer said as he drove through Mostar's small streets, "I really can do nothing else, I am terribly sorry."

Rebecca's eyes stared through the window. She said nothing, her thoughts turning to that cursed day she left her husband. She should never have left him. She should have stuck with him. Together they should have gone as a family to the work camp. Whatever came, they would have faced it together.

She should have listened to her heart.

The officer looked at Benjamin. "How old are you, boy?"

Benjamin clenched his jaw.

"I, too, have a son, back in Rome." The officer took a deep breath as he saw the police station at the end of the street. He slowed the car down.

"Listen," he said, and something in his voice made Rebecca attentive, "I will go inside the station to arrange for your detention, and you will wait here, alright?"

He turned his head to look at her. "Yes? I will go inside, and you will stay here until I arrange everything, you understand? Do not leave!"

Rebecca nodded. She saw the expression on the officer's eyes. Could it be?

The officer parked the police car, opened his door in a large gesture and left it open as he ran up the stairs into the police station.

Holding onto little Tova, Rebecca instantly looked at Benjamin and grabbed his hand. "Come!"

CHAPTER 18

The knock was extremely loud. Zaynab hurried to the door, hearing Bahriya's voice, "Zaynab! It's me, open up!"

Zaynab opened the door to her crying sister-in-law. Bahriya had left two hours earlier to go to the market in the snow.

Bahriya entered, sobbing. Zaynab hurried to close the door. "What happened?"

"I saw him…." Bahriya cried, unable to speak clearly.

"Who? Abdul?"

Bahriya shook her head 'no.'

"Then who?! Speak!"

"Joseph!"

Zaynab's heart sank. "Where?"

"He was… he was… chained, in a row with other prisoners…."

"Where!"

"At the King's Street, clearing snow, with other prisoners…."

"How did he look?"

Bahriya shook her head and began crying.

Zaynab took her coat and quickly put on her veil.

Bahriya tried to protest, "You can't! There was a soldier there…."

"Take care of Babo, he is not feeling well. I'll be back. King's Street you said?"

There were no prisoners cleaning the street on King's Street. Zaynab walked quickly, the sound of the snow crunching under her feet. There were no people on the streets. She turned to Cathedral Street and there she saw them. A group of prisoners, about ten of them, clearing the snow with shovels. A disinterested soldier guarded them.

She walked closer and then stopped. She did not want to be seen by the soldier. She tightened her coat, looking at the prisoners from afar. Bahriya must have imagined. Joseph was not there.

Or, was that man Joseph? No, impossible. A thin man made his way through the snow with the shovel. He looked much older than Joseph.

It had only been two months since Joseph had left their house. Could it be that he looked so….

Then she saw his eyes.

Joseph.

The kind, joyful man. The man who played for hours with little Aisha and Kemal and stayed with baby Salih when she and Bahriya left to go to the market. The man with the good smile, who became a member of the family.

He looked broken. She could see from the distance that his hands were blue, his skull looked odd, as if beaten.

He stopped.

He looked at her at the end of the street.

He bowed his head.

The soldier turned toward her.

She ran.

The following day Zaynab swore Bahriya not to tell.

Bahriya whispered, "You are mad!"

"I may be," Zaynab said as she took the pot of potatoes in her hands. "But I cannot sit here knowing he is there like that."

"Mustafa will kill you, Zaynab! There was a soldier there, you are playing with fire!"

"Swear to me, Bahriya!"

A long moment passed. Zaynab's deep brown eyes penetrated into Bahriya's soul, forcing her to nod.

"Good," Zaynab said. "I'll be back in an hour."

The snow was unbearable to walk through. A narrow pathway was made by the few pedestrians who dared step outside. Never had Zaynab experienced such a winter. As if Allah was punishing man for his cruelty.

She saw them on King's Street, and waited until Joseph caught her glance. She wondered how he could recognize her through the veil. But he did, and nodded slightly at her.

She gestured at the pot. She walked the street, daringly passing in front of the oblivious soldier.

She continued walking, and at the snowy mound at the corner of the street she fell gently, her pot dropping the potatoes into the snow. She got up, took the pot, and continued walking toward Cathedral Street, afraid of the soldier calling her, or worse, shooting her.

But nothing happened.

She entered one of the residential buildings on Cathedral Street. She walked into the building's corridor, leaving the door slightly open.

She stood there for half an hour. Fortunately, no one came in or out of the building.

Then she saw the group of prisoners advancing toward the corner, slowly clearing the street from the deep layer of snow. Joseph was there, attentively examining the corner with his shovel. Then he found it.

Joseph took a potato, glanced at the soldier, and bit it like a madman. It was pitiful for Zaynab to look at. Here was the head of a factory of dozens of workers, eating a potato like a starved animal.

He then took another potato with his shovel and slowly made his way toward the prisoner next to him, always with his back to the soldier.

Zaynab nearly laughed when she saw the look on the other prisoner's face. He took the potato and bit it hurriedly.

Then Joseph took the other potatoes and slowly but surely he passed them to the other prisoners. Zaynab loved him so much in that moment. She knew him to be a God-fearing man.

For three weeks this ritual continued. Until one day Zaynab came, especially excited about the seasoning of the potatoes she had brought—and saw that they were gone. No prisoners were to be found there, or in any of the adjacent streets. Not the following day nor the day after.

Zaynab was distraught. Joseph was gone. Was he taken to Jasenovac?

No news came from him. Zaynab was worried.

No news came from her little brother either. And the city felt empty, hollow, dark.

A surprising piece of mail came from a woman in Bogodol. Mustafa opened the letter and was bewildered. Bogodol was a small town in the Prenj mountains, near Mostar. The letter inside had nothing but a picture of a woman, a son and a daughter. He hurried upstairs to show it to Zaynab. She cried tears of joy. Rebecca was safe.

CHAPTER 19

"There were ten of us," Joseph told them all, as they stood above his bed. He looked so frail, Zaynab was afraid he would die then and there.

But he smiled. He looked at Ahmed and then at Mustafa, Izet, Zaynab, Bahriya, and Nadia, all wanting to hear the full story.

He shivered. "The heavy snow—they wanted to take us to Jasenovac, but the snow—the trains couldn't enter Sarajevo. So they had to keep us here doing something."

Ahmed clapped his hand. "The grace to Allah for sending you all this snow! Now I understand!"

Joseph laughed, but the pain in his ribcage brought sudden discomfort to his face.

Mustafa said, "We should let him rest."

It was half past one in the morning, and the knock on the door a few minutes earlier scared everyone in the house. Now the fear turned into a celebration.

Sipping hot soup as he rested against the pillow, the frail and gaunt Joseph Kabilio shared his horrifying experiences over the past three months.

"So they used us to clear the snow, and then they took us in a truck to Zvornik to help build an army base there. We worked as much as we could, but we were all starving. So they said we'd be heading to the firing squad. But then an officer, a Croat, was good to us. I think he left the cabin unlocked intentionally. We all ran. I came here."

Mustafa's eyes widened, "From Zvornik? On foot?"

"I hid in barns and fields during the day, and walked by night. I thought—" his voice broke, "I thought you would be here for me. I don't know where the other prisoners went."

"You thought right," Mustafa said. "Now," he gestured to everyone, "the council is over. Our brother needs rest."

Everyone saluted Joseph and exited the room. Mustafa was left alone with him. Joseph shivered. Mustafa sat by his bed. "Don't worry. We'll take good care of you. You came to the right place."

"I…" Joseph said, his voice cracking, "I don't want to put you in danger again."

"Danger is not from men, Joseph, but from Allah. People can do nothing to us. Now you rest."

"Oh, Mustafa," Joseph said and began crying. His thoughts turned to the abuse, the investigations, the torture he experienced in detention, and then in Zvornik, hearing and seeing things that were unbearable—rape, killing in cold blood—

"Joseph," Mustafa said, sniffling, his eyes also wet, "I have something for you."

Joseph's eyes fixed on Mustafa.

Mustafa pulled out an envelope, and took out a photo. "This is from a woman hiding in Bogodol, near Mostar."

Joseph's shriek of joy brought both men to tears.

A month later Joseph left via the forest to Konic with a fake ID. It was a dangerous journey. From Konic he would have to take the train to Mostar. Being rather well known as the owner of a large plumbing factory, it was even more dangerous for him. Yet he knew staying with the Hardaga's was not an option. The mere thought of risking the lives of the entire household, especially his old friend Ahmed as well as the children, was more than he could bear.

CHAPTER 20

The war raged on without end in sight. The entire Jewish community was gone, and the Serbs had disappeared. The local regime became bored and began to round up the Communists. Anyone who remotely opposed the New Independent Croatia was taken.

The city became quieter. Though summer had come, people were locked in their homes. Only soldiers and police officers roamed the streets, looking for the glory war had promised them.

Summer turned into winter again, and there was no sign of the end of the war. The Russians retreated. British Foreign Secretary Eden reported mass executions of Jews by the Nazis to the British House of Commons, according to the underground newspaper that Mustafa had found. He told none of it to Zaynab.

Winter came again, 1943. The city of Stalingrad had been under siege for months. In Sarajevo business was slower than ever. Ahmed, tears in his eyes, had to close his furniture shop after nearly twenty years. Nearly two decades of hard work left no money for the family. He had to be supported by his son-in-law, who was also in financial difficulty. The new government had taken over the pipe factory and were not paying rent. An army officer told Mustafa he should feel lucky for being able to help the war effort.

Finally, in February, in Stalingrad, the Russians were able to push Hitler's armies away and the Nazi forces there surrendered.

"This," Mustafa said at the dinner table, "is what we've been waiting for. Now it is only a matter of weeks. Hitler's whole 'New Europe' will crumble."

Ahmed sighed. "Do not celebrate too early. You were children, but in the Great War the same was said."

Mustafa grew tired of having the entire family in his house, including Ahmed and young Nadia. "Babo," he said, forcing a smile, "We must find a cause for celebration! It's been four years!"

"Four and a half," said Zaynab. She remembered it well. Her mother's death marked the Germans invading Poland.

Izet tried to intervene. "Whatever Allah wants will happen. Let it be His will."

Little Aisha was now nearly four years old, and little Salih two and a half. Zaynab was often assisted by Bahriya, and sometimes by Bahriya's mother, who would come to visit. But Zaynab longed to have the aid of her own mother.

Motherhood made Zaynab realize how committed her own mother was. How, without complaint, she would stand in the kitchen for hours on end, making food that was better than Zaynab could ever make. And in one word of command, Aisha could straighten all the crooked places, solve any unsolvable situation and bring peace to a feud in the entire Sadik family.

Zaynab missed her terribly. "Mama," she whispered in her mind, "have you seen little Aisha? She looks like you, with those lips, and the royal nose. She is also clean, and neat, she is very organized and does not like crumbs on her shirt, or disorder on the kitchen table. She is more like you than me. You should see her, Mama, she is so bright!

"And little Salih, Mama, he is... such a brat. And he loves getting all the attention, just like Abdul used to fight for attention at the table. Then at the very moment we'd all look at him, he'd become shy and shrug his shoulders saying, 'Oh nothing....'

"Oh Mama, where is Abdul? And why does Babo look so sad? I try to make him happy. He spends time with Aisha and little Salih, but there is sadness in his eyes. He is not as buoyant as he used to be. He is constantly worried about Abdul, and looks through the window constantly waiting for him. Oh Mama, make Abdul come back. Make the war end, Mama."

To add to the strife, Nadia was growing quieter. When Zaynab tried to probe her, she found her sister's answers to be short, polite and revealing nothing.

The only joy was the children. They seemed oblivious to the war. They thought that this was the way it had always been.

One day, as Zaynab was taking Salih to her mother-in-law, the boy saw the soldiers on the street and said, "Mama, one day I will be a soldier too!"

Zaynab pulled on her son's hand firmly.

"Mama, it hurts!"

"Salih," Zaynab whispered, kneeling in the middle of the street, "don't you ever say that! These are infidels, you hear me? They are not God fearing! Don't you ever say that again; you hear me?"

With her veil covering her entire face but the eyes, her eyes looked bigger than they ever looked.

She jerked Salih's arm again. "You hear me?!"

"Yes Mama," Salih said quietly, his chin quivering.

"Good. Now let's go to Grandma's. We're late."

CHAPTER 21

Summer came again. The Germans were defeated in Tunisia. People's greetings in the street became more hopeful. Some of Ahmed's old friends, passing each other on the streets, said, "With the help of Allah, the Day of Judgment is coming."

It sounded like a religious conversation, but everyone knew what it meant. The Muslim community was suffering under the brutal Nazi-sponsored Croat government.

Germany's defeat, first in Stalingrad, then in Tunisia, made the Germans more upset. A Jewish uprising in the ghetto of Warsaw was crushed, and the news reported the ghetto was set on fire with thousands of people being burnt alive.

The forests of Sarajevo became unsafe and more attacks were launched from the mountains and forests by Partisans. The group consisted of Serbs, Muslims, Jews, and even some Croats opposing the regime. They were led by a man called Tito, who molded together the separate Partisan groups into the collective Partisan Army.

These small attacks of the Partisan army made the soldiers at Sarajevo more anxious, impatient and violent. The streets remained vacant. Women were never seen. Only men did the little shopping necessary to keep families from starving.

Rumors began about soldiers taking Muslims, anyone they perceived to be aiding the Partisans or support the Allies.

No words were exchanged in the house about Abdul, especially not in front of the children, who could say something foolish to someone, not understanding what "Partisan" meant. The consequences could be devastating for the family.

Five years had passed since the beginning of the war. People became weary of hoping. Perhaps Hitler should get what he wanted and at least the war would end. Hitler himself survived an assassination attempt by German Army officers, said the rumors.

The Hardaga family listened to the news attentively. While they were limited and filled with pro-Nazi propaganda, they still reported the 'realignment' of Germany on various borders. Everyone knew what realignment meant. Withdrawal. Defeat.

Yet in Sarajevo the local government of Independent Croatia only tightened its grip. People were forced to salute all soldiers when passing them in the streets. Some killings were performed in the streets of the city. Dissidents were beheaded.

It began like a regular evening when, in January 1945, harsh knocks were heard on the Hardaga door.

Mustafa turned the light on. So did Izet. The children woke up and began crying. The banging persisted and a loud man's voice was heard, "Open up! Army order!"

Zaynab took crying Salih in her arms. Her heart beat fast. What was going on? Had Abdul been caught?

Mustafa put his slippers on. Nadia, Ahmed, Bahriya and Zaynab looked at each other in the hallway, pale.

Mustafa hurried downstairs, mumbling to himself the prayer of protection: "O Allah, Lord of the Seven Heavens, Lord of the Magnificent Throne, be for us a refuge lest anyone abuse us or do us wrong. Mighty is Your patronage and glorious are Your praises... Amen."

With that he opened the door. Four soldiers stood at the door. "Are you Ahmed Sadik?"

Mustafa's heart sank. He did not know what to say.

Izet rushed down and stepped forward. "No, officer. He is not. Why are you coming here?"

"Ahmed Sadik needs to come with us."

Izet swallowed his saliva. "He does not live here. His house is at the Tobacco Factory Street."

Mustafa put his hand on Izet's chest, quieting Izet down. Messing with the army was not a wise thing to do.

The soldier clenched his jaw and shouted, "We've been there and the neighbors directed us here. Show us your IDs!"

Commotion was heard upstairs.

Zaynab was pushing her father into his bedroom and urging him to hide in the closet. Ahmed refused to hide. Baby Salih was crying.

Mustafa swallowed hard. "Gentlemen, we will cooperate with you. Our IDs are upstairs. Izet, stay here, I will come back in a moment."

As Mustafa climbed the stairs, Ahmed's voice was heard, "Let me go Zaynab! I shall not hide!"

Ahmed pushed his way past Zaynab, Nadia and Bahriya and saw Mustafa's face up the stairs. Mustafa's eyes were wide as if he had seen a ghost.

Ahmed nodded. "I heard it all."

Mustafa shook his head 'no,' but could not utter a word. "Babo," he whispered, "no."

Ahmed put his hand on Mustafa's shoulder and then pushed his son-in-law aside.

Mustafa reluctantly moved against the wall to allow Ahmed to walk downstairs. Zaynab looked at her husband in disbelief. She handed Salih to Nadia, grabbed her veil and ran downstairs.

Ahmed arrived at the door and looked at Izet and then at the soldiers. "I am Ahmed Sadik."

"You need to come with us," said the soldier, who looked not at Ahmed, but at Izet. "Didn't you say that Ahmed Sadik was not here?"

Izet's mumbled, "I… did not… know…."

The soldier snorted and turned to Ahmed, "Come!"

Ahmed glared at the soldier and pushed his shoulders back. The soldier could have been his son. "May I ask at what charge?"

"Were you in Konic two years ago?"

Ahmed's face betrayed nothing. "I may have. I travel a lot."

Zaynab ran down the stairs and held on to her father's waist.

The soldier glanced at the veiled woman and then at the old man. "Did you hide a family of Jews in the room you rented there?"

Ahmed's face did not budge. "I did."

Zaynab's cry rattled the entire street, "No! Babo, no! He is lying, officer! He is mentally ill, he does not know what he is saying! He was here, he was here all along!"

"Zaynab," Ahmed said calmly, "let me go. Justice is not at the hands of men, but at the hands of Allah."

The soldiers reached to take him.

Zaynab pushed herself in front of her father, "No!"

Izet turned to look at Mustafa, who stood frozen on the stairs.

The soldier shouted at Zaynab. "Move!"

"No!" Zaynab hollered, "He's my father! He did nothing wrong! Shame on you!"

The soldier nodded to the three soldiers standing behind him, and they pushed Zaynab inside. Mustafa instantly ran from the stairs and jumped in between them, "Get your filthy hands off her!"

The first soldier grabbed Ahmed's arm, meeting no resistance. The children cried upstairs. Zaynab fought the soldiers until one of them pulled his pistol and shot in the air.

The sound of the shot rattled Zaynab and made her stop, panting in the soldier's arms. Mustafa grabbed her and pushed her into the house. The soldiers took Ahmed and headed to the street, then, at the command of the first soldier, two of them came back and took Izet too.

"Me?" Izet mumbled.

"You lied to an officer!"

Izet did not know what to say. Stunned, he did not resist the soldiers who dragged him away.

Zaynab howled, launching forward. Mustafa's strong arms held her as she fell onto the floor, screaming, "No! No! Don't take them... Babo! Babo! Babo!"

CHAPTER 22

The following day Izet returned home. He had signs of being beaten on his face, back and hands. He said nothing, and refused to say anything for weeks.

Zaynab and Mustafa went to the old cinema house, but were sent to the prison. They hurried there.

Mustafa tried to bribe a clerk, who took the money and disappeared. Another soldier appeared after twenty minutes and said that they should come next week.

They kept coming each day, Zaynab's face growing older by the hour from lack of sleep and food.

On the fifth day they were told that prisoner Ahmed Sadik had admitted to all the charges. He was sent to a work camp.

Jasenovac.

CHAPTER 23

Zaynab's spirit died. Bahriya took over the household, Zaynab being unwilling to come out of the dark, shuttered bedroom.

Nadia tried to comfort her. After all, Ahmed was her father too. But Zaynab could not be comforted.

"You'll see," Nadia tried, "Babo is a strong man. Soon the war will end and he'll come back stronger than before."

Zaynab's eyes, always big, now seemed so large that it was unpleasant to look at her. Her eyes galvanizing her whole face, looking at you but not really at you, past you. Searching.

Aisha's school drawings did not help. Nor her Qur'anic recitations, which used to make Zaynab's heart melt. Now Zaynab would nod and mumble, "Good girl," and then stare into space. Aunt Bahriya would then say to Aisha, "Let Mama rest."

Weeks turned into months, and no news came about her father or her brother. Life seemed not worth living. In the past she used to converse with her mother in her mind, and have better conversations than she used to have with her while Aisha was alive. But no conversations were held in her mind now. There was no use.

Mustafa was broken, too. He felt less than a man for not standing up to the soldiers, for not punching them, or killing them. In his eyes, the respect of his family, the respect of his name, was gone. He had failed as a son-in-law and as a husband.

This was unfortunate, as the news got better every day. Tito's Partisan army was now recognized by the allies, who dispatched by planes, packages of food and weapons into the forests. The Partisan's assaults on the Independent Croatia Army became more frequent and more intense.

In Poland, Russian troops were pushing the Germans back. Warsaw was liberated. A camp, Auschwitz, was liberated as well.

The German city of Dresden was destroyed by a firestorm after bombing raids by the Allies. The Russians were quick to advance toward Berlin.

"Zaynab," Mustafa cried one night, "please! We need you. I need you!"

His words made their way past fog of Zaynab's sorrow. "Mustafa," she whispered.

"I need you, Zaynab. The children need you. Aisha wants to show you how well she reads. She needs you. Salih asks me all the time, 'Is Mama sick? When will she get healthy?'"

"I am sorry, Mustafa," came Zaynab's whisper.

"You deserve a better woman."

Mustafa's eyes streamed with quiet tears. He longed for his wife's reassuring hands to wipe his tears, kiss him and say, "I'm here."

But she did not. She heard him crying in the darkness of their bedroom, and remained quiet.

"Come," Mustafa said one day to Zaynab, opening the shutters. Spring was coming. Some light might help her. Mustafa had been consulting with everyone about what to do. It had been four months since that night, and his wife had yet to leave her room. He tried everything he could. Finally, Zaynab's old aunt Surayda told him he had not tried everything. "Try this," she said.

Zaynab was reluctant. "I need to rest," she mumbled as she covered her eyes from the light coming through the open window.

"No." Mustafa said. "Dress now!"

"I can't."

"Dress now I tell you!"

Obediently, Zaynab got up.

Aisha entered the room. "Mama, Mama, wear that silk dress that you like!"

Zaynab reluctantly did as her daughter suggested. The dress felt odd and uncomfortable. She had worn only her nightgowns for so many weeks.

She was a little dizzy going down the stairs, leaning on Mustafa.

Only when they stepped into the street did she ask, covering her eyes, "Where are you taking me?"

"Come." he said and held her arm.

They walked for a long time. Zaynab looked around her. The streets were still empty despite the good weather. The city was still in hiding.

They turned the corner past the mosque near the clock tower and continued walking. Finally, Mustafa stopped near a three-story building. "It should be here."

Suddenly Zaynab recognized where she was. The house of old Hakima. "No!" she pulled away from Mustafa.

Mustafa looked puzzled. "But..." he thought of Aunt Surayda's words, 'If that old wretch can not help her, then only Allah can save our Zaynab.'

Mustafa pulled on Zaynab's arm, "Come!"

"No!" Zaynab shouted and pulled away with an unusual force. "She hates me!"

"Who? This lady?"

Zaynab nodded.

Mustafa frowned, "But your aunt said that you were her favorite student!"

Mustafa was exasperated. "Come!"

"No!" Zaynab screamed, her eyes wide like a haunted animal. "She..." she lowered her voice into a whisper, "she is upset. I promised I'd come to her after the wedding. I did not. I let her down. She hates me!"

Mustafa took a deep breath in, and then decided to lie. "But she invited you."

"She did?" Zaynab's eyes widened. The look in her eyes reminded Mustafa of the good old days, when Zaynab's animated personality would often make him smile.

"Yes," he lied again, "she really wants to see you."

Something softened in Zaynab's face, and for a long moment she stood there holding Mustafa's arm. Then she suddenly frowned and shouted, "You're lying to me!"

Mustafa shook his head adamantly, "Zaynab! Zaynab!" He was on the verge of tears, "Enough already! Come now!"

Something in his tone made Zaynab yield. He opened the building's door and dragged her inside. They climbed the stairs. At the second floor Zaynab stopped, "It's here."

Mustafa did not wait, and knocked on the door.

Not a sound was heard.

He knocked again.

Zaynab looked at him, suddenly grabbing his arm, "Mustafa, let's go. She is not here."

Mustafa banged on the door. "Open up!"

Zaynab hissed at him, "You said you talked to her!

You lied? Mustafa, did you lie?"

Mustafa banged on the door harder. Zaynab managed to pull away from him and descended the stairs when suddenly they heard a door lock, then another door lock, and a third. The door opened slightly, the door chain preventing it from opening wide.

An old, contorted face filled with wrinkles looked at Mustafa. He stepped back, taken aback by the wretched face of a witch leaning on a cane.

The old lady placed a veil across her face. Her hand shook, "Who are you?"

Mustafa looked down helplessly at Zaynab, who stood at the stairs where the old lady could not see her. He looked at his wife, "Come, Zaynab!"

"Zaynab?" Hakima said slowly, wonderment in her voice.

Zaynab stood on the bottom stair, frozen.

"Zaynab?" Hakima cleared her throat, "Zaynab Sadik?"

Mustafa nodded. "Now Hardaga. I am Mustafa," he smiled.

The old lady frowned at him, her face turned in disgust. "Is she here?"

Zaynab nodded.

The door closed and then opened again, the door chain released. "Is she here?!"

Zaynab found herself walking up the stairs, nodding like a little girl.

"Zaynab!" Hakima's face lit up when she saw Zaynab.

Zaynab did not know what to say, but Hakima fell onto her in an embrace that turned into a mutual sob. "Why?" Hakima shook her head, "Why? Why?"

Zaynab shrugged as she cried in Hakima's embrace, the old lady clutching to her firmly, painfully so.

Mustafa did not quiet understand what was going on.

"Enough, enough," Hakima mumbled, "how impolite of me, I should have invited you in. Come, my Zaynab, come."

Zaynab nodded, tears streaming down her cheeks, and followed Hakima inside. Mustafa was about to follow suit when Hakima closed the door in his face. He stood there, stunned.

Then the door opened, "Come back in two hours!"

He nodded, speechless.

The door closed and then opened for the second time. "No. Three."

When Mustafa returned nervously after three hours, Zaynab was there. She was *there*. Her eyes were red from crying but they were bright. Her smile broke through her face; a beaming, hopeful smile.

Hakima hugged her by the door and said, "Now, come back next week, you hear me? I'll be waiting for you. Don't let one week turn into six years again you fool!"

Zaynab laughed and nodded, "I promise."

Mustafa looked at her with astonishment, and then at the old lady with the cane. She stood at her door and looked at him, raising her eyebrows, her forehead wrinkled into deep lines. She nodded ever so slightly, in what he knew to be a sign of approval.

CHAPTER 24

Spring was here, and so was Zaynab. She played with her children, cleaned the house, and cooked for the first time since her father was taken. In her mind Hakima's words kept repeating themselves. "Do it for him."

"But I can't, Hakima!"

"Stop lying to me, fool! Of course you can. Do you remember Rabia or have you forgotten it all?"

Zaynab's memory instantly flashed with the story about the woman who was sold into slavery, but kept praying and praising God. One day the slave owner witnessed her bowing in prayer, surrounded by a bright light. Fearing the consequences of enslaving a saint, he released her, granting her freedom, and subsequently bringing to life one of the greatest Sufi poets, who along with Rumi and Hafez spread Sufi poetry through the world.

Hakima closed her eyes, "My Love. My joy. My hunger. My shelter. My friend! My food for the journey. My journey's End. You are my—"

Zaynab completed the words, as if in a trance, "You are my breath. My hope. My companion. My craving. My abundant wealth."

Hakima nodded, pleased. "Without You—my Life, my Love—I would never have wandered across these endless countries. You have poured out so much grace on me. Done me so many favors, given me so many gifts—"

Zaynab began crying uncontrollably.

Hakima ignored her tears, her voice penetrating Zaynab's soul, "I look everywhere! Everywhere for Your love—Then suddenly I am one with it."

Zaynab, sobbing, nodded incessantly.

Hakima exclaimed, "O Captain of my Heart! Radiant eye of yearning in my bosom! I will never be apart from You as long as I live!"

Zaynab nodded.

Hakima repeated, "'I will never be apart from You as long as I live!' Just like you are with Allah, so is your father with you, Zaynab! Can you not feel him?"

Zaynab hesitated, and then began crying again, nodding her head repeatedly.

"Then do it for him! Be his living legacy, Zaynab! Make him proud. And come back to me next week, or Allah will punish you and turn you into a pig in your next life, you hear me?"

Now, Zaynab, walking about the house, tending to the cleanliness, the food, the clothes, kept talking to herself. "Make him proud. Be his living legacy, Zaynab!"

One day Mustafa ran into the house, "Quick, turn the radio on!"

Bahriya hurried to turn the radio on, Zaynab came from the kitchen.

Mustafa grabbed Zaynab and kissed her, which was not proper to do in the presence of his sister-in-law, but he did not care. The radio blared, "This is the station of New Yugoslavia, brought to you from Belgrade, with the direction of our beloved Tito, President of the Democratic Federal Yugoslavia...."

Zaynab lifted Salih in her arms. Shouts of joy came from other houses in the street.

Within hours, soldiers were gone. They were called to the hill of Poljana to join 30,000 other men in the last stronghold of the battling Independent Croatia.

The following day, May 8th, Germany officially surrendered to the allies. Rumors circulated that Hitler had committed suicide.

People went out to celebrate in the streets of Sarajevo.

But it turned out that the celebration was too early.

Days passed and the entire continent of Europe was finally breathing the air of peace. All battles had ceased, except for one.

On the hill of Poljana thousands of members of the Independent Croatia government were fighting Tito's Partisan army.

At dinner, Izet buried his face in his hands. "The whole continent is celebrating, and only here in Yugoslavia we are still fighting!"

Mustafa reassured him. "These are only the last flames."

On May 15th, the Battle of Poljana, the last battle of the Second World War, ended with the victory of the New Social Yugoslavia Army, formerly the Partisan Army.

Six long years of war had ended.

To add to the celebrations, the following evening a knock was heard on the Hardaga door. Unafraid, Mustafa rushed downstairs.

"Abdul!"

The joy in the house was greater than words could describe. Izet rushed to buy meat, and that night everyone, including Nadia, talked into the wee hours of the night. Abdul had already heard about his father. The rumor of Ahmed Sadik being taken to Jasenovac made it all the way to a Partisan friend of his.

Mustafa, not wanting to ruin the celebration, asked quietly, "Do you think he might return?"

Abdul frowned. He did not want to tell them of the horrors he had seen when helping liberate the camp at Tenja, one of the 26 camps built by the Nazis around Yugoslavia. The skeletons, the dried blood, the mounds of bullet shells at the firing squads, the piles of corpses, it was all too much for him to recall. And rumor had it that Jasenovac was worse.

Izet quickly shifted the conversation. "With the help of Allah he'll return. Now, Abdul, eat, you probably haven't eaten properly for an entire two years!"

Zaynab sat close to her young brother, as did Nadia. Zaynab never imagined that she would be so happy to see her brother. Tears of joy kept streaming from her eyes throughout the whole night.

CHAPTER 25

Life slowly returned to the way it was before the war. Coffee shops opened again. More people came to the market.

When Zaynab walked near the Jewish quarter, she was taken aback by the ruins and neglect. A few Jewish families returned, but Joseph and Rebecca were nowhere to be found.

The old grand synagogue was in complete ruins, burnt to the ground, showing nothing of its old glory.

The Jews that did return to the city walked sheepishly, spoke quietly, avoided the looks of the Muslims and the Croats of the city.

Some Serbs returned as well. Now, under Tito's new Socialist Federal Republic of Yugoslavia, it was safe for them to return.

There was still animosity in the street, one could sense it. Serbs who returned were suspicious of both the Croats and the Muslims. During the war some Serbs had joined the Partisans, some hid in the mountains, and most fled to Belgrade. Now, returning to their city, they found many of their houses taken by Croats.

Tito, in his speeches, called for "brotherhood" and for "putting the past behind us."

But no one would, or could.

The scars were too deep. Zaynab witnessed the look in the eyes of those who returned. Haunted, constantly looking behind them expecting danger.

A few weeks after the war was over, a knock sounded on the Hardaga family door.

Mustafa, upon opening it, fell to his knees and shouted, "Allah is great!"

Joseph laughed. Rebecca offered a bouquet of Golden Lilies. Benjamin and Tova hid behind her.

Izet rushed downstairs. "What is happening?"

Mustafa kept bowing on the ground, "Allah is most merciful!"

Joseph shook his head, laughing. "Come now! Get up off the floor!"

Izet clasped his hands, "Welcome, welcome!" searching for other words he kept repeating, "Welcome! Welcome!"

Mustafa finally stood up and embraced Joseph in a strong, long embrace. As they grabbed each other's arms, smiling at one another, Joseph noticed a cloud passing on Mustafa's face. "Mustafa? Is everything alright?"

Mustafa brushed that thought away. "Of course everything is alright. You are here! Zaynab!" he shouted, "Zaynab, we have guests!" To Rebecca, who stood at the door, he said, "Well come in, Rebecca. Oh, Zaynab will be so happy!"

Zaynab, followed by Bahriya, rushed downstairs. "Rebecca! Joseph! Thank God you're here!"

Rebecca smiled. Behind her, 15-year-old Benjamin stood, looking at the ground shyly. Six-year-old Tova clung to her mother's legs.

Zaynab, always somewhat reticent, now overflowed with words, "Well come in already, why are you standing there like that, come, come, oh Benjamin! Look at you! You are a little man aren't you! And Tova, so big! Do you remember me? Do you remember our song about the bird and the spring? Izet! Go buy some Baqlava! And sweets! Rebecca, you lost weight! Are you well? Oh thank God! Where were you all this time? Why didn't you write? Joseph, you can have the factory back, can he not, Mustafa? Oh Tova, look at your beautiful braid!"

Sitting in the dining room, the celebration was great. All the food in the house found its way to the table. Salih impressed the strange guests with his recitation, and Aisha boasted of her ability to read almost all letters already. Tova and Benjamin kept clinging to their mother, but upon seeing the sweets brought to the table they filled their mouths. They hadn't eaten like that in four years.

Mustafa interrogated Joseph and Rebecca about how they managed to survive, where, how, with whom, for how long? Seriously? The Partisans did that? The good Partisans!

Mustafa boasted of his brother-in-law having fought with the Partisans. "We are very proud of Abdul. Had I not a family of my own, I would have joined as well, I'm telling you!"

Rebecca asked, "And where is Nadia? How is her school?"

Zaynab exclaimed, "She is getting very good grades. She is already in the 11th grade!"

"Oh my, how the years have passed!"

"And your father," Joseph asked, "how is our dear Ahmed faring?"

Everyone became silent.

The children noticed the look on the adult's faces.

Joseph looked at Zaynab. "Where is he?"

Mustafa took a deep breath.

Bahriya said to the children. "Go play downstairs. You can go outside, but stay near the house."

Little Aisha was excited, an approval to go outside was not an everyday occurrence. She rushed downstairs, followed by Salih and Tova. Benjamin did not want to go with the younger children, but Rebecca gave him a severe glare. He headed downstairs unwillingly.

Joseph's heart nearly missed a beat. "Tell me!"

Mustafa bit his lip and looked at Zaynab. Tears welled in her eyes.

Mustafa took a deep breath. "They took him."

Rebecca looked at Joseph.

"When? Where?" Joseph asked.

Mustafa looked at Zaynab again. "Just eight months ago, in January."

"Where to?"

Mustafa did not want to say the name.

Finally Izet uttered the word. "Jasenovac."

The subsequent wail coming from Joseph's mouth was so loud, that even the children on the street could hear him. Staring in horror and disbelief at Mustafa as Mustafa confirmed the information with a nod, Joseph began pulling on his shirt near the collar. The shirt tore in his hands.

Mustafa looked at Zaynab, who sat there with her eyes closed, trying not to cry.

Izet swallowed his saliva, surprised by Joseph's strong reaction.

Rebecca tried to console Joseph, all the while smiling politely at the four.

Joseph sobbed for a long time, shaking his head in disbelief. Eventually he sniffled and gained his composure. "Have you mourned already?"

Zaynab bit her lip. She did not want to mourn. Mourning would mean her father was gone for good. In her heart she still had some hope.

Mustafa coughed and spoke quietly. "We cannot mourn if... we do not know for certain... of his...."

Joseph, his face contorted, looked at them in amazement. "But you said he was sent to Jasenovac!"

They looked at him blankly. Joseph turned to Rebecca with a questioning look. Did they not know?

Rebecca put her hand on Joseph's shoulder. "My entire family was sent there. None returned." She wanted to say what the Partisans told them about Jasenovac. But she couldn't.

Mustafa looked at the table with all the sweets, feeling extremely uncomfortable. More than anything, he did not want his wife to become morose again. He cleared his throat and told Joseph, "Let us drink some coffee." He nodded at Bahriya and she got up to boil a new pot of coffee for them all.

Later, in the living room, Joseph took a moment to converse with Mustafa. "But you must mourn, it is a deed, a mandatory deed."

"We've mourned for four months, Joseph. We've mourned for six years, ever since this hateful war—"

"No, Mustafa!" Joseph nearly cried, "A deceased person must have the prayers and ceremonies—"

"We do not know if he indeed is—"

"Mustafa! Mustafa! They took him to Jasenovac!"

Mustafa's heart pounded, "Listen, Joseph…."

"Tomorrow, Mustafa, you and I shall go."

"Go where?"

The look on Joseph's face said it all. Mustafa shook his head. "No. Never."

CHAPTER 26

The train from Sarajevo left at seven in the morning. Mustafa and Joseph were aboard, not wanting to speak. Each was lost in his own thoughts. Rebecca stayed at the Hardaga house, along with the children. She apologized, saying, "Only until we get settled again." Zaynab said nothing, hugged her, and then held firmly to her hand. "Our home is yours. You will have your old room."

The train took two hours to reach Travnik. They changed trains to a smaller one; two and a half hours later they arrived at Gornji Ribnik. They approached the counter at the train station, Joseph explaining to the clerk behind the ticket counter that they wanted to go to Jasenovac.

The clerk's eyes nearly came out of his head. "There are no trains there. Not anymore!"

Joseph insisted, "But we must get there."

The clerk shrugged. Then he began shaking his head. "You do not want to go there."

Mustafa looked at Joseph. "He is right."

Joseph shook his head. He was determined.

An hour later they were on a truck leading toward Bravsko. The village was not too far from the camp.

From Bravsko Joseph and Mustafa walked by foot along the train tracks. The smell was foul. Small hills with green grass were scattered along both sides of the tracks. Finally, they saw tall walls and a fence surrounding what a large military camp.

In the distance they saw a man in uniform walking near the gate. Joseph stopped in his tracks, ready to launch and run back, as he saw the man wearing the frightening red and white armband, but then he glanced again and realized he was wrong. The red and white armband was that of the Red Cross.

They kept walking toward the camp. Mustafa shook his head, dismayed at the proximity he found himself to the place whose name sent shivers down people's spines. What was he doing here, following Joseph's crazy, unexplained behavior?

Joseph saw that the man in uniform had noticed them. He stood and called someone. Another man came from the booth near the gate.

Joseph waved his hands, trying to show he and Mustafa were not armed. He shouted, "Good day!"

The two men in uniform nodded. "You can't come in here," shouted the first. "It's a closed zone."

Joseph nodded but kept walking toward them. The walls were extremely tall with curled wires at the top. No one could have climbed up and gotten out of here.

"Gentlemen," Joseph said, extending his hand as he approached the two men, with Mustafa walking behind him. "I am Joseph, this is my friend Mustafa. We have come all the way from Sarajevo."

The man shook his head. "Have you heard me, Mr. Joseph? This is a closed zone, not open for civilians."

Joseph nodded, "Of course, we do not wish to enter."

"Oh," the man said.

Joseph noticed the man's Swiss accent and said, "Do you prefer speaking French? Je parle français, je voulais seulement...."

The man's face softened, and they switched to speaking in French. Mustafa, who did not understand, waited patiently.

The man in uniform introduced himself as Jean and the other man as Louis.

Joseph put his hand on Mustafa's shoulder as he spoke to the two men.

The men's faces turned into frowns and they shook their heads.

Mustafa whispered to Joseph, "What are you telling them?"

Joseph did not respond.

The first man, Jean, took a deep breath and asked Joseph a question.

"Sadik. Ahmed Sadik," Joseph answered.

The second man, Louis, asked another question.

Joseph turned to Mustafa, "Do you remember the date he was taken?"

"January. January fourth."

Louis asked Mustafa in Bosnian, "Of this year?"

"Yes, 1945."

Louis looked at Jean for approval. Jean nodded and said, "We'll look. We don't usually do it, but we'll do it for you. Yet you'll have to wait outside."

Joseph nodded. He and Mustafa remained by the gate made of thick metal rods and barbed wire. The view offered them a glimpse of the inside. Long, narrow huts were built in rows to the horizon. It must have been a huge camp. A hill on the left was green, almost picturesque. It felt unthinkable that at this beautiful hillside man would turn into a killing machine.

They eventually sat on the ground by the booth.

They did not say a word.

Mustafa's thoughts turned to his father-in-law. How he was taken in the midst of winter, at night. What cruelty! Snatched from his family, from his two daughters. It was then that he realized that he knew Joseph through Ahmed.

"My father-in-law," Mustafa said to Joseph, "introduced the two of us, didn't he?"

"Yes, a decade ago," Joseph said.

Mustafa nodded. They said nothing, each was lost in his own thoughts. Though it was only September, the sky began to form clouds. Cold wind blew on their faces. A foul smell followed.

A few minutes later Louis came out. Mustafa and Joseph stood up.

Louis took a deep breath, and spoke to Joseph, though he knew that Mustafa was the son-in-law. "Ahmed Sadik, born 1884? Taken from Sarajevo?"

Mustafa nodded.

It began drizzling.

"He arrived here on January fifth, 1945."

Silence followed.

Mustafa mumbled, "And?"

Louis said nothing.

Joseph murmured, "Firing squads?"

Louis shook his head, "No."

Mustafa pressed, "How?"

Louie looked at the two of them. "Come inside."

Joseph and Mustafa sat by the desk. Louis and Jean brought them coffee. In the office there was a third man.

Louis sat with a thick pile of papers, all hand written with crowded lines. Names, numbers.

Mustafa and Joseph did not drink the coffee.

It was raining outside.

"Tell us," Joseph asked. "There were rumors about gas...."

Louis shook his head. "Not here." He looked at Jean, who then looked at the other man and nodded. The other man took a wooden box, pulled something out and threw it on the table.

A small knife attached to a wristband lay on the table.

Joseph thought it was a joke. But the look on the men's faces told him it was not.

"The Croats called it Srbosjek," said Jean. "Srbosjek. Meaning, 'Serb-cutter.'"

Mustafa shook his head in amazement. "With this?"

Jean pointed at the wooden box, in which dozens of these knifes lay. The leather straps attached to the knifes were all red. From use.

Joseph wetted his lips. "But they could not have possibly killed so many with these—"

Jean interrupted him, pulling a list from a brown leather binder, and read, "Transport of 29 August 1942, prison guard Ante Zrinusic-Sipka: 600. Prison guard Mile Friganovic: 1,100. Prison guard Petar Brzica: 1,360."

Mustafa got up, "I'm going outside."

Joseph called after him, "But it's raining."

Mustafa said nothing and went out into the rain.

Joseph hesitated, wanting to go with Mustafa. But he had another question. "Could I please look at the transports from Sarajevo in winter 1941?"

Louis looked at Jean, who nodded.

Louis left the room. He returned a few minutes later with a wooden box. "Begin here."

On the many sheets of paper, Joseph read the crowded rows of names, written in meticulous handwriting. Names. More names. He knew so many of them; there was the name of Julia Batino, the famous women's rights activist. And the famous sculptor, Slavko Brill. The chief rabbi, Mavro Frankfurter. The head of the hospital, Slavko Hirsch. The famous chess master, Izidor Gross, who used to represent Yugoslavia in chess competitions. The names kept going and going. Memories came with each.

Then he saw them.

His sister-in-law.

Her husband.

Their children.

His parents-in-law.

His aunt and uncle.

All of the names were there.

His entire family.

His only thought was that he should have saved them. Or had gone with them.

Jean, Louis and the third man, Philippe, stood in silence. Soon Jean pulled out a cigarette and offered one to Joseph. Joseph, who did not usually smoke, took the cigarette and smoked in silence.

It stopped raining. Joseph thanked them and walked outside. Mustafa stood there, his coat wet, his eyes red.

They thanked the three men. Jean said, "I'll walk with you to Bravsko."

On the way to the village, as they walked, Jean said in French, "We did not know what we'd come to. They said these were work camps. This was a killing camp."

Joseph said nothing.

"How could people do it?" Jean mumbled. "How could they?"

Joseph said nothing again. In the four years of fleeing he had seen the other side, too. The Partisans doing horrible things to their captives.

Jean continued speaking. "The files show 20,000 Jews were killed here. As well as 20,000 gypsies."

He kept reporting the data, as if speaking about it might make it more comprehensible. "Muslims, too. Some 12,000. But the majority were Serbs."

Joseph was surprised. "The majority?"

"Oh yes. Some 50,000. All slaughtered around the camp."

Joseph asked, "Around the camp?"

Jean pointed at the small hills surrounding them

on both sides of the tracks. Joseph suddenly saw body parts sticking from the grass. He regretted asking.

They arrived at Sarajevo that night with the last train. Joseph was relieved. So was Mustafa.

Rebecca hugged Joseph that night in bed. "What did you see?"

Zaynab asked Mustafa the same question.

Both men said nothing. For decades neither of them would say anything.

CHAPTER 27

Zaynab was hesitant about Joseph's instigation that a proper Muslim mourning period, a *Hidaad*, be held for her father. She did not want to bring up old pain, pain that was too fresh to be tampered with.

Abdul also resisted, saying, "We do not need a proper mourning. We mourn daily."

But Joseph insisted. And the new imam, whom Mustafa consulted with, said that even without Ahmed's actual burial, proper *Hidaad* mourning should take place.

The Hardaga house turned into a mourning house for three days and nights. People from the community came to share their condolences.

Three brothers, merchants from Mostar, who saw the notice in the Mostar newspaper, travelled all the way in the train to pay respects. Ahmed, they said, used to sell them furniture for their store. "An honest man," they said, "Allah will embrace him unto His kingdom."

An old shoemaker that Zaynab recognized from the store next to Ahmed's, came the second morning and said nothing, but he stayed until evening, nodding his head all-knowingly.

Men came from the merchant's association, and praised Ahmed to his children. "He cared not only about his own business, but about the cleanliness of the neighborhood, the good relationships between merchants. All public matters were also his own."

Zaynab, Abdul, and Nadia learned that their late father was also an arbiter. Two men came, both of whom had their grocery stores in the same neighborhood. "Ahmed made us begin the meeting with a prayer," said one of them. The other looked at Abdul, "He then told us to say one good thing about the other. We sat there in silence, but he waited. The meeting was over within half an hour, after we had gone to several people asking for mediation."

Abdul nodded, "Where did he meet you?"

"At the back of his furniture store."

On the third day came a Jewish man and his wife. They seemed very timid. "We are not sure if we came to the right place."

Joseph, who sat among the men, hurried to greet them. "Are you here for the mourning of the blessed Ahmed Sadik?"

"Well," said the man, who introduced himself as Izidor, "we are not certain. We were aided by a man called Ahmed Sadik, but it was in Konic."

Joseph's eyes widened.

Izidor continued. "We were returning from Dubrovnik to Sarajevo, and had to change trains in Konic. There Mr. Sadik approached us and asked us where we were going. We told him, and he said that we must not come here, that the transports had taken all the Jews. He gave us shelter in his room while he searched for IDs for us."

Abdul, sitting with the older Muslim men, got up, "Hello. Welcome. I am Ahmed's son."

"Our condolences," said Izidor. "Was your father in Konic in the winter of 1942?"

Abdul shrugged. "I think so. Here," he pointed to a photo of Ahmed placed on the table at the back of the room.

Izidor saw the picture and began sobbing.

"We owe our lives, and our children's lives, to your father."

At the end of the Hidaad mourning there was a different atmosphere in the Hardaga house. Before there was an odd silence with an underlying feeling of victimhood. Now, there was pride. Ahmed Sadik proved to be not only loved by the community, but he was also a hero.

Joseph searched for a home to rent. He also petitioned the government to receive back the ownership of his factory's machines.

A night before Joseph and Rebecca were to move out of the Hardaga's house into their new rented apartment, Mustafa announced a special dinner to celebrate their new home. At the dinner table, which had a special amount of meat and sweets, Mustafa said, "You know, Joseph, Rebecca, you always have our home as your home. Our families are intertwined forever."

Joseph offered a toast. "To better times," he said and raised his glass. "To life!"

"To life!" everyone toasted.

Abdul added, "And to make proud our beloved ones that have gone."

CHAPTER 28

Life slowly returned to how it was before the war. At least to a certain extent. The cinema across the street opened, showing Russian films that were translated into Serbian; old Turk films were less in vogue nowadays.

Tito's posters were hung everywhere. People were proud of the new Socialist Yugoslavia. Old schools were reopened, including the four Serbian schools in town. The Jewish school opened as well, but instead of seven classes in each grade, it only had one.

From the 10,000 Jews who lived in Sarajevo before the war, some 1,000 managed to survive. It was little, but in comparison to other communities that perished entirely, Sarajevo was well off. The synagogue was slowly rebuilt. The Jews called what they had gone through during the war 'The Catastrophe.'

While many had hoped that the end of the war meant the end of anti-Semitism, truth proved otherwise. In Krakow, in August of 1945, months after the liberation, the small Jewish congregation gathering in a synagogue was attacked, and the synagogue was set on fire.

In the small Polish town of Kielce, Jewish refugees were attacked by Polish civilians, soldiers, as well as police officers, after a blood libel, claiming Jews had killed Christian boys to use their blood for Jewish rituals. Forty-two Jews were killed.

The news rattled Sarajevo's small Jewish community. Though the numbers of casualties in Kielce was small, the mere fact that such a pogrom would take place after the end of the war shocked everyone.

No one dared to speak about the war, and the camps, and the killings, and the lost family members. It was out of limits for the small community of survivors who were trying to heal. No, not a word could be spoken about the atrocities of the war. But after the Kielce pogrom, all that the Jews of Sarajevo could speak about was the details of the pogrom: the exact number of adults, of children, what the police did or did not do, and most importantly, what it meant.

Joseph and Rebecca adjusted to their new apartment, and soon invited the entire Hardaga family to dinner. After dinner Mustafa lowered his voice and expressed his amazement. "The Poles are simply not God-fearing. Muslims would never do such things."

But then, at the end of that year, news came of another pogrom. This time in Libya's capital, Tripoli. This was a Muslim nation, a Muslim city, with a

Jewish community dating back hundreds of years.

Joseph was heartbroken. The news of the Tripoli pogrom was all that everyone in the Jewish community could talk about. In the synagogue, prayer was pushed aside as the traumatized small Sarajevo community tried to comprehend the reason for the attack.

The pogrom in Tripoli lasted three days.

Mustafa came to the factory in the late evening, as Joseph prepared to close the door. Sixteen-year-old Benjamin was there with him.

Mustafa seemed unhinged. "Joseph, have you heard?"

Joseph smiled bitterly. Had he heard? That was all that everyone, including Rebecca, were speaking about. First Krakow, then Kielce, now Tripoli. The world was a dangerous place for Jews.

Mustafa mumbled, "I was… astonished, this is not Islam, I cannot understand…."

"Mustafa, my brother, don't be bothered. This was a mob. I hear there is hunger in Tripoli."

"Hunger does not justify killing!" Mustafa shouted.

Benjamin looked at Mustafa.

Mustafa shook his head and fell into a chair by the door. "What is happening to the world?"

Joseph put his hand on Mustafa's shoulder, as if Mustafa was the one to be consoled. "Don't you worry, it's all temporary. This too shall pass."

Benjamin thought otherwise, however. In the small Sarajevo Jewish community, young men and women spent evenings talking together. In Palestine, the British Mandate was losing steam. Since the end of the war there were rumors of the British leaving. The small Jewish population would be the responsibility of the local Arabs. A second Holocaust seemed around the corner.

"We must not let this happen," said Moshe, a friend of Benjamin, who had spent the war years hiding in an Orthodox convent near Belgrade. His entire family was killed in Jasenovac. He was the only one remaining.

Benjamin was silent. So were the others.

Moshe clutched his fist. "Without defending our people there, our nation is doomed! Where else can we go to? To Kielce? To Krakow? To Tripoli? Or to America, that has closed its gates to us? Where?"

Along with a couple of other friends, Moshe made contacts with a budding Jewish organization called The Haganah, or "defence" in Hebrew. The Haganah recruited Jewish refugees who survived the camps, and trained them in armed combat.

Moshe was told that the youth of Sarajevo could begin working on physical training, discipline, and moral code. No weapons would be sent for training.

Yet.

In the Hardaga house, Zaynab thanked God everyday that the war was over. Sarajevo was rebuilding, the market was vivacious again, and a spur of life was felt everywhere.

Everywhere—that is, except in a small apartment not far away from the clock tower, where an 80-year-old lady slowly became sicker and weaker.

Zaynab had been visiting Hakima since the end of the war, consistently, at least once a week. The meetings with Hakima were always invigorating, and would leave Zaynab pondering such diverse things as Muslim law, women's suffrage, Sufi poetry and world history. Zaynab always looked forward to her meetings with Hakima, who was like a mother to her. And a father. And a counselor.

Zaynab did not know much about Hakima's private life. Why hadn't Hakima ever married? Or had she? Was she a widow? Did she have children? Had they died? Was she born in Sarajevo? How old was she exactly?

Hakima never shared words about herself, and Zaynab never dared to ask. This proved odd at night when Mustafa asked her about the meeting she had that day with Hakima.

"What did you talk about?"

"Oh, we read some poetry together. We compared Rumi to Hafez and Saadi. You must read this poem by Hafez called—"

"Does she have children? How come no one comes to visit her?"

"I don't know."

"Zaynab, you should ask her! You always say how open she is, and modern…."

"Yes, you are right."

But Zaynab would never ask.

Two summers after Zaynab had begun to visit Hakima, the old lady started coughing. It was a hot summer, and the cough was odd. Hakima brushed it off, and after each coughing-fit she would hurriedly whisper the rest of the sentence she was saying earlier, as if nothing happened.

Zaynab became worried. Hakima refused to see a doctor, saying, "I can take care of myself. Can you find me a doctor who has read Avicenna's 40 books on medicine? No. I read them, I know it all. Did you know that all European medicine is based on his writings, all from the eleventh century! He lived in Persia and was quite a polymath…."

One day Zaynab did a daring thing. She went to Hakima's and brought with her, Dr. Teodora Krajewskathe, the first female doctor in Sarajevo.

Hakima threw a fit when she saw the lady in doctor's clothes, and only after reprimanding and scolding Zaynab for nearly half an hour, did she allow the quiet doctor to examine her.

The woman checked Hakima's heartbeat,

breathing and temperature, and asked her several questions.

Hakima exclaimed, "It's just a cold, a regular cold!"

"How long have you had this 'cold?'" asked the doctor.

"About six weeks now."

The doctor took a deep breath. "I'm afraid you have whooping cough."

Hakima frowned, "As in *Bordetella pertussis*?"

The doctor looked surprised. "Are you a nurse?"

Hakima snorted. "Every child should know this. Isn't this what Sokmen Artuqid died from, in Turkey in the 12th century?"

The doctor mumbled, "I... do not know..." she turned to Zaynab and said, "Can I have a minute with you outside?"

When Zaynab returned, her face was pale.

"She told you I'm dying!" Hakima exclaimed.

"No, she didn't," Zaynab said.

Hakima squinted, examining Zaynab's expression. Zaynab looked overwhelmed. Hakima nodded and closed her eyes. "Very well."

Zaynab cried the whole night. Here she had finally found a person who understood her, who valued her brain, who listened to her concerns about her children and always gave a wise advice. Here was this brilliant woman whom Zaynab had nearly lost, and now the doctor said that she'd be lucky if she survived two more weeks.

Zaynab protested. "There must be something we can do!"

It was too late for a vaccination, the doctor explained, and antibiotics would probably kill her. She should keep warm and breathe fresh air.

Zaynab was crushed.

Mustafa did not know what to do or say. He feared another wave of depression from his wife.

Zaynab began visiting Hakima daily in the mornings, bringing little Salih, who was too young to go to school, with her. In the beginning, the boy was afraid of the scary-looking woman. But soon he took a liking to her, especially when she commanded his mother to give him candies.

Zaynab saw with concern that each day Hakima felt weaker. She lost her appetite, and her face became whiter. She did not look well. She needed help sitting up on her bed and walking to the bathroom. The cane was not enough anymore.

Zaynab brought a wooden walker with her. Hakima refused to use it, shouting with her scruffy voice, "What am I? You think I'm an old lady!"

But soon Hakima began using it; she had no other option.

Zaynab feared leaving the old woman alone during

the nights.

"Could I?" Zaynab asked Mustafa.

Mustafa looked at his wife's big eyes. "Do what you need to."

Zaynab moved in with Hakima, seeing the lady who once was a powerhouse slowly wilt before her eyes.

Two days after Zaynab moved in with Hakima, a knock was heard at the door. Zaynab hurried to open, but Hakima told her, "It's probably a mistake, don't get it."

Zaynab opened it anyway. She gasped.

Before her stood a crowd of women that filled the hallway down the stairs. Wafaa, who she hadn't seen in years, stood there, smiling, with a bouquet of flowers. There was Aminah, and Khadijah, and Jasmine, Maryan, Lubna...everyone was there.

Hakima coughed from her bed, "Who is it? What's the silence, Zaynab?!"

Zaynab began tearing up. All the weight on her shoulders for the past days and weeks... She saw all the smiling faces and turned to Wafaa, "How did you know?"

"Your aunt Surayda told me." She shrugged. "I thought we should gather like the good old days."

Zaynab nodded, her chin quivering.

Hakima somehow sat up, pulled the walker toward

her, and began walking to the door.

Zaynab whispered to Wafaa and the other ladies, "I am not sure how she will receive you all, she's been…."

"Who is it, Zaynab?!" Hakima shouted, her body shaking. She came to the door, and her mouth opened.

"Hakima!" Wafaa called, followed by the other ladies. "Surprise!"

"Allah shall curse you!" Hakima said, wetting her lips, trying to adjust her night-gown. She felt sloppy and quite ugly. "Allah will punish you for coming and disturbing an old lady…." Her eyes teared up as she looked at all the faces, "Now come inside, you fools!"

They boiled tea, and the women filled the little apartment with boisterous laughter and glee. They all concealed the concern they felt for one who was their great teacher.

Hakima surprised them all by remembering not only their names, but the names of their husbands and children. Many had had new children born. A few of the older ladies had grandchildren too. Hakima asked for the names of the newborn, each time nodding her head, as if blessing the the new soul emerging on this earth. "Very good," she said, "very good."

The women also tried to conceal the immense feeling of guilt. During the war years each tried to somehow take care of her own family. The shortage of food, the high prices, the closed schools…. Jasmine, one of the youngest women, asked, "How did you survive the war, Hakima?"

Everyone looked at Hakima. This was a question that was on everyone's mind.

"I survived. What was there not to survive? My house was not bombed, though at times I sure wanted it to be and bury me with it."

Silence followed. Uncomfortable smiles. Khadijah asked, "But food? How did you manage to get food?"

"There is this man, Abu-Sufyan, from the market," Hakima said and smiled sheepishly. "He liked to come and… talk. So he came every other day and brought something. I did not need much."

The women nodded. For most of them, it was their first time in Hakima's apartment, and the endless number of books from floor to ceiling was difficult to grasp.

The conversation turned into gossip about how the vendors in the market were trying to outsmart the customers, and how some of the Serb ladies who had returned since the end of the war began to dress in a promiscuous way, showing shoulders and—"

"Enough!" said Hakima. "Wafaa, bring me the Hafez book. We shall read something together."

Khadijah, one of the elders among them, protested. "But Hafez wasn't a woman!"

Everyone giggled. Everyone but Hakima. She stared straight at Khadijah. "We should not discriminate against him for not being a woman."

"Of course, Hakima," answered Khadijah, "I was just kidding."

"From this kind of kidding wars begin." Hakima said and glared at 65-year-old Khadijah, who lowered her gaze. Hakima was still Hakima.

Hakima opened the small book, flipping through the pages, her fingers quick and experienced. "I caught the happy virus last night," she read. Everyone became silent. The words seemed ominous.

"I caught the happy virus last night. When I was out singing beneath the stars. It is remarkably contagious," she read and smiled, "so, kiss me!"

Smiles appeared on the women's faces. Some clapped. Zaynab bit her tongue to stop herself from crying.

Hakima sat up in her bed. She looked reawakened. She flipped through the pages of the book. "Oh, this is suitable."

She cleared her throat. The coughs, magically enough, were gone for the moment.

"Leave the familiar world for a while. Let your senses and body stretch out. Like a welcomed season onto the meadow and onto the shores and hills."

The way Hakima read, articulating each word, devouring each sentence, was spellbinding. "Open up to the Roof! Make a new watermark on your excitement, on your love! Like a blooming night flower, bestow your vital fragrance of happiness upon our intimate assembly."

Hakima looked at the women and then continued reading. "Change rooms in your mind for a day! All the hemispheres in existence lie beside an equator in your heart. Greet Yourself, in your thousand other forms, as you mount the hidden tide and... travel back home."

Hakima's face filled with pleasure, as if just tasting a sweet dessert. She took a deep breath, "Now, let's talk about this poem. Zaynab? What did it make you feel?"

The women decided to take shifts to be with Hakima by her bedside. They each brought food with them. Delicious food, that the small apartment had not seen in decades. Hakima's appetite was limited, but the food brought her comfort, as did the company.

Bahriya was happy to have Zaynab back home. The few days of being in charge of all the children, the cooking and keeping the household all alone tired her. Salih and Aisha were thrilled to have Mama back home, as was Mustafa.

But Zaynab kept returning, at least once a day, to Hakima's apartment. She summoned Dr. Teodora again, and the doctor's prognosis was the same. She was surprised at how Hakima continued to survive.

Hakima slept longer and longer each day, apart from sudden cough spurts. Her body ached. She moaned and groaned. And whenever she could utter a word she would always say, "Go away, I can manage on my own."

A week later her state worsened. She had not eaten for two days, and her fingertips turned blue. Her face had a tinge of grey.

She had a hard time breathing. The women put hot compresses on her chest, and massaged her hands and feet. Khadijah insisted on putting hot pepper on her feet and chest. "This will burn," she promised.

But Hakima did not even feel it. Khadijah's expression said it all. She had never seen a person not scream from the heat. But Hakima's body seemed to lose all senses.

The following day Hakima took her last breath. She was 81 years old.

The small apartment had never seen so many people as it did during the Hidaad mourning. Mourners came from all over the community. The imam of the small mosque came, and recalled the day when Hakima, then in her forties, insisted on opening a "Quran class for girls."

He immediately gave his blessing and offered the mosque for its weekly meetings. "She has raised a generation of intelligent women versed in our holy book," he said.

The women found no reason to tell him about the extra-curricular nature the classes Hakima took. The Qur'an was often referred to, but calling the classes Qur'an classes was not precisely the truth. It was a celebration of all of Islam, of Muslim women, of womanhood, and of the human race. It was a celebration of life.

The women stayed in the apartment late into the evening. No one wanted to go home. They read poetry, and tried to make impressions of Hakima. At first they were sheepish about it, but soon laughter swept them all, and each attempted to do an even more dramatic imitation, filled with pauses, eye glares, and scary looks. They laughed and cried.

Each morning they all met by the fresh grave at the old Muslim cemetery in Sarajevo to leave new flowers. Then they walked together back to Hakima's old apartment. They wore no jewelry or ostentatious clothes, as was the tradition for mourners. But somehow they did not feel overly sad. They felt a part of something bigger than them. And they felt grateful. Grateful for having known such a great soul.

A few men came to visit the Hidaad as well. A few vendors from the market, a few religious scholars, and two university professors. But all the men felt intimidated by the large crowd of women, and within a few minutes excused themselves and left, blessing the mourners with cordial condolences, and then rushing down the stairs.

When no guests came, the women, feeling like teenagers, would lock the door and unveil themselves, talking and sharing how they first came to meet Hakima. The elder women in the group spoke of Hakima's extraordinary beauty. She wasn't beautiful in the common sense, they said, but she had presence that was hard to ignore. "I kept looking at her," Khadijah admitted, "and I felt that she could see through me."

The other women agreed. "She always knew things from the other world."

"Now she is in the other world. She must be happy."

When the third evening of the Hidaad came, the women were morose. These days had been a blessing. No men, no household to take care of, no children or grandchildren running around. Only good food and friendship.

"We must keep meeting," said Wafaa.

"Yes!" Lubna said, "We must! I don't want it to be another six years again before we get together like this!"

"Zaynab," Khadijah said, "you should lead the class now."

The women cheered, but Zaynab's face turned red, "I'm not Hakima! I can't possibly—"

"We'll help you!" Wafaa called. The women were enthused about it. "We will."

A few shrugged, thinking that this was just a passing excitement that would wear off in a few days or weeks. Little did they know that this same group, with some minor alterations, was to last nearly five more decades, witnessing passing of members, and embracing   daughters,   nieces,   and   even granddaughters.

CHAPTER 29

"But Joseph, Sarajevo is your home!"

Mustafa looked indignant. Three years passed since the end of the war. Everything seemed better, did it not? The factory was doing well, selling great amounts of pipes to the government. Why did Joseph want to leave for Palestine of all places?

Joseph shrugged. They stood at the entrance to the factory. Mustafa shook his head, "Is it because of Benjamin? Write to him to come back here at once! He'll listen to you, you're his father!"

Joseph tried to smile. Mustafa simply did not understand. Benjamin had left a year earlier to help the Jewish community in the Holy Land prepare for when the British left. The recent UN partition plan proved Benjamin was right. Violence spread through Palestine in new records. Muslims were fighting Jews. Jews were fighting Muslims. The inevitable seemed to be happening, and all hell was breaking loose.

Mustafa continued, "What do you have to look for there? That's the Levant, the Middle East, people are backwards there. Sarajevo is in the heart of Europe. In Palestine there'll be no demand for pipes, only for camels!"

Joseph took a deep breath. Rebecca also had similar fears, and they were torn as to what to do or where to go. But so many families had already left Sarajevo for the Holy Land. Only there, they promised, could they walk erect, could they be protected.

Not that protection was offered now. There was a full scale war, with several Arab armies fighting what was perceived as Jewish colonialism that would only be a worse replacement of the British colonialism.

And Benjamin was in the midst of it all.

Mustafa was upset when Benjamin left Sarajevo a year earlier. "You are not a fighter," he told Benjamin, who sheepishly came to say goodbye to the family that hid him as a child seven years earlier. "Benjamin, you should not fight! The Jews are God-fearing!"

But all that Benjamin could say is, "I must, Mustafa. I must." That was the phrase the young man repeated, "I must. I must."

Mustafa was profoundly hurt then. But now, standing in front of the man who had rented his factory for years, the man who was like a brother to him, his heart broke.

"Why, Joseph, why? Why throw away everything you've built? The government is now your largest client. You can't throw that away!"

Joseph did not want to say, 'Yes, the government

is my largest client, but it forces me to sell to them at cost, and constantly threatens to nationalize the factory. There isn't certainty here either.'

He said nothing.

"Joseph, have I done anything bad to you? Have I upset you?"

"Mustafa!" Joseph said, "You are my brother, my family! But there, in Palestine, I also have a family!"

"Call him back here! Command him! He'll listen to you—"

"Not only my son, also my cousin from Belgrade has moved there. And an offshoot of the family that escaped Berlin before the war are settled in Jerusalem, and wrote to me that they could help."

"Jerusalem is under siege!" Mustafa cried, "I read of casualties every day! You couldn't have possibly survived this war here just to go and..." Mustafa could not utter the words.

Joseph felt as if he could simply say nothing to convince Mustafa. He sighed and said, "I wanted to give you notice as early as I could."

Mustafa's face betrayed how hurt he felt. "Very well." Joseph was treating him like a landlord. "I don't need a notice. You are free to leave when you wish."

"But Mustafa, I don't want to....,"

"I'm tired. I'm not feeling well. We'll continue talking another time. It's not like you're leaving tomorrow, right?"

Joseph, Rebecca and Tova remained in Sarajevo for another year. The news of the establishment of the State of Israel made them rejoice, but the constant reports of casualties reminded them of the war.

Benjamin wrote a long letter to them detailing the battles with the Jordanian forces. The exhaustion, the casualties. His friend from Sarajevo, Moshe, was killed in the battle of liberating Jerusalem from Arab siege. He was buried near the battlefield, along with eight other young men, six of whom were Holocaust survivors.

Finally, in the beginning of 1949, Israel signed armistice agreements with Egypt, Lebanon, Jordan and Syria. Peace seemed to be around the corner.

Joseph was still hesitant about uprooting his small family and leaving for the new nation in the heart of the Middle East. He spoke little Hebrew, and had no illusions as to the state of industry there.

Yet Sarajevo seemed like a graveyard. Passing through the newly rebuilt Jewish quarter, he could not help thinking of all the people who had perished. This building was where his sister-in-law lived with her husband and children. This building was where Rebecca's aunt used to live. This is where the famous artist who married Joseph's best friend's sister lived. The neighborhood felt like a memorial.

In addition, the few families who composed the Jewish community were all leaving. Some received visas to Britain. One family received a lucky invitation from America. And a few families had already left for the newly founded Israel.

Joseph remained on the fence for another year. Benjamin enrolled in university in Jerusalem, and was not planning on returning to Sarajevo. "Father," he wrote, "your place is here, with your people. In Jerusalem."

Eventually it was the state that helped Joseph make the final decision. With growing demands on the new socialist order, Tito's government nationalized the large factories. Joseph's was one of the last. Seeing the officials coming, wearing government uniforms from the Ministry of Commerce, Joseph knew.

The following month Mustafa and Zaynab escorted Rebecca, Tova and Joseph to the Sarajevo train station, from where the Kabilio family was to take a train to Belgrade, then an airplane to Tel Aviv. The women were warm to one another, Rebecca and Zaynab embraced and cried in each other's arms. The men were reticent, each cocooned in his own hurt. They shook hands. Mustafa said, "Farewell. Have a safe journey."

Joseph thanked him. "For everything, Mustafa. You are like a brother to me."

Mustafa pointed at the train at the platform. "Go, you don't want to miss the train."

CHAPTER 30

Life in Sarajevo continued. The Museum of Sarajevo underwent construction and reopened. Many residential blocks were built in the new parts of town, copying communist building style, accommodating the growing population of the city.

A new source of pride opened the year that Joseph and Rebecca left. 5,263 bound manuscripts in Arabic, Persian, Turkish, and Hebrew, along with thousands of Ottoman-era documents, were gathered in one unique, world-class museum. The Oriental Institute brought much pride to Sarajevo, as well as an opportunity for researchers from around the world to look at the ancient manuscripts.

As for the Hardaga family, little Aisha, now in fifth grade, brought much pride to the family by winning a school competition in Qur'anic knowledge. Mustafa kept saying to the proud relatives, "It's not from me! It's from her mother!"

Abdul was beginning second grade in school. He was slower than others, but Zaynab spent hours with him, perfecting his knowledge of the alphabet.

Mustafa wanted more children. Zaynab did not. "I have already so much work with the two of them, and with leading the Wednesday study group, can you imagine having a crying baby around?"

Mustafa did not push it. "Whatever you wish," he said. But he dreamed of having a new baby.

Once every few weeks they received a letter from Israel. Joseph would open each letter with "My dear brother and sister."

Every few letters, Joseph would also attach a picture. Tova in scout's uniforms. Benjamin's graduation from university. A professional photo of the four family members in a studio.

Zaynab would send pictures back. A photo from Nadia's fancy wedding. A photo of Abdul near the furniture store he opened in Belgrade. A photo of Aisha winning a competition in school.

Zaynab wrote back on both of their behalfs. Mustafa had no patience. "Write to them that we are well, and that the factory awaits them when they decide to come back!"

Zaynab did not write that. She wished them health, success and prosperity. She shared a few anecdotes of what the children were doing, how Aisha was reciting Qur'an passages, how Salih was improving with his reading and enjoyed the new comics books that Abdul brought from Belgrade.

The years passed quickly. Aisha became a teenager, and Salih an energetic child. Zaynab cleaned the house, preparing excitedly for Ramadan. Her little brother was coming back for the last days of Ramadan to celebrate Eid with the family.

Abdul, who had moved to Belgrade, came with good news. He was marrying next summer. A good Muslim woman, he said, from Belgrade. The joy was great. Zaynab clapped her hands together, "You couldn't have brought me better news!"

On the second day of Eid, the entire family went to visit the cemeteries, along with the whole community. This was one of the only times that Zaynab allowed herself to cry. Aisha and Salih were taken aback, seeing their 34-year-old mother fall on a grave and cry. Big letters were written on the grave. Aisha Sadik.

Then they proceeded to a large grave in another cemetery. This one had many flowers on it. As Zaynab, Abdul and Nadia fell onto the grave, Salih asked his father, "Babo, is that where grandpa is buried?"

"No, son," Mustafa answered with a heavy heart. "This is just a place to remember all the anonymous casualties."

"Where is grandpa buried, then?" Salih pressed.

Mustafa could not answer.

Joseph, though far away in Israel, kept in touch with

the small Jewish community of Sarajevo. He and other Sarajevo-born immigrants in Israel collected money for a monument to be built. They wanted a memory for all the families who were lost in the Holocaust.

The list of family names was long and depressing. Nevertheless, in meetings in Jerusalem and in Tel Aviv, Joseph collected the names, and sent the list along with the money to Sarajevo. The rabbi in Sarajevo met with the mayor, offering the list as well as the collected money.

On a spring day, the monument with all the names was unveiled at a city ceremony. Joseph wrote to Mustafa and Zaynab that he wished he could have come. He urged them to go and visit the monument, and to look at the names beginning with the letter S.

Puzzled by Joseph's urging, Mustafa visited the monument. He came back home with teary eyes. All hard feelings he had toward Joseph for leaving Sarajevo melted. He told Zaynab, "Come. Come now!"

The children stayed with Bahriya, and Zaynab hurried with Mustafa. "What is it?"

Finally, when they arrived at the monument, she saw it. Her father's name. "Sadik, Ahmed."

The following letter to Joseph was filled with both gratitude and reprimand. "Thank you from the bottom of our hearts," Zaynab wrote, "you shouldn't have!" and again, "We are most grateful," and "really, this was too much. I imagine it took much work to create the large monument. How could you hide this from us?!"

In their tiny apartment in Jerusalem, Joseph was filled with glee as he read the letter proudly to Rebecca.

He wrote back, "This is the least we could do. We owe our lives to the kindness of your family."

In 1957 two celebrations were celebrated, and many letters exchanged. In Israel, Benjamin married the daughter of a family that had lived in Jerusalem for 12 generations. "We are honored," Joseph wrote to Mustafa and Zaynab, "to have our family tied with this family. The bride, Malkah, is wonderful. We wish the young couple many years of joy."

In Sarajevo, a surprise came to the Hardaga family when Zaynab, now 39-years-old, became pregnant. Mustafa was ecstatic, "I knew it! Allah wanted to bless us with another child!"

Zaynab was apprehensive, thinking herself too old to carry a successful birth. "Pray for us," she wrote to Joseph and Rebecca, "that the child will be healthy, and the birth easy."

And it was. A beautiful baby girl was born to the Hardaga family. Her name was Aida.

"A blessing took place in our house," Mustafa's shaky handwriting told Joseph in a short letter, "a baby girl by the name of Aida. She is healthy, and we are thankful to Allah for remembering us."

Rebecca hurried to sew a tiny baby dress for little Aida. The parcel, arriving in Sarajevo just as Aida turned three months old, brought much delight to Mustafa and Zaynab, who, as new parents, suddenly felt much younger.

Two years later another parcel made its way across the Mediterranean, this time in the opposite direction. "Dear sister and brother, you must be so pleased to be grandparents now! Who could have thought of Benjamin as a father! I still remember his shy glance when we first met. Please send him and Malkah our best wishes. We love the name Gabriel, as it is also the name of the angel who brought our prophet the message of the Qur'an. What a pretty name. Attached is a suit made for baby Gabriel by Bahriya (I myself am not particularly talented with the sewing sticks, as you may remember, Rebecca!) Bahriya sends her love, and so do Izet and everyone."

The years kept passing quickly. "Time flies, does it not?" wrote Joseph to Zaynab and Mustafa.

"Yes, it does. We are looking for a proper match for Aisha. She, however, thinks us to be outdated, and that matches are a matter of history. Many young ladies in the community prefer to choose their own husbands. My mother would have strongly disapproved. How could they know whether they fit or not, based only on a temporary infatuation? The parents know better."

"We are growing old, Zaynab," Joseph wrote back. "Perhaps the children do know better. I have learned to keep my nose out of things, if you understand what I'm saying. Both Tova and Benjamin want no advice from us. We help with Benjamin's son, but are careful not to say anything."

"Dearest brother. They are making a mistake, not counting our opinions, Joseph. The years are the best teachers, and so is the experience. I long for the days when children listened attentively to their parents. On a more positive note, Izet is celebrating his 65th birthday next month. We plan a trip together to Mostar. We shall take a photograph and send it to you."

"Thank you for the photo, dear sister. I hoped to see little Aida in it, but I guess she stayed home with someone and allowed the adults to travel for the day? Seeing the old Mostar bridge brought so many memories to me and Rebecca. She is not feeling well these days, but we keep praying. I heard of Tito's meeting with Nikita Khrushchev on the news. I was not pleased with the new alignment of Yugoslavia with the Soviets. I think Tito was right about staying independent. With this alignment with the Soviets, you and I will soon find ourselves on different sides of a stupid conflict."

"Dear Zaynab, have you received my last letter? I sent you a photo of our newborn granddaughter Rachel. Please do send me a letter back."

"Dear Zaynab, it's been over a year since we heard from you. Have I done anything to offend you?

Please send me a letter back! Your brother, Joseph."

Joseph knocked on the door of the Jewish Agency Office in Jerusalem. He introduced himself as a former community leader in Sarajevo, and asked to speak with the head of the Soviet Department.

Over coffee, Joseph poured his heart. "I've been sending letters, with no reply. I have a feeling my letters do not get through to them."

"Have you written anything to criticize the regime?"

"No, of course not!"

"Well, if you wish to send a simple message, you can leave it with us. Once a month we pass a parcel to the small remaining Jewish community there, perhaps they can forward the letter."

"Dear Joseph and Rebecca! We were so glad to receive the letter from you! We were quite worried about you. I am so happy to hear everyone is well. We too are praying here for Rebecca's renewed health. Aida turned five last week. She is beautiful and very bright. We also have good news! Our daughter Aisha is pregnant. With the help of Allah, we too shall become grandparents soon. We miss you and think of you often. I shall send this letter to the synagogue, hopefully this time you shall receive my letter. Mustafa sends his warm greetings. Yours, your sister in Sarajevo."

CHAPTER 31

"April 5th, 1972.

Dear sister,

I was saddened to hear of Mustafa's passing. Mustafa was the bravest of men: kind, honest, caring, respectful of everyone. I can imagine there were many at his funeral and at the mourning. I remember walking with him to a coffee shop once, and every moment someone stopped us to greet him. What a great man. My deepest, deepest condolences.

Now you and I are both alone. I miss Rebecca terribly. But I have the children and grandchildren to worry about. Gabriel is now in the fourth grade and little Rachel is now in the second. Tova's son, Michael, has just celebrated his third birthday and I went to the celebration in the kindergarten. We also have good news, Tova is pregnant again. I visit them almost every afternoon. Do write to me, I long for your letters. Remember your brother in Jerusalem. Joseph."

"Dear Joseph, your words touched my heart. Thank you for your kind and warm words. Not every woman is lucky to have such a husband. I was fortunate to have Mustafa by my side for thirty-two happy years.

I must confess that I am worried. I am worried about little Aida. She is ten years old now, and her father's death has been difficult on her. She placed his old coat by her bedside and she hugs it every night. I hope she will be okay.

My greetings to Tova, Benjamin and the families. Your sister in your loving hometown, Sarajevo."

"October 8th, 1973

Dear Joseph.

Please respond to my letter as quick as you can. I tried telephoning you from the post office, but the call did not go through. I was shocked to hear of the Arab armies attacking Israel, and of all days, in your Ramadan, your Youm Kiper (I hope I have spelled it correctly). It is a shame. I am praying for you and your family. Please tell me everyone is safe."

"Dear sister.

These are difficult days for us. Golda Meir has stepped down from her position as the Prime

Minister. Investigations are being carried out by the government about the lack of preparation for the war. This seems to be our deadliest war. Even Benjamin was called from reserve duty. God bless, he is well, but two people he knew died in the battle on the Sinai Peninsula, and another one in the Golan Heights. These are sad, sad days. We hope that the new Prime Minister, Rabin, can help us come out of this dreadful situation. I am sorry to write this, but something in the atmosphere here reminds me of Sarajevo, winter 1941."

CHAPTER 32

The years passed. Zaynab was growing old. Younger generations refused to wear head coverings. She could see no reason why a woman would want to expose herself that way. But Aida rebuked her mother. "Mama, you are so old fashioned!"

She *felt* old fashioned. She also felt misaligned with the general sentiment of other young people. Some identified strongly with the Soviet Union and others aligned with nationalistic sects, asking for separate autonomies for Bosnia, Croatia, and Serbia, hoping to split her beloved Yugoslavia.

"But Mama," Aida persisted, "you are either a Soviet, and support all of what it means, including the lost freedom of speech, the attack on religions and faiths, or, you believe in free autonomy for each of our country's unique populations."

"Aida, why must you put me in an either/or situation? I despise the Soviets and much of what they are doing. But I also do not want to split our country. I know what it means. You were not born yet. I know what factions fighting one another means."

"But it can be done peacefully, Mama."

Zaynab had bitter memories. Before WWII the Nazis were said to be civilized. No one knew what was to come. Now people were speaking about a peaceful partition of her country. It sounded ominous to her.

Tito's health was slowly failing. Now in his 80's, he refused to relinquish power to the younger generation.

In her small, dwindling study group held in the old mosque near the clock tower, Zaynab, now 62, asked Nur, a younger member of the group, to lead a presentation. Nur presented the importance of democracy. That subject was on the mind of many youngsters.

"Islam supports it, too," Nur said, speaking passionately to the whole group, now consisting of only ten women despite Zaynab's invitation to others. Young people were not interested in reading, in conversing from one's heart.

But Nur was a different. Adjusting her glasses, she spoke passionately. "Islam and democracy are not just compatible. Their association is inevitable! The Islamic political system is based on the concept of *Shura*. Due to the *Shura* tradition, democracy is only natural—"

Zaynab interrupted. "Nur, clarify what the word means. Do not rush."

Nur smiled gratefully at Zaynab. Moments like this made Zaynab feel that she was somehow continuing Hakima's legacy.

"The word Shura means 'consultation.' The Quran and Prophet Muhammad, peace be unto him, encourage Muslims to decide our affairs in consultation with those who will be *affected* by any decision. Nowadays the word is used as the names of many parliaments in the Muslim world. Basically, to work according to Shura is to take into consideration the opinion of the majority. Therefore, Islam supports Shura, and it also supports democracy."

Jasmine, now in her sixties, challenged Nur. "Democracy is the sure path to anarchy. Look at what happens in America. Promiscuity, lack of respect for parents, a lost generation is being raised there!"

Nur listened patiently, noticing the nods of some of the elders in the group. "I do not condone promiscuity or loss of values. But claiming that democracy is related to a degeneration of values is like claiming that Islam is not friendly towards democracy. These are assumptions that are not based on true facts."

Zaynab noticed the women each taking a stance.

Wafaa, now in her late seventies and the eldest in the group, said, "Do you prefer democracy over socialism? In America many people are left homeless, on the streets."

Nur shook her head, "Leave America alone. America isn't necessarily the best example of a well executed democracy. A true democracy is not one where people vote once every four years, but one in which the citizen is constantly involved in policy setting, like in the concept of Shura, constant consultation. True democracy means peace; democratic countries tend to never fight one another."

"Mind you," Wafaa retorted, "that it was your 'democracy' that used an atomic bomb, not socialism…"

Nur interjected and Zaynab had to intervene. "Ladies, ladies, we shall listen respectfully to each other. Nur, you are praising the concept of Shura, consultation with the many. Practice true Shura by listening, respectfully, genuinely. It may be that the elders have some experiences that you do not have. And ladies, do not attack her! Her ideas are important for us to listen to. We do not come here to spew our opinions, but instead to challenge ourselves, to learn and to develop."

The women nodded meekly.

Zaynab nodded. "Now, Nur, you were saying…."

Zaynab's study group was not the only group that held tension. People longed for a regime change.

When Tito finally died in 1980, at the age of 87, his funeral, though long anticipated by many, left the country in shock. It drew many world statesmen, and was the largest state funeral in history. Four kings, 31 presidents, 6 princes, and 22 prime ministers were present. They came from both sides of the Cold War, from 128 different countries.

Reporting on his death, The New York Times commented: "Tito sought to improve life. Unlike others who rose to power on the Communist wave after WWII, Tito did not long demand that his people suffer for a distant vision of a better life. After an initial Soviet-influenced bleak period, Tito moved toward radical improvement of life in the country. Yugoslavia gradually became a bright spot amid the general grayness of Eastern Europe."

But now Yugoslavia was at a loss. Speculation began about whether Tito's successors could continue to hold Yugoslavia together. Ethnic divisions and conflict grew.

The country was on the verge of disintegration. But people still had hope of a united future. Zaynab witnessed how preparations began for the Winter Olympics in Sarajevo. At first it sounded to everyone like a joke. "Our little Sarajevo could host the Olympics?"

But soon everyone took part in making it happen. People volunteered their time to make the preparation complete, constructing new buildings and stadiums to make the Olympics represent Yugoslavia well in the eyes of the world. New stadiums were built. The shining Zetra Olympic Hall, the Zetra Stadium, and the Olympic Bobsleigh and Luge Track, were all reasons for pride for the people of Sarajevo.

When 1984 came, the Winter Olympics in Sarajevo demonstrated the continued vision of brotherhood and unity as the multiple nationalities of Yugoslavia remained united in one team.

Never had Sarajevo witnessed so many visitors of so many nationalities. To Zaynab, walking hand in hand with her teenage granddaughter Gabriella, this was a true miracle, a sign of a better future.

But difficulties began to appear. Yugoslavia's big sister, the Soviet Union, crumbled. The Yugoslav government, under immense debt from Tito's time, attempted to transform into a market economy. Efforts were made to privatize sections of the economy, which immediately led to massive layoffs. The government lost popularity due to rising unemployment. The winds of change were blowing through the Sarajevo streets.

And Zaynab did not like it.

CHAPTER 33

Zaynab's life was complicated enough without the talks of disintegrating her beloved nation into smaller republics. Her leg had started to bother her, and she went from one doctor to another trying to find an answer to the immense pain.

Financially, these were difficult times. Without a husband or savings, she, like so many others, had to move into smaller quarters. Luckily, all her children now had their own lives. But not so luckily, some of her children—and grandchildren—made decisions that she knew would make their lives difficult.

First came her granddaughter, Gabriella, Aisha's daughter. Gabriella fell in love with a Serb, a Christian. Zaynab's pleas did not help. "Nana," Gabriella cried, "you don't understand, I love him!"

Zaynab was dismayed, "How will you raise your children? Muslim? That would be impossible with a Christian father!"

"We will raise them as God tells us to raise them. They can be both, both Muslim and Christian! Nana, please! Would you prefer that I married a Muslim who I did not love?"

Zaynab pouted her lips. "No," she said, but she could also not approve of such a thing.

Then, her very own daughter, her young rose, Aida, came home at the age of 24, admitting that she fell in love with a Serb. "I want your blessing, Mama."

Zaynab began sobbing. "Why are you doing this to me, Aida?"

"Mama, you always say that we should never judge a person by their religion, color, or anything! You say it yourself!"

Zaynab was now at a loss for words. She could see the truth in her daughter's words, but she could also see all that Aida could not see: the strife, the difficulties, and possible alienation from both communities.

"Mama," Aida cried, "I want you to give me and Braunmir your blessing!"

Zaynab felt her heart being torn from its place.

"Mama, please! It is you who always wrote letters to your 'Jewish brother!' You cannot be hypocritical when it comes to your own *family*, when it comes to your own *daughter*!"

Zaynab, crying, pulled Aida closer. "Why… why are you making my life so difficult… Of course I will give you my blessing, but why do you choose such a difficult life for yourself, I cannot understand…."

"My dear brother.

I cannot believe you have celebrated your 85th birthday. Joseph, are we getting old or what? You have been unjustly silent in the past year. Do write to me.

As to us, life continues. I celebrated my 67th birthday a month ago. We had all the children and grandchildren over at my new apartment. We have a beautiful view of the Sarajevo hills. From the seventh floor we see everything. I wish you could come and see it for yourself.

Aida recently married a Serb. I gave my blessing, as you can imagine, but I also dread when I think of their future. They say I am old fashioned. But I foresee troubles. Do you too feel uncertain about the future? I am not sure whether it is a general pessimism that comes with age, or whether I simply have learned better than to hope for the best. Our country is in disorder. Unemployment is rising, especially since the end of the Winter Olympics here in Sarajevo. I see many youngsters just spending their days on the streets, aimlessly, looking for trouble. It would be a sin if I put in writing what these scenes remind me of.

Do write to me. I long to hear your wisdom. Why have you been hiding for so long?

Your sister, Sarajevo."

What Zaynab did not know was that with failing health, 85-year-old Joseph was laboring on his last will: to get recognition for his friend's courage.

Joseph made his way to the Israeli Holocaust Museum. He told his story to the director of the prestigious international prize granted by the Holocaust Museum and the State of Israel. The prize, recognition as Righteous Among the Nations, was given to a select few people who during the Holocaust endangered their lives in order to save Jews.

"She and her husband saved my life!" Joseph pleaded to the director, Mr. Reichman.

Mr. Reichman was an Israeli-born man in his sixties. He looked at the 85-year-old with a sad look, "I'm afraid we can not help you with this."

"But why not? I filled out all the forms!"

"Mr. Kabilio, the title, Righteous Among the Nations, is not given easily. We conduct thorough investigation, with our partners at the Jewish Agency in Europe, and I simply do not see how this… family you mention… is deserving to win this title—"

"They saved my life!" Joseph cried, "They also saved the lives of my late wife and my two children! They hid us in their home, they hid me twice! For months! The Nazis outside were killing anyone who hid a Serb or a Jew!"

"But Bosnia wasn't 'Nazi.'"

"The Independent Croatia was Nazi like any other

German occupied territory!"

The director looked again at the forms, filled with Joseph's shaky handwriting. He read through the testimony again. "Did they charge money for hiding you?"

"No, nothing!"

The director pouted his lips. "But you were renting your factory from them, were you not?"

"I was, but—"

"You see, Mr. Kabilio, the title, Righteous Among the Nations, cannot be given to anyone who received any payment in return for their assistance."

Joseph was flabbergasted. Why was the director so adamant about not examining the request properly? Joseph knew what pride it would offer to Zaynab and her family. He imagined them, too, planting a tree in Jerusalem's Mount of Remembrance, where hundreds of trees were planted in honor of the brave Righteous Among the Nations. Why was the director so uncooperative? "I am telling you the truth, Mr. Reichman. They received nothing. They did it out of the goodness of their heart. Across the street the Gestapo's investigation headquarters were located, and I saw with my own eyes how they tortured and threw people from the top floor to die on the street. The Hardaga family was risking their lives!"

The director pouted his lips, feeling awfully tired of the relentless old man. "You see, Mr. Kabilio, we have never given the title to a"—he measured his words carefully— "a family of... of the Islamic tradition."

Joseph's eyes widened. "So, is that what it is all about? You can be sure that they were devout Muslims, and they kept saying it was their faith that instructed them to hide us—"

The director was exhausted. "Mr. Kabilio, our board will examine your request thoroughly. I can assure you that."

CHAPTER 34

No word was heard back from the Holocaust Museum, and Joseph was extremely disappointed. At a Friday night's Shabbat dinner at Tova's house, his daughter noticed that her father was distracted.

"What is it, Papa?"

"Oh, nothing," Joseph tried smiling.

"Any news from the Holocaust Museum?"

Joseph shook his head.

Tova's husband leaned forward, "I don't understand what their problem is."

Joseph shrugged; he was tired of the whole process. He never liked speaking of the Holocaust, nor did he like trying to convince other people, let alone such suspicious and sly people as Mr. Reichman.

Later, when dinner was finished and the grandchildren were in bed, Tova brought up the subject again. "Papa, tell me what you wrote them."

Joseph, reticent and bitter, said, "I told them everything, about Zaynab and Mustafa, Bahriya and Izet, how they hid all four of us in that summer and autumn, and how later they hid me alone. I even mentioned Zaynab's food carrying to me while I was doing hard labor cleaning the snow that winter."

"Did you mention Zaynab's father?"

"Ahmed? No, the secretary told me that 'bundling' them all was not a good idea, and that applying for the recognition of four people was already too big of a list."

"Papa, Zaynab's father was killed in Jasenovac. That can be easily proved."

Joseph shrugged, his eyes becoming watery. He felt old and incompetent. "Tova, I can't do it anymore. It's proven too difficult. They don't understand. The man there said they have never given the Righteous title to any Muslim—"

Tova's face became red. "Papa, I'll go with you. We'll go first thing next week."

Mr. Reichman was not pleased to see the elderly man, escorted by a woman who seemed rather feisty. He looked at the old man and feigned a smile. "Mr. Kabilio, how pleasant to see you. I did promise you that we would get back to you, but unfortunately we have concluded that—"

"Mr. Reichman," Tova interrupted, "we want to update our request."

"Update?"

"Yes. Update! We want to include Mrs. Hardaga's father, Mr. Ahmed Sadik."

"Now you want to add another person? Listen, friends, this is not a market—"

"You better listen to us, Mr. Reichman."

Tova's tone made the eyebrows of the director stretch across his forehead.

Tova continued. "Mr. Sadik, Zaynab Hardaga's father, was hiding a Jewish family, two parents and their two children, in Konic. He was reported to the Gestapo. They took him and he died in Jasenovac, for hiding Jews."

Mr. Reichman frowned. "He died in Jasenovac?"

Tova and Joseph nodded. Tova pulled out the statement she had devised over the weekend and pushed it across the table.

The director seemed puzzled. Lost in thought, he looked at the request. "And he did not receive monetary compensation for his services?"

Joseph shook his head. "No."

"Well," the director sighed, "we'll have to research it. The lists of Jasenovac include some one hundred thousand names—"

Joseph interjected, "Mr. Sadik was taken on January 22nd, 1945. The records include his name."

Mr. Reichman hesitated. "Mr. *Ahmed* Sadik, you are saying?"

Tova did not like his tone. She stood up. "We expect to hear from you in the coming week."

Mr. Reichman laughed, "Madam, this process takes months!"

"Well," Tova straightened her dress, "I'm sure the press would be very intrigued by why the Holocaust Museum would not recognize the righteousness of a Muslim family who together saved not one Jewish family, but two. It sure sounds like an interesting story, perhaps tinged with some racism or political—"

"I beg your pardon!" Mr. Reichman stood up.

"We shall expect your call, Mr. Reichman, this coming week." Tova reached her hand over for a handshake. Never was Mr. Reichman so reluctant to shake someone's hand.

CHAPTER 35

The doctor's face said everything. "Mrs. Hardaga, I'm afraid we'll have to amputate."

Zaynab said nothing. Her face sank.

Aida looked at the doctor, rocking a baby girl in her arms. "Surely, there must be another way to help my mother, isn't there, doctor? Isn't there a medicine, or some treatment?"

The doctor shook his head, his eyes sad. He would much rather have entertained the baby than explain to her mother about the old lady's leg. He took a deep breath. "The infection is in an advanced stage. We've tried antibiotics without improvement. The thickening of the nerve tissue, here," he pointed at the purple area on the leg, "shows an advanced neuroma—"

"Neuroma?" Aida asked. Her mother seemed lost in thought, lamenting over the bad news. What would she do without a leg?

"Yes, neuroma," the doctor continued, "a tumor

of nerve tissue." Seeing Aida's face, the doctor hurried to say, "Not a cancerous tumor, but a benign one. The nerve tissue, including the nerve fibers and their myelin sheath, are all under genuine neoplasms. If we don't amputate quickly, the neuroma can spread upwards."

Aida stood up. "We will have to see other doctors in another hospital." With her free hand, she helped her mother stand up. Baby Stella began crying. The doctor looked at them with a sad face. He wished he could do more.

CHAPTER 36

Mr. Reichman had a wide, fake smile on his face. "Mr. Kabilio, Mrs. Grinberg! Please have a seat." Joseph and Tova sat down.

Next to the director stood two of the Museum researchers in their seventies. One of them reached his hand out to Joseph. His arm showed a number etched on his arm. Tova immediately nodded with reverence. Much was said, though unspoken, in those instants.

Mr. Reichman introduced the two men, and said that they would need to find more information. Joseph and Tova nodded. Mr. Reichman looked at Tova, "I'm afraid that, as you are a witness too, we'd need to take both your testimonies separately."

Tova looked at her father and then back at Mr. Reichman. "My father is old; I'd rather remain with him—"

"Tova, it is fine," Joseph said.

Reluctantly, Tova stood up, raised her chin, glared

at Mr. Reichman and stepped outside the room.

Nearly three hours later Joseph came out. He was rattled, his eyes red.

Tova looked at him worriedly, "Papa?"

He smiled. "They listened. They understood."

"But why so long? What did they ask you?"

Mr. Reichman stood by the door, "Mrs. Grinberg," he said, his demeanor more respectful than before, "we are ready for your testimony."

In Sarajevo, Zaynab was healing from her operation, her amputated stump resting on the bed, when she heard the phone ring. Aida, who had recently moved with her husband and daughter to her mother's apartment to help her recuperate, put baby Stella on the carpet and hurried to the phone.

"Yes?" Aida picked up. The sound was bad. "Hello?"

"Zaynab? Zaynab?" the manly voice came through the noise of the international call.

"It is her daughter, Aida."

"Aida! You don't know me; my name is Joseph—"

"Joseph? From Israel?"

The man laughed. His voice shook, "Yes! How wonderful that you know! Forgive me for my bad Serbian, I haven't spoken it for a... long time...."

"Of course, of course."

Zaynab, from the bedroom, heard the excitement in her daughter's voice, as well as the name Joseph mentioned. "Who is it, Aida?!"

Aida extended the phone line so it could stretch from the living room into the small bedroom, "Mama, it is from Israel, Joseph!"

Zaynab's eyes lit, she reached her hand and took the receiver. "Joseph?"

"My sister Zaynab!"

Zaynab began sobbing. "Oh, Joseph!" She tried to sit up, and yelped as a surge of pain climbed up from her hip.

"Zaynab? Is everything alright?"

Zaynab bit her tongue. Aida looked at her worriedly. Her mother clutched the receiver. "Yes, yes. I am just... excited... to hear you! You are in Israel? In Jerusalem?"

There was a little delay in the line. "Yes. Yes, in Jerusalem! I have news for you. Happy news!"

"Another grandchild?" Zaynab asked, smiling at Aida knowingly.

"Oh, no," Joseph laughed. His voice trembled, "We, the Israeli government... we wanted to honor you and your family for..." his voice broke. He swallowed, "For all that you did for us. There is a ceremony, in Jerusalem, and you are invited."

Zaynab shook her head, "Oh, Joseph, no need, what for? What have we done? We should have done more!"

"Nonsense," Joseph's voice came choppy from the other side. "You are a hero, and Israel wants to honor you. The ceremony is in May. Will you come?"

Thoughts ran through Zaynab's mind quickly. She felt she did not deserve the honor. And she also knew that she could not afford the travel. "Joseph, you are very kind. But," she hesitated, "the Ministry of Foreign Affairs here, they do not allow people to travel. Let alone to a country out of the communist block...."

"Nonsense," Joseph said, his voice betraying his glee, "We have taken care of that through the Jewish Agency. They have arranged with the Ministry in Belgrade for two visas for the ceremony."

Zaynab's heart began beating fast. Was he serious?

"Zaynab? Are you there? Hello?"

"Yes, yes, Joseph. I just...."

"The Israeli government will pay for everything, your flight, your accommodation, that is, if you would like to stay in a hotel. I thought perhaps you could stay in my apartment in Jerusalem, it's nothing grand, but.... Zaynab? Zaynab? Are you there? Hello?"

CHAPTER 37

The airplane's wheels met the tarmac and the plane rattled. Zaynab held her hand firmly to her young sister's hand. Nadia looked through the window, "Zaynab, we are in Israel!"

The Tel Aviv airport witnessed a unique scene that morning. Two head covered old Muslim ladies, one of them in a wheelchair, were greeted with hugs and kisses by a large Jewish family led by an old man, his son and daughter, as well as numerous grandchildren and great grandchildren.

When the kisses were over Joseph turned to Zaynab and pointed at the wheelchair. "What happened?"

"Oh, my leg," Zaynab waived her hand dismissively. "They had to amputate it."

"You didn't tell me!" Joseph protested.

Zaynab smiled. "And you didn't tell me you were cooking all this!"

The Yugoslav government only approved a two-day visit, for the mere purpose of attendance to the ceremony. Though short, those two days were packed with kisses, hugs, tears and laughter. Tova and Benjamin practiced their lost Serbian, and Nadia and Zaynab were ecstatic to visit Jerusalem. Zaynab explained to Joseph and his entourage, "Not only am I happy to be with you, and with all this honor, but this is also a religious obligation for me, that you are helping me fulfill."

Questioning looks probed her to explain. "In Islam, one of the commands is that one shall strive to visit Mecca at least once in a person's life. It's called the *haj*. But even a visit to Jerusalem is recognized as holy, as a *Ziyarah,* or a holy visit. You helped me fulfill my *Ziyarah,* my holy visit to Jerusalem."

Later that evening, Zaynab and Nadia sat on Joseph's balcony, watching the sun set over Jerusalem. Every few moments Zaynab would shake her head in disbelief, "Who would have thought… who could have dreamed…."

The following day was a busy one. They wanted to see Jerusalem, but only had a few hours before the afternoon ceremony at the Holocaust Museum. With a wheelchair, elderly Joseph walking slowly, and several cars of the entire Kabilio family, including all the grandchildren, they managed to only visit the Dome of the Rock on the Temple Mount. But Zaynab's face streamed with tears as she recalled her father's stories about the Prophet landing with his flying horse on that very spot, on his night's journey.

In the afternoon the four cars made their way up the Mountain of Remembrance, to the grand Holocaust Museum overseeing the Jerusalem Mountains. Zaynab was surprised by how green it was. "We truly reached heaven," she whispered to Nadia. Nadia smiled back, she, too, trying to take it all in. The two of them had never left Yugoslavia in over six decades of life. Now they were in the Holy Land. It felt surreal.

They were surprised by the number of guests at the ceremony. Zaynab adjusted her head covering, embarrassed to see all the cameras and the dignitaries in suits. Tova pushed Zaynab's wheelchair as Joseph and Nadia walked hand in hand at the head of a long procession, followed by the Kabilio family. The first stop was to plant a tree in honor of the Sadik and Hardaga families.

They walked on a trail outside the large museum, winding through hundreds of trees, some old, some new. Silver plaques were raised from the ground near each tree. Zaynab glanced at names such as Archbishop Damaskinos and Mr. Oskar Schindler near two of the trees. She shook her head; she felt that she did not deserve this respect.

The long procession stopped by a clearing in the woods, where a hole was already dug in the ground. Photographers and reporters hovered around them. A man from the museum came to Joseph and handed him a small tree. Joseph trembled, with Benjamin supporting him, towards Zaynab and Nadia.

Zaynab, with the help of Nadia and Tova, stood up, balancing herself on her prosthetic leg. Joseph handed the tree to Zaynab, and she nodded for Nadia to take it. Nadia knelt on the ground and placed the tree in the hole. Cameras flashed. Benjamin, knowing Zaynab was unable to lean forward, brought some soil to her hand. She gratefully took it, said a prayer, and then threw it into the hole.

The Kabilio family and some of the dignitaries quickly helped fill the hole in the ground. It was then that an Israeli dignitary brought a silver plaque, just like the ones that Zaynab saw near the other trees. She looked at it, written in Hebrew and Latin letters, and began sobbing. The names were written clearly, boldly, proudly.

"Mustafa and Zaynab Hardaga—Izet and Bahriya Hardaga—Ahmed Sadik."

After taking too many photographs standing along with the Kabilio family near the newly planted tree, the procession made its way into the museum.

The reception at the large auditorium was grand. Zaynab felt embarrassed to be the cause of all the commotion. Many people spoke, and Joseph sat beside her and Nadia and translated the entire ceremony. The translator who was hired for the purpose found herself idle for some time while Joseph translated all that the dignitaries said. Beautiful words were spoken, about unity of mankind, and of religions serving as a bridge between people.

Then, to Zaynab's surprise—and seemingly, to the

surprise of many of the people present there—an older man wearing traditional Muslim clothes was escorted to the microphone. He was dressed like an imam. Was this planned?

The old man, who Zaynab later learned was the imam of the Muslim town of Abu-Gosh, began with a blessing. "In the name of Allah, the most merciful."

Zaynab and Nadia's eyes filled with tears as they mumbled, "Amen."

The imam proceeded to speak in Arabic and in Hebrew, reciting the Qur'an and quoting from the spoken tradition. "In our holy scriptures, in *Sahih Muslim,* we say, 'Kindness is a mark of faith, and whoever is not kind has no faith.' You, Zaynab, Nadia, and your family, have proven the most faithful of all. You have pleased Allah by being his messengers, carriers of human kindness, as a mark of your deep devotion."

Zaynab wiped the tears from her face.

The imam continued, "Our Holy Qur'an says clearly in chapter five verse 32, that 'Whoever kills one person, it is as though he has killed all mankind. And whoever saves a life, it is as though he had saved all of mankind.' You, and your family have not saved one person, or one family, or even two families. According to the Qur'an," the imam said and raised the Qur'an in his hand, concluding his speech, "you, most faithful Muslims, you have saved all of mankind."

Applaud followed again, and suddenly people stood up, clapping for Zaynab and Nadia. The two of them looked at the floor. Tears streamed down Zaynab's eyes.

The conductor of the ceremony came and whispered to Joseph, "Now the Mayor of Jerusalem will speak, and then Mrs. Hardaga." Joseph nodded and translated to Zaynab. She nodded back.

As the mayor spoke, Zaynab unfolded her one-page speech, which she wrote with the help of her daughter Aida in her apartment in Sarajevo. She wondered whether she would succeed in reading it without bursting into tears. She closed her eyes and nodded to herself. She added a short prayer. "Babo, this is for you."

The mayor finished his speech and the conductor called Zaynab to the stage. She insisted on standing up, supported by Nadia and Joseph, both helping her walk slowly to the podium. She placed her written speech in front of her.

She was about to begin when suddenly she remembered Hakima, and how Hakima would have liked for her to speak. Proud. Loud. Erect.

"I would like to express my deep thanks," she began, "for the great honor of being here."

The translator hired by the Museum quickly translated her words.

Zaynab continued. "I would like to thank you for adding the Hardaga family to the international family of Righteous Among the Nations." She then added, not from the written speech, "I am also proud that I was privileged to plant a tree on the Mount of Remembrance, here, in the country where our friends, with whom we have a shared fate, live."

She looked at Joseph and his children while the translator translated.

Zaynab continued, "The friendship between the Kabilio and Hardaga families began many years before World War II, when Joseph Kabilio built his pipe factory—the second largest in the entire state—in our courtyard. This friendship was sealed almost in blood on April 14th, 1941. On that terrible day when the synagogue was destroyed by an air raid, houses were on fire and people ran to the forests."

The translator interpreted. Zaynab's thoughts wandered to that day, little Salih in her arms, little Aisha clutching to her legs, as they were hiding in the bedroom. She remembered the sight of the grey airplanes through the window.

She took a deep breath and continued. "When they returned they found destroyed homes, looted shops, and wounded and injured people. When we learned that the house of our friends Kabilio was also hit, and saw how destitute they were, we brought the entire family, Joseph, his wife and both their children, to our home."

She remembered Mustafa's insistence. How she loved him at that moment. Her Mustafa.

"It was the first time," she recalled, "that a male stranger spent the night in our house. This was forbidden for us women, who according to tradition and religion had to veil our faces. But our husbands Mustafa and Izet received the Kabilio family with the words: 'Our home is your home; feel at home. Our women will not hide their faces in your presence, because you are like family members to us. Now that your life is in danger, we will not forsake you.'"

She suddenly began crying. She did not know why. The audience was perfectly quiet. Some wept too. Zaynab quickly sniffled and gained her composure. She glanced at Joseph's reassuring smile and continued. "I would like to say a few words about our father. Our father, Ahmed Sadik of blessed memory, was born in Celine and was close to the Mostar community. He came to Sarajevo in 1913 and immediately found friends among the Jews. When the persecution started, he was in Konic. We knew he was helping Jews, but he told us only of one case."

The auditorium was completely silent. Zaynab waited for the translator to finish, and continued. "It was in the beginning of 1942. Our father happened to be at the Konic railway station, which is an intersection. Suddenly he saw Izidor Papo, a Jewish agent from Sarajevo, with his wife and two children, who were getting off the train that had arrived from Dubrovnik and getting on the train to Sarajevo. My father approached them and asked where they were going. They said, 'Home, to Sarajevo!'

"My father told them that there were no more Jews in Sarajevo, that all had been taken to the camps, and that if they showed up in Sarajevo, the family would be taken to Jasenovac. They did not know what to do, but my father did."

Tears began streaming down her face again. She kept speaking, ignoring them, wishing to finish the last paragraph of her written speech. "My father took the entire family to his lodging, got papers for them and passed them to an area under Italian occupation. They were all saved, only—" she gasped for air— "only my father was not. He was denounced, and taken on one of the last transports to… Jasenovac… where he was executed for saving Jews."

She folded her speech and waited for the translator to finish. She looked at the audience, at the surprised look on the people's faces. She wished to add one more thing. "The name of our father, Ahmed Sadik, is among the Jewish names on a large monument that was erected in the memory of the victims and fighters in Sarajevo. His burial place is unknown. It is…" she choked her tears, "a great pleasure for me to commemorate my late father, especially here, among the Righteous from all over the world who risked their lives and the safety of their families to rescue their Jewish friends. This, now, here, is to me his burial place. Here, in Jerusalem. Thank you."

An emotional standing ovation followed. Zaynab smiled and reached her hands to Nadia and Joseph who helped her back to her wheelchair. People kept clapping. She took a deep breath in, sitting in her wheelchair, and thought of her father. She felt a sense of completion.

The farewell at the Tel Aviv airport that night was difficult. Joseph, who managed not to cry the entire visit, suddenly clutched Zaynab's arm and they hugged, him whispering to her in Serbian, "Sister, will you come visit again?"

Zaynab laughed, "In your dreams!"

Joseph laughed, "Write to me more often, will you?"

She promised.

The family hugged her and Nadia. Over the course of these two days, the Kabilio family had grown fond of the two old ladies. Nadia and Zaynab, in return, fell in love with the grandchildren, who now gave them shy goodbye kisses. Everyone seemed sad that the visit could not be extended.

"Don't worry," Joseph said when they were about to go through the boarding gate, "we'll meet again soon."

Zaynab and Nadia nodded. Zaynab knew very well that Joseph knew this was their last meeting. She was approaching her 70s, he was in his 80s. She smiled at him all knowingly. "Allah shall bless you and your family."

Joseph responded with the Bosnian greeting, "And He shall bless you and yours."

Tova hugged her father as the two ladies disappeared through the boarding gate. Benjamin patted his old father's shoulder. "Well done, Papa. Mama would have been proud of you for making it all happen."

Joseph smiled with teary eyes.

The following summer Joseph, age 88, died. He passed away peacefully in his sleep in his apartment in Jerusalem.

Tova did not have the heart to break the news to Zaynab over the phone. She instead wrote a long letter to Zaynab, attaching pictures from her and Nadia's visit.

Two months later came the letter from Zaynab, in an envelope from the Jewish Agency.

"Dear Tova,

Your words stunned me. It seems like only yesterday your father was greeting us in the airport, teasing me about my leg, hugging me like an old family member. To me, too, Joseph was somewhat of a father.

It took me several days to digest the terrible news. I was happy to know that he died peacefully, bless Allah for His mercy. I did not know what to write to you. Many thoughts troubled my tired old mind. Please forgive me for taking so long to write back.

Your father was a special man, Tova. He and your mother were the most grateful people I have ever met. Even when hiding in our house, with you running and playing around us, they were grateful. Not a day passed without your mother saying to me, quietly, "Thank you, Zaynab." Sometimes in a whisper, sometimes with a nod. Your mother was an angel.

As was your father. He treated her so

respectfully. I remember telling Mustafa, "You see? Joseph never raises his voice at Rebecca."

It is no wonder that my late husband took a liking to your father. He was an honest man, a good man, with whom everyone enjoyed doing business and being in his presence. I remember the first time I met him. My memory is vague, as I was still a girl, but I remember him bringing candies to my father's store to celebrate a holiday. I think it was Passover. And when he left my father told me, "That man is a good man."

It is a blessing to me that our families' lives were intertwined the way they were. Undoubtedly, this was part of Allah's plan in bringing us together so that we could be stronger together. The Qur'an says, "Hold firmly to the rope of Allah all together and do not become divided." It means, to me at least, that our families must never be divided. In the war it was not only us who helped your parents. They helped us too. I do not mean by cleaning and spending time with the children. I mean through their example, through their encouragement, through their manners and strength.

We say that what a person does is more important than what a person says. Your parents, not only in their words but also in their actions, showed their devotion to God. I feel honored to have played a minor part in their lives. And I am blessed to have known your mother and father.

In these days of mourning, please send my condolences to the entire family, and especially to you and Benjamin. I know that your father was very proud of you and of the families that you have raised.

I hope I did not tire you with this letter. Please do write to me. And remember that Sarajevo is still your home, and my home is yours, always.

Sincerely,

Your aunt, Zaynab."

Tova and Zaynab continued to correspond, though not with the fervor that Zaynab and Joseph had. Tova sent pictures of the family, especially of the grandchildren. She informed Zaynab of her older brother's failing health. Benjamin, now in his sixties, was diagnosed with liver cancer. Zaynab promised to pray for his health.

Meanwhile, in Sarajevo, the atmosphere in the streets was difficult. Though she was now in her early 70's, Zaynab was not disconnected from the pulse of the city. Taking the elevator from her 7th floor apartment, she pushed her wheelchair in front of the building, and conversed with the youngsters. She understood that difficult days lay ahead. Unemployment was rampant.

In the study group all the women could speak about was the state of the Soviet Union. The new General Secretary, Mikhail Gorbachev, announced plans with fancy names such as Glasnost and Perestroika. The women in Zaynab's study group did not understand what these words meant specifically, except that changes lay ahead. Everyone felt that the glory of the Soviet Union was fading.

As was the glory of Sarajevo. Only a few years before was Sarajevo a world hub during the winter Olympics. Now, as the eighties reached their end, the huge construction projects that had employed so many Sarajevo citizens stood empty and abandoned. The shining Zetra Olympic Hall, the Zetra Stadium, and the Olympic Bobsleigh and Luge Track, were now neglected, paint peeling off, piles of garbage collecting on their outskirts.

Zaynab watched her color TV with worry as news came from Berlin. The Wall was falling. In Sarajevo people were celebrating on the streets. But Zaynab was worried.

Her daughter Aida was ecstatic. "Mama, you should celebrate too! It means the end of political repression, of authoritarianism and of religious persecution. It is a spring, Mama, an awakening of the people!"

Zaynab wanted to be happy. The look of families reunited around the Berlin Wall made her shed tears. Yet something disturbed her. As she watched independence from the Soviet Union achieved gradually in Poland, Hungary, East Germany, Bulgaria, Czechoslovakia and Romania, all she could think about was her beloved Yugoslavia. She knew her father would have strongly disapproved of what was happening. Though she had had much criticism toward Tito decades earlier, now she missed the leader. She missed the man who reunified Yugoslavia after the Second World War.

In the past, politics were not a welcomed subject at the Hardaga house. Mustafa never liked to speak of politics. But now, Zaynab and Aida talked about politics constantly, often to the dismay of Aida's husband, Braunmir.

There was no escape from politics. Everyone in Sarajevo spoke only of politics. Whether in loud dinner conversations, or in quiet murmurs on the street, people felt the tides changing.

While Aida was enthused about all that it meant for Sarajevo and for the Bosnian people, Braunmir felt more aligned with his mother-in-law's views. "Zaynab is right," he said, "unity is better than any division."

Aida shook her head. They were sitting by the small dining room table in Zaynab's apartment, with five-year-old Stella drawing with crayons. Aida could not understand her husband. "Braunmir, don't you see that more autonomy for each region in Yugoslavia would mean more freedom, less centralization and adherence to some remote federal dictation, and more decision making at the local level? It means more freedom of expression! More individualism! More mixed couples like us. Think of all the good it entails!"

Braunmir looked at Aida and then at his mother-in-law. "I don't know. People in the city are speaking about a free Bosnia. Does a free Bosnia have a place for me, a Serb? And say, in Belgrade, would a free Serbia not outcast the Muslims? The Croats? Yugoslavia was meant to be one nation."

Zaynab agreed. "Whatever happens, it needs to happen slowly. I don't like the speed of what is happening in Poland, in Romania, everywhere."

"Mama, don't be so negative!" Aida smiled, "It will be alright. Better times are ahead."

With the fall of communism, elections were held in November 1990. The parties contending for power were mostly based on ethnicity: Serbs, Muslim, and Croats. They formed a loose coalition and ousted the communists from power.

As people celebrated in Sarajevo, northern parts of Yugoslavia, namely Croatia and Slovenia, declared independence from the country.

Violence in those regions, in which the Yugoslav army tried to seize control, soon brought an odd atmosphere to Sarajevo.

"You hear that?" Zaynab said to her granddaughter as they sat in front of their building. The street was quiet.

"Do I hear what, Nana?"

Zaynab took a deep breath. She wanted to say, "The quiet before the storm." But instead she smiled, her wrinkled face twisting with hope mixed with fear. Empty streets reminded her too well of another period in her life.

The warfare in the north placed Sarajevo and its three constituent peoples in an awkward position. The Serbs in the city championed the importance of staying with the Yugoslav federation. The Muslims and the Croats, however, favored independence for the region; a new state, to be called Bosnia and Herzegovina. A new state meant new hope, and a feeling that the people of the region were directing their fate, rather than being dependent on a far away Yugoslav government in Belgrade, with its own agenda.

The new government, ruled by the three groups, did not last long. Soon Serb members of parliament abandoned the central parliament in Sarajevo, and formed the Assembly of the Serb People of Bosnia and Herzegovina. With all the changes in the air, the public called for a referendum. Should Bosnia and Herzegovina remain a part of the shrinking Yugoslavia, or should the region, like Slovenia and Croatia, declare its own independence?

The referendum was planned for the first of March, 1992. The Muslims and the Croats were excited about it. The Serbs, however, were not. They knew well that, together, the Muslims and the Croats formed a majority.

It was a beautiful morning on March first. Though it

was cold, the sun was out. Zaynab and Stella were sitting outside the building, Zaynab in her wheelchair, and Stella reading a children's book. Zaynab was happy to see people out. Aida dressed up excitedly to vote in the referendum. People dressed in their finest clothes as if it was a holiday. After decades of very little practice of democratic procedures, this day of the referendum was nothing short of a holiday.

Aida saw her mother downstairs. "Mama, are you sure you don't want to come and vote? Everyone is going to vote! It's our civic duty!"

Zaynab pouted her lips. "Does your husband intend on voting?"

Aida took a deep breath. Like most Serbs, Braunmir thought the referendum was just a formal procedure to sustain a process he did not support. To him, as well as to many other Serbs, the word "Independence" reminded them all too well of World War Two and the government of "Independent Croatia."

Aida looked at her mother. People were coming out of the building, and greeting Aida and her mother, "Happy referendum day!"

"Happy referendum day!" Aida smiled. She turned to her mother. "Alright. I shall go. If you change your mind, the ballots will be open until the evening, and all you need to bring is your ID."

Zaynab said nothing. She saw her daughter leave and took a deep breath. She then looked at her granddaughter reading. "Good, Stella, keep reading. It's good for you."

Zaynab was surprised to see, among the people passing in front of her, a couple dressed in fine clothes. The Gardovic family were Serbs, she knew them. Could they be going to vote? "Good morning Mrs. Gardovic, Mr. Gardovic!"

"Good morning, Mrs. Hardaga!"

Stella took her eyes off her book, looking at the finely dressed older couple.

Zaynab looked at them. "Are you going to vote?"

Mr. Gardovic frowned. "No, of course not! My brother Nicola's son is getting married today. They planned the wedding months ago, before this shame."

"Oh," Zaynab said. "Well, congratulations! May the young couple know many years of happiness and joy!"

Mrs. Gardovic smiled, "Thank you Mrs. Hardaga, God bless you. Come, Alex, we don't want to be late."

Zaynab watched them walk toward the old city. She felt bad for having asked them about the referendum. She should have known better. In Sarajevo one had to be sensitive, especially these days. This was the beauty of her city, making everyone feel invited.

An hour later it was growing colder. Zaynab thought of going upstairs and getting a blanket. She enjoyed sitting in the sun, though now it was hiding behind the clouds.

It was then when she suddenly heard it.

Shots. Several shots. In the distance.

Stella kept reading, unaware of the sounds. But Zaynab's heart began racing. She knew those sounds all too well. In her twenties, during the war, they were all too common.

"Come, Stella, fast. Let's go home."

"But Nana, it's nice outside—"

"You heard me. Come now!"

Stella reluctantly joined her grandmother as they took the elevator upstairs. Zaynab hurried to turn the television and the radio on.

Nothing.

Her heart was pounding. But the news said nothing. Could she have imagined? She rolled the wheelchair toward the window. She could see nothing in the streets in front of the building. She looked at the beautiful hills and took in a deep breath. She must have imagined. She turned her gaze to Stella, who was lost in her book. "God, please," Zaynab murmured to herself, "make our crooked places straight. Please God, do not forget your obedient servant."

The radio began blaring. "Breaking news from Sarajevo. We repeat, breaking news. You are listening to radio Sarajevo, 93.5 FM. A few minutes ago, shooting was heard in the old city in the Muslim quarter. Eyewitnesses report a few injured. We will be bringing you the details as we find out more. The police request all people to remain calm. Stay with us as we find out more. I repeat, a few minutes ago a shooting was heard in the old city in the Muslim quarter. Eyewitnesses report a few injured. We will be bringing you the details as we find out more. The police request all people to remain calm...."

Stella looked at her grandmother. Zaynab's eyes were open wide, like an animal in the forest, hearing danger in the bushes. Alert.

"Nana, what happened?"

Zaynab took a deep breath, "Go to your room. Take your book and go to your room."

"But I just finished the book Nana!"

"I don't care, go to your room Stella!"

The news kept blaring. Stella went obediently to her room. Zaynab looked through the window at the street.

Only in the evening did all the facts begin to unfold. A Serbian wedding was held at a church in the old city. Could this be the wedding that Mr. And Mrs. Gardovic were going to? The news did not say. All the news could report was that after the wedding, the guests walked to have the wedding meal in another church, the Old Orthodox Church. The father of the groom carried the Serbian flag in the procession, as the procession made its way through the Muslim Quarter. Carrying the Serbian flag was interpreted as an act of deliberate provocation on the day of the independence referendum. A Muslim, outraged by the provocation, began shooting at the flag carrier. The father of the groom was rushed to the hospital, and the shooter was taken by police.

At dinner Zaynab could not eat. She kept mumbling to herself. Braunmir tried to console her, but Aida whispered to him, "Let her be. She won't speak to you when she's in this state."

After a few minutes, Zaynab, tears in her eyes, said, "I'm going to go to the Gardovic's on the fifth floor."

Aida said, "Mama, are you sure?"

Braunmir said, "I'll come with you."

The apartment of the Gardovic family was open. Several neighbors were there, all of them Serbs. Braunmir pushed Zaynab's wheelchair out of the elevator and through the corridor. When they knocked on the open door, the quiet murmurs inside stopped. Zaynab saw Mrs. Gardovic weeping in another woman's arms, and Mr. Gardovic standing near the kitchen with red eyes. She saw other people who she did not recognize. Zaynab instantly understood that what she feared was true. The father of the groom who was shot was Mr. Gardovic's brother.

She swallowed, feeling everyone looking at her, wearing her head covering. "Mrs. Gardovic, Mr. Gardovic, I'm so sorry. I'm so terribly sorry." She began crying.

No one stepped toward her or motioned for her to enter.

Mrs. Gardovic, on the sofa, consoled by two women on both sides, sobbed. "Nikola is dead! My brother-in-law is dead! On the day of his son's wedding! How could they, how could they, God?"

Zaynab's eyes widened and she quickly turned to look at Braunmir. She did not know that the father of the groom was shot *dead*. Wasn't he only injured?

People's backs were turned to her. Mr. Gardovic disappeared into the kitchen. One of the other neighbors came and knelt before Zaynab. "Mrs. Hardaga, I do not think this is a good time."

Zaynab, tears in her eyes, mumbled, "I see. I did not mean to disturb."

She motioned to Braunmir to take her back into the corridor. As they took the elevator upstairs, Braunmir and Zaynab said nothing.

Inside the apartment, Aida hurried to them, "Is everything okay?"

Zaynab seemed as if she had seen a ghost. Braunmir looked at his wife and shook his head 'No.'

In the morning Zaynab had no appetite, again. "Mama," Aida pleaded, "please, eat something!"

Zaynab shook her head. The bags under her eyes showed she had not slept. "I want to go to the Gardovics again."

Aida, who heard from Braunmir how cold the family had been to him and Zaynab, said, "Mama, I would wait if I were you."

Across the kitchen table, the radio kept blaring the news. "An outcry in the Serbian community. Slobodan Milosevic, President of the Assembly of the Serb People of Bosnia and Herzegovina, said "the bloody wedding is a great assault aimed at the Serbian people. Serbs will not live as second-class citizens in a Bosnia dominated by Muslims and Croats. The shooting yesterday was a call for war."

Zaynab began rolling her wheelchair toward the door.

Braunmir hurried to put his utensils on his plate and follow her. Aida shook her head and said to Stella, "Come, we'll all go together."

They all crammed in the small elevator and descended to the fifth floor.

The door of the Gardovic family was closed. They rang the bell. There was no answer. Zaynab leaned forward and knocked firmly. "Please, Mr. Gardovic, open the door. We are friends, are we not? Please!"

She kept banging on the door until, across the hallway, a door opened. "Stop shouting!" the lady called.

They all turned around. Braunmir helped Zaynab roll her wheelchair around. "Mrs. Brankovic, why do they not open—"

"They left, Mrs. Hardaga! They left early this morning!"

Zaynab rolled her wheelchair across the narrow corridor. "Left to where, Mrs. Brankovic?"

"To Belgrade. It's not safe here in Sarajevo for us

Serbs." Mrs. Brankovic raised her eyebrows and stared at Braunmir across the hallway, as if he was a traitor.

Zaynab saw an open suitcase in the living room. "No! No, please, why... where are you... please, Mrs. Brankovic, this was a mistake, a terrible mistake—"

"Well this 'mistake' cost the life of a father, and now our priest, Radenko Mikovic, is lying wounded in the hospital from this 'mistake!' How dare you, Mrs. Hardaga!"

The door slammed in their face.

Zaynab buried her face in her hands and began sobbing. "God, God...."

They returned to the elevator silently.

That morning Zaynab was glued to the window, looking at the street with tears in her eyes, listening to the radio, in which politicians were bashing one against the other with declarations that sounded ever so frightening.

Finally, Zaynab wiped her tears, and said. "I am going outside. We must do something."

Aida, who had decided not to send Stella to school that morning, said, "Mama, I don't think it's wise. The government will announce the referendum's results later today and—"

"I will go by myself, then."

Braunmir stood up and looked at Aida. She nodded at him helplessly.

"Where to, Mama?" Braunmir asked Zaynab when they exited the building.

"To the flower shop on Karnica street."

The streets were quiet as they walked toward the flower shop. They entered and Zaynab pulled out her purse and said to the young lady, "A large funeral wreath. Very large. The largest."

The lady nodded and began assembling the circle of flowers. "With a black stripe across it, Madam?"

"Yes."

A few minutes later they exited the flower shop, Zaynab carrying the large wreath on her lap. "Where to, Mama?" He feared he already knew the answer.

"To the Old Orthodox Church in the old city."

"But Mama, this is… it is dangerous."

"You'll either come with me or I'll go there myself."

Braunmir pushed her wheelchair silently. He headed toward the tram station.

"No, no, Braunmir, I want to go through the streets. I want everyone to see me."

Braunmir swallowed. What could he do?

They walked through the quiet streets: Braunmir, a Serb-looking man, pushing a traditional Muslim lady, with a large wreath of mourning in her hands.

The looks of the shop owners said it all. The Muslim shop owners were upset at this sign of weakness. After all, what happened yesterday was inevitable. The Serbs knew what they were doing walking with the Serbian flag. It was a provocation.

Croat shop owners felt the same.

The few Serb shop owners who opened their shops that morning looked with disapproval. No wreath of flowers could serve as an apology for what was a calculated assault on a married couple and their family on a wedding day. The Muslims were going to be punished. And they deserved it.

Braunmir found it hard to avoid the stares through the shop windows, as well as through the building's windows. Zaynab, clutching the wreath, kept her chin raised.

As they approached the older section of town, she felt a thickening of the atmosphere. The stores were closed, but faces were seen behind almost every window.

A Serb couple with a suitcase crossed the street and looked at the Muslim woman with the wreath. They shook their head. The woman spat on the ground, carrying her suitcase behind her hurriedly.

From a window above them a Muslim lady yelled at Zaynab. "Allah will punish you!"

Zaynab shook her head and murmured, "Allah will praise me."

Braunmir felt the tension building in his body as they approached the Muslim quarter. "Mama, let us go to the Orthodox church from Kings Street."

"No Braunmir! They need to see us, my people,

shame on us. Shame on us."

They walked through the street. Zaynab recognized an older man who had once been a friend of Mustafa. He looked, wide-eyed, at the man pushing Zaynab's wheelchair. Then he saw the wreath. He shook his head.

Zaynab glared at him and did not take her eyes off him until they had passed.

Finally, after the third turn, Braunmir saw the Old Orthodox church. A police car stood there, along with a few clergymen and priests. Braunmir spotted blood on the pavement.

Near the church's fence there were a few bouquets of flowers. The police and the clergymen stopped speaking and looked at the Muslim lady in the wheelchair and at her caretaker.

Zaynab, her chin still held high, nodded at them. Braunmir approached the fence, and Zaynab placed the wreath among the others. Her shoulders rattled. She began crying.

One of the older priests came to them. He said a word of greeting to Braunmir and then knelt near Zaynab. "Thank you. Thank you."

On their return home they took the tram. Braunmir was tired, both physically and emotionally.

Climbing on the tram, they saw many people with suitcases. Braunmir placed Zaynab at the stroller's place near the back door and locked the wheels, sitting on the seat behind her. Zaynab looked with sorrow at all the people with suitcases. There were whole families there. Her heart ached.

When the tram reached the train station, everyone began getting off. One woman was getting off as she noticed Braunmir was still sitting. She told him in Serbian, "Brother. You better come too."

Braunmir said nothing.

"Did you not hear me, brother? They will butcher everyone here! Did you not see the news yesterday?"

Braunmir coughed and pointed at Zaynab. "I'm her son-in-law."

The woman looked at Zaynab with a terrified look that instantly turned to disapproval as she disembarked the tram.

The tram continued towards the residential blocks and the new neighborhoods. Beside Zaynab and Braunmir there was only one other man on the tram; the driver.

At home Aida was grateful that her husband and her mother returned. "You were crazy to go out like that," she mumbled frantically. The radio blared along with the television. From all apartments in the building, from every house in Sarajevo, people were listening to the news, holding their breath.

The television blared: "Following the results of the referendum, Serb leaders announced the establishment of the Serb Republic of Bosnia-Herzegovina. As of an hour ago the roads leading out of the city are blocked by haphazard barricades led by armed gangs of masked Serbs that are blocking roads in protest of yesterday's killing at the bloody wedding. The government of the new Independent Republic requests all people remain calm."

Images of masked men with long rifles kept replaying on the screen, the men standing near a makeshift checkpoint, examining the cars on the road. Braunmir looked at the screen. "That's near the intersection out of Sarajevo toward Konic."

Stella began crying, sensing the fear in the living room. Aida embraced her, "Sweetie, it's nothing. You'll see. Everything is alright."

An hour later they heard the first shells falling.

CHAPTER 38

The following days were frightening. The city, the news reported, was completely sieged by the Serbian controlled gangs and members of the former Yugoslav army.

Wednesday came and it was time for Zaynab's weekly study group. Since her amputation seven years earlier the meetings had moved from the small mosque to her own apartment.

Zaynab looked forward to the meeting the whole day. But when evening came, no one showed up.

That was why Zaynab rejoiced the following day, when, on Thursday, several friends of Aida and Braunmir came to visit. Admira and Bosko, who, just like Aida and Braunmir, were a mixed couple: she was Muslim, he was a Serb. Two other young women arrived, Suada and Olga, friends of Aida from university. Finally, Zaynab's granddaughter, Gabriella, and her husband, Anton, came along with their two young children, Michael and Ella, Zaynab's great grandchildren, Aisha's grandchildren.

Zaynab greeted everyone as they entered. After three days of people staying at home, fearing to go outside, a truce was declared that morning, and the Muslim president called for everyone to go out and relax.

People were still afraid, however, to go to coffee shops. Aida's invitation for friends to come over to the small apartment they were sharing with her old mother, therefore, was warmly appreciated.

Zaynab tried entertaining the children. Rolling around in her wheelchair, she brought out crayons and a puzzle, and began playing with them on the kitchen table, wishing to give their parents some quality time after being stranded at home for the past three days.

Everyone in the living room was in their 20s or 30s. Between them, they represented the unique blend of the city. Aida was Muslim, Braunmir was a Serb. Gabriella was Muslim, Anton was a Serb. Admira was Muslim, Bosko was a Serb. The three mixed couples had always felt very comfortable in each other's company. While some older members of their families did not approve of their spouse, here, along with other couples who made the brave decision of putting love over tradition, they all felt at home. Their friends from university, Suada, a Muslim, and her best friend Olga, a Croat, added to the mixture. The eight of them, four Muslims, three Serbs and one Croat, were a mirror of their city.

Olga said, "We cannot allow the situation to disintegrate this way. We must do something. They say there's a peace rally being organized tomorrow.

We should go."

Braunmir was more reserved. "It's still unsafe, Olga. We should be careful."

Olga shook her head, "If we, the young people, won't show our solidarity with one another, if we don't show our belief in fraternity and unity, then the gangs and the army generals will take over!"

Suada agreed. In university she was the head of the interfaith dialogue group. Like many other young Muslims, she did not wear a head covering, and believed that everyone should follow his or her own conscience, as long as they respected other people's choices. She said, "We need to remind ourselves, to remind the nation, what Yugoslavia is all about. People need to see couples like you," she said to Admira and Bosko, "who put aside differences and allow friendship to be the ruler. We must go and demonstrate. I agree with Suada; we can't just hide in our homes!"

Zaynab, from the kitchen, heard the youngsters speaking passionately. She prayed in her heart that they would lead the way.

The three men were more reserved. Bosko said, "They came to our house yesterday, a group of Muslims, shouting at Admira to leave the 'traitor' and 'infidel.'" He seemed rattled. So did Admira.

Aida put her hand on Admira's hand. "Don't you worry. This is just a passing thing," she smiled and whispered, "sometimes when Stella is just about to fall asleep, she begins crying and messing around. But it's just a sign that soon she'll go to sleep. It's the same in our situation. All these religious outcries are just the cries before they go dormant and disappear for good, you see?"

Admira nodded. They were all scared of what was happening. The previous night Serbs and Muslims clashed at an ammunition barracks on the hills outside Sarajevo. Five were killed. The pictures of the bodies in the newspapers were horrible. Torn faces.

"It's surreal," Gabriella whispered, not wanting her children to hear her, "Anton was just telling me yesterday that it feels like we are in the Middle East or something. The gangs with their faces covered, the checkpoints, the blockades over the entire city! It's crazy."

They all agreed. Bosko, who was the youngest of the men, said, "What they are trying to do is to frighten us. As a Serb, I'm embarrassed about Miloshovic's rhetoric. Saying that he is willing to fight to secure Serb territories is just... it's against Orthodox Christianity. It's not right."

Bosko continued, holding Admira's hand, "We should not be frightened. We should go out, hand in hand, for everyone to see and be reminded of the beauty of Sarajevo. This could not happen elsewhere, this beautiful blend. This is what we are about. We should fight for it."

The following day Zaynab served as a babysitter for Stella, Ella and Michael while their parents went to the peace rally. Zaynab hoped that all was coming back to normality. From the window, she could see people on the street again. She was encouraged.

The television showed footage of the peace rally. Many youngsters were there. Zaynab was proud of all of them. In World War Two there were no such things. Then, people hid in their homes. Now, many felt courageous enough to step outside and demand peaceful negotiations by all parties.

The television stated that similar peaceful protests were also gathering in Mostar and Belgrade. A young Serb man, in Belgrade, held a sign, "Muslims and Croats are my brothers."

Seeing that sign on the television, Zaynab began weeping.

"Nana, don't cry!" Stella said.

"No, sweetie, these are tears of joy."

A helicopter camera on TV showed how protesters were marching all over Sarajevo, crossing bridges over the river toward the parliament square. The news reporter said, "We see tens of thousands of people, possibly one hundred thousand. In these days, considering recent calamities, these numbers are nothing but staggering. Sarajevo demands peaceful negotiations."

Zaynab, unable to take her eyes off the television screen, felt encouraged.

Until she heard the shooting.

Only at two in the morning did Zaynab hear the banging on the door. Aida and Braunmir were hysteric. Braunmir was pale. Aida was sobbing in his arms. Behind them, Gabriella and Anton followed, hurriedly taking Michael and little Ella. "Thank you, Nana," Gabriella said with tears in her eyes.

Zaynab grabbed her granddaughter's hand, "What happened, Gabriella, what happened?"

Gabriella could not explain. Words were too painful. She pointed at Braunmir and Aida, and hurried to take her children outside along with her husband.

The door closed. Stella ran and clung to crying Aida. "Mama? Mama?"

Aida sobbed and hauled in Braunmir's arms. He led her to the sofa trying to reassure her.

Zaynab, helpless, rolled her wheelchair toward them. "What happened? Tell me!"

Through tears and sobs, Aida mumbled, "Snipers... From the roofs, they shot at us. We ducked. Suada and Olga were in front. They were...they were shot...."

Braunmir, pale, was unable to speak. He just held on to Aida, his eyes wide. Zaynab asked, "Are they in the hospital?"

Aida shook her head and howled, choking on her own tears. "We went there, after the ambulances. Eight people were injured, but... Suada, and Olga... they were... they were... oh Mama, they were pronounced dead..."

CHAPTER 39

The following days were a blur. Everything happened so fast. Muslims and Croats attacked Serb outposts. Serbs shot endless numbers of bullets and shells at various government and police structures. Numbers of fatalities escalated each day in the besieged city.

The phone rang. Zaynab was too exhausted to pick it up. She had not slept in days.

Stella ran to the phone. An older lady speaking funny Serbian asked to speak to Zaynab. "Nana! It's for you!"

Zaynab did not respond. From her place near the window she gazed at the empty street. Not a soul was out.

Her granddaughter nagged her, pulling on her sleeve, "Nana! It's a phone call for you!"

"Who is it?"

Stella ran back to the phone. "Who is it? Tova? From Israel? I will tell her. Wait."

Zaynab, as if reawaken from a spell, pushed her wheelchair toward the phone. She took the receiver, her hand shaking. "Tova?"

"Oh, thank God, Zaynab! I have been calling you for the last four days!"

"The phones were disconnected, but now they are working again."

"I've been watching the news. I'm so concerned! Are you okay? Is everyone safe?"

Zaynab hesitated for a moment, not wanting to scare Tova. "I am fine. We are all fine. It's... not easy, but we are well. How are you. How is the family?"

Tova answered and then pressed again. "Are you certain that you are well? Do you need anything? I can call the Jewish Agency, perhaps they can get—"

"We are fine, Tova, we are fine. Thank you."

Tova's voice broke. "I was so concerned... Is there anything I can do?"

"Just pray, Tova, pray for us that this bloodshed will end."

"I will," Tova said, "I already am."

Aida and Braunmir were both heart-stricken. They feared going outside, especially Braunmir. Serbs walking the city were shouted at and sometimes even publically attacked.

A few days after the peaceful rally that turned deadly, the phone rang again.

Zaynab picked up this time. She heard her daughter's voice. "Aisha?"

Aisha was crying. "Mama?"

"Aisha? What's wrong?"

"It's Gabriella and Anton and the children. They were threatened at their home two days ago, so they came here—"

"Two days ago? Why didn't you tell me?"

"I was…I did not want to scare you. They came here and they stayed with us, but an hour ago some people came and warned us that if they find Anton here tomorrow they will kill him." She began sobbing.

Zaynab cursed. She rarely did. "Allah will punish them. Where are Anton and Gabriella now?"

"They packed again and left with Ella and Michael. I told them to come to you. You live far enough away from the center, I was hoping—"

"You did well." Zaynab said.

"But Mama, don't tell the neighbors. Don't tell anyone. It's dangerous now."

"I won't. Of course not."

With shells constantly shot at Sarajevo from the surrounding hills, and with Muslims and Croats attacking the Serb outposts, death tolls were rising quickly.

The apartment on the seventh floor became crowded. Gabriella, Anton, and their two children were sleeping in the small living room. Zaynab tried to be cheerful. "Now we get to spend more time together, the whole family!"

But the truth was that she was frightened and tired. She had not expected to go through such dark times at age 74. She kept praying to God, but her prayers often turned into accusations. "What do you want from me? Has not your servant done enough? Have I not suffered enough?"

She searched her heart for answers. She found none.

On the living room wall, her father's photograph was staring at her. Ahmed's dignified eyes. His confident look. She mumbled to herself, "Papa, what is happening? Why is all this happening?"

But even her father could not help her. She was at a loss for what to do. She kept putting on a smile and tried to be jolly, especially for the young children. But inside she wanted to disappear. She even thought of dying. Seeing the agony in her children and grandchildren's eyes was too much for her to bear.

The phone line was gone again, now for nearly a week. Price of food became more expensive due to supplies being kept out of the city. Serb checkpoints stopped anything from going through.

Anton was outraged. "How can the world allow it? All they sent is a few UN ambulances. How can the world allow this aggression to happen?"

The kitchen table was too small for everyone. They sat in the living room, each holding a plate in their hands. Braunmir rarely spoke these days. It seemed like the incident at the peaceful rally shaken him to his core. He ate little.

A knock was heard at the door. Each knock frightened Gabriella and Anton, who remembered the knocking on their own door, and then on their parent's door. No one moved.

"Zaynab!" the voice called from behind the door. It was a voice of a girl. "It's Nur! Open the door! I brought you some food!"

Zaynab rolled her wheelchair to the door. Braunmir and Anton hurried to stand up and go hide in the bedroom. Zaynab turned to them. "Don't. Stay out. She's my student."

Zaynab opened the door. Nur, who had been with Zaynab's study group for over a decade, stood there, smiling. "Zaynab! I was worried about you!"

"My Nur! I'm so pleased to see you. Come in!"

Nur entered, carrying a sack of rice, "There was a UN convoy bringing some food, and I thought you must be—" Nur froze in her tracks as she saw everyone in the living room. The two men standing were clearly Serbs.

Zaynab saw her face. "Nur, meet my son-in-law

Braunmir, and my grandson-in-law, Anton."

Nur's face betrayed her fears. "Well, I just wanted to bring you the...sack."

"Come sit with us," Zaynab said. Aida stood up, "Please, Nur, join us!"

But Nur hurried to the door, forcing a smile. "I'm sorry, I have to go. Good bye!"

When the door closed, Anton buried his face in his hands. "We should have hidden. Who knows if she might tell someone."

"She won't!" Zaynab exclaimed. "She won't!"

The voice from the other side of the phone was choppy. The phone company's headquarters were bombarded, and now phones were connected through temporary cables. Zaynab strained to hear, "Hello? I can't hear anything!"

"Zaynab? Zaynab? It's me, Tova! Can you hear me? Zaynab? It's Tova. From Israel."

"Tova!" Zaynab exclaimed. There was something so relieving in hearing that voice.

"I have phoned you so many times. Did someone from the Jewish Agency visit you? I spoke to their representative here. They said they'd contact the synagogue in Sarajevo."

"No," Zaynab said, forcing a smile, "But why should they. We are still here."

"I've seen the shelling on the news. It's horrible! How is the family? How are you faring?"

Zaynab glanced at the messy living room, at the makeshift beds on the floor. Anton and Braunmir were reading the news. Stella was playing with Ella. "The family is fine. Closer than ever."

"Oh, good," Tova said and began crying, "I'm so happy to be talking to you! I thought something had happened. Listen, I spoke to several people, in the government too, and they said that there is a possibility we could get you out."

"Get me out? Where would I go?"

"You can come and stay with me until things calm down in Sarajevo. You and I don't know how long this is going to last."

"I cannot leave. Sarajevo is my home. My children and grandchildren are here."

"Zaynab, just give me their names and IDs and I could apply to the—"

"No, Tova, no, no. You are so kind, but we shall not flee like refugees...."

The voice on the other side of the phone became choppy. "Think about it, Auntie... Please... I'm... so concerned.... I'm... when—"

"Tova?" Zaynab called into the phone, "Tova? Can you hear me? Tova!"

The line died. Zaynab tried punching the phone keys. There was no line.

She put the receiver back and sighed.

Anton looked at her. "Nana, what did she say?"

Over dinner, the conversation in the small house became argumentative. Anton and Gabriella seemed adamant. Gabriella was outraged. "It's been five months now and it's not getting any better!"

Anton joined her, "If we stay here eventually we'll get buried alive. You saw how they brought down the television building?"

Zaynab felt horrible, especially about the children hearing their parents speak that way.

Aida objected, "We cannot leave Sarajevo. That is exactly what they want! We can't just play into their hands that way!"

Zaynab had to interject. "We are not to judge one another. If Anton and Gabriella wish to leave, I will give them my blessing. We all will."

Anton and Gabriella looked at each other. This decision was the hardest one they ever had to make.

The Jewish community in Sarajevo had dwindled over the years. Nevertheless, several hundred families still lived in the city. Like many other Jewish communities, they were assisted by the Jewish Agency. Being a minority in so many places around the globe had taught the Jews to support one another in times of need.

Now, with the siege, Jews around the world were sending money and food for the small Jewish community. In Sarajevo, people were volunteering at the synagogue, cooking, trying to serve as a safe shelter for everyone.

As Gabriella approached the building, two guards stopped her. "Where to?"

"The… synagogue," Gabriella answered, bewildered.

"Are you armed?"

"No."

They looked at her for a long moment. Then they let her enter.

She hurried inside.

Opening the door, she was puzzled to see dozens of people, standing near long tables, organizing food parcels. Within seconds she could see that they were not Jewish at all. Some were Jewish, but most were Muslims or Croats. She even spotted two Serbs. What was this place?

An older woman came to her, "Darling, did you come to volunteer?"

Gabriella stuttered, "No, I'm… I'm sorry, I… my grandmother, she was told by her friend in Jerusalem that perhaps… we could join the convoy out…."

The older woman smiled at her and took her hand, "I'll take you to the office."

A rabbi in his fifties was sitting in the office next to papers, passports and phones, yelling into one of the phones in English.

He motioned for Gabriella to sit down and smiled at her. She sat down quietly and the woman behind her left.

When the rabbi finished the conversation he said, "Forgive me. It was from America. I'm Rabbi Levinger."

"I'm Gabriella, Gabriella Markovic, Hardaga-Markovic."

The rabbi nodded all knowingly. From the mere combination of family names, he could tell the entire story. Hardaga. Markovic. Muslim. Serb.

"My grandmother," Gabriella said, "has a friend in Jerusalem, and she told her that she might be able to arrange—"

"Is that friend's name Tova?"

"Yes!" Gabriella said, on the verge of tears.

"Well," the rabbi said and pulled a pile of faxed letters, "you sure have someone caring for you."

When the plane landed at the Tel Aviv airport, Tova and her children greeted Gabriella, Anton, and little Michael and Ella. "Welcome, welcome!" Tova said in old Serbian, hugging the strangers as if she had known them for years. "Without your grandmother I would not be here today, and neither would all my children. Come now. You must be hungry. How was your flight?"

CHAPTER 40

In Sarajevo things were only getting worse. Braunmir became sick. Though only 37 years old, he began losing his sight in one eye, felt constant fatigue, and complained about his muscles hurting.

The doctor who visited the seventh-floor apartment looked very grim. He asked Braunmir a series of long questions. He then had Braunmir perform several physical tasks to test his coordination and physical strength. Finally, the doctor sighed. "I'm afraid it is Multiple Sclerosis."

"What is that?" Braunmir asked. Aida leaned forward to hear the doctor's quiet voice.

The doctor began explaining the disease, the attacks in relapsing forms, and the neurological problems as the sickness advanced.

Zaynab was beside herself. How could Braunmir get sick, being so young! It must have been the siege that brought this disease. They'd been stuck in the apartment for over a year. Most of the building was abandoned now. The elevator had stopped working, and often the electricity was gone for days.

In addition, Zaynab's own health was failing. The cold winter of 1992-1993 was too much for her to bear without proper heating. Though they were all sleeping in the same room next to a wood-burning stove, it still did not feel warm enough for her.

With Braunmir's health slowly deteriorating, and Zaynab losing her strength, more responsibility fell on 35-year-old Aida. She had to clean, entertain, and most importantly—cook. Cooking with recurring electricity outages, depending only on a small gas stove was a challenge. Trying to oversee Stella's schooling at home with a few books was also difficult. The atmosphere at the apartment was testing.

The whole building became abandoned. All the Serb residents had fled over a year earlier. Even among the Muslim and Croat residents, everyone who could somehow leave or flee, did. Many moved to safer quarters within the city, leaving the building, which was exposed to the Sarajevo hills.

Aida would go alone to buy wood on one of the street corners—those street corners that were protected by a tall building. Any street corner that was visible to the hills surrounding the city became an easy target. Innocent pedestrians were targeted from a distance, sniper bullets aiming straight at running people.

Cemeteries were filled quickly. Soon the dead were

buried in makeshift graves in public parks and gardens throughout the city. The international community kept "expressing concerns" and "strongly condemned" the aggravators on all sides. Yet the few UN ambulance forces and food distribution units they sent were not enough to change the situation in the city.

Mostar had also been besieged, but the joined forces of Croats and Muslims in Mostar managed to push the Serb militia away. Mostar was liberated. At the dinner table Aida reported the good news. "It means that we are next!"

Braunmir smiled. Stella glanced at her grandmother. Zaynab was not so optimistic. "How did they liberate Mostar?"

"They managed to push the Serb siege away!"

"By which means, Aida?"

"By force, of course."

Zaynab shook her head. "It's not good. It's not good. Using force will only bring more force." She said nothing else.

One day there was a knock on the door. Aida hesitated. Apart from the Jewish doctor who came from the synagogue once a week or so, no one else had come to visit them in months.

The knock came again. Aida hesitated. Zaynab was resting in her bedroom. Braunmir was staring through the window at the empty street. Without turning to her, he said, "Don't open it."

There was another knock.

Aida reached to the door and peered through the peephole. "Admira!"

She hurried to open the door. She hadn't seen her friend from university in months. Ever since that hateful peace rally.

Admira looked thinner and not well. "Aida!" she said with a big smile, "I came to say goodbye!"

"What do you mean? Where are you going? Come in and let me fix you some tea."

Stella hurried to join them, happy to finally have a visitor in the house. Admira hugged 9-year-old Stella and waved at Braunmir. "Hello, Braunmir!"

Braunmir nodded and said nothing.

Aida tried to be cheerful. "Let's go to the kitchen." She brought the kettle to the tap, but no water came out. Another water shortage. She hurried to open a jerrycan and pour water into the kettle. She turned the gas on and sat by the table. "Tell me, where are you going?"

"I don't know. Anywhere but here... Bosko hasn't been out of the house for 14 months. That's not life."

Aida turned to her daughter. "Stella, go play in the living room with Papa."

"But Papa doesn't—"

"You heard me, Stella!"

Stella reluctantly left the kitchen.

Aida turned to Admira, "How will you exit the city?"

"We'll try one of the roads. They announced a cease-fire last night—"

"You know very well what these 'cease-fires' are worth!"

"Aida, we can't stay here. It's... too dangerous. It's dangerous for Bosko. It's dangerous for me. It's dangerous for you, too."

Aida got up to the boiling kettle.

Admira's eyes watered. "Aida, they killed my cousin, Brana, while she was putting her two sons to sleep. A 60-millimeter shell hit their house."

"Admira, I'm so sorry!" Aida mumbled. "I didn't know!"

Admira looked around, as if haunted. "It's not safe here anymore. I, too, like you, wanted to save our city. To face everything with Sarajevo-pride. But our lives are more important than staying here and getting killed."

Aida nodded. She poured the water into the cups and began crying. Admira hugged her. They wept together.

In the hallway outside the kitchen door, Stella was listening.

Aida wiped her tears and whispered, "You are right, Admira. Go. If it was not for my mother, I would have done the same as well. Go."

They embraced again.

"When this madness is over," Admira said, "we'll return. Keep safe, alright?"

Aida pointed at the tea cups, "At least stay for the tea, Admira!"

"I... we want to leave today, before it gets dark. I..."

"Go. Go. You are right. May God be with you."

Seconds later Admira was out of the apartment.

Aida stared at the two cups of tea. Her heart weighed heavily.

That same day a couple was shot while trying to cross the Vrbanja bridge. They were Admira and Bosko. They died in each other's arms on the bridge, their picture making it to news reports around the world.

Aida heard of it only two days later when she was buying wood. Upon hearing the news in passing she fell on the road and could not bring herself to stand. An older woman came and sat next to her. They did not know each other, but they cried together.

Once a week, the Jewish community sent the doctor to visit Zaynab's apartment. Zaynab's health was failing her. She developed bronchitis. The doctor tried to do what he could but he knew the war was wearing the 75-year-old lady down quickly.

It was only after bullets came through the kitchen window one evening that Aida decided this could no longer continue.

The following day she went to the synagogue. She spoke to the same rabbi who helped Gabriella and Anton leave with their children. Since then, news came from Jerusalem, that they had lived with Tova for four months. Then Anton received a visa to work in Sweden, and took the family with him. Aida, though she hated it, was envious of Gabriella. She had been wiser.

The rabbi leaned back in his chair, and looked exhausted. "I am very sorry. The situation has changed in the last couple of months."

"What do you mean?" Aida's voice betrayed her fear.

"I mean that even if we get an official invitation from the Israeli government, we need the approval of both the Bosnian authorities and the Serb army. It's almost impossible. We have labored for weeks just to get approval for the names of the remaining Jews in the city."

Aida broke into tears in his office. "My Mama saved a whole family in the war, and now you are telling me you can't help us? You flew her there eight years ago!"

The rabbi exhaled slowly. "We'll do what we can. I promise."

With phones no longer working in the city, the rabbi's communication with the world depended on radio only. After sending in the information on Zaynab, Aida, Braunmir and Stella, he was alarmed at the response he received through the radio. "Only Mrs. Hardaga gets a visa. Her daughter will have to stay behind."

The rabbi found it hard to break the news to Aida.

"My mother cannot travel alone!" Aida protested. "She is in a wheelchair, and very weak!"

The rabbi explained that he had already petitioned the Israeli Minister of Foreign Affairs for help. He knew things were only getting more complicated. The following convoy may be the last. Arranging it took coordination between ten organizations and four languages. Adding four more people to the convoy was impossible.

At home, Zaynab was resolved. "I won't leave you," she told Aida. "If we need to die together we'll die together. I am not afraid."

With wind blowing through the broken window in the kitchen, the apartment became unsuitable for the winter. They had no place else to go.

Each day Aida would travel the dangerous streets to the synagogue, the rabbi said he still had no news. He was doing his best to get all four on the list, he said, but Aida must have patience.

It was a week after a shell fell on the street in front of their building and killed five people, that Aida found herself again walking, scared, on the street. It was January, and the snow was piling up.

She had three trips that morning. First, to get water. She took four jerry cans with her on a small wagon. It was light to carry when the jerry cans were empty. Coming back would require some pulling.

Later she would go and get some wood for heat. They had run out of wood yesterday. She would also visit the synagogue, where she hoped to get a food parcel. Then she could finally return home and rest. Also, the doctor was supposed to come later that day for her mother.

As she exited the building she saw a snowstorm outside. She tightened her coat and stepped out of the building, pulling the small four-wheeled wagon behind her. Though she had gloves on, her fingertips felt numb.

She walked the streets, turning right and then left. Three streets away, at Austrijski square, she would find the UN water truck, and could fill herjerrycans.

In the distance she heard bullets and shells. She ignored it. She, like so many others in the city, had become used to it.

She saw another man walking with two jerry cans in his hands. She nodded to him, and he nodded back. The people who stayed in Sarajevo developed a sense of comraderie. After all, so many had either left or died. And everyone, rich or poor, Muslim or Croat, was in the same predicament.

They walked along in silence, quickly, until they turned the street to the Austrijski square. There were a few people filling their jerry cans and bottles by the

UN water truck. Aida waited, noticing the conversation one foreigner had with an older lady. He had a big camera hanging on his neck. He was probably looking for an opportunity to make a name for himself.

Aida saw the old lady refusing, shaking her head 'no.' People did not want to be photographed in their dismal state.

The photographer nodded and was coming now toward Aida. He was a young man.

He spoke in English. "Excuse me, Ma'am, my name is Edward. I'm a photographer from the United States. Would you mind me taking—"

"No, thank you." Aida said. She was in no mood to pose for some American.

The photographer nodded and left.

Aida's turn came, and she took off her gloves so they wouldn't get wet. She'd put them back on in a second, but there was nothing worse than wet gloves in such weather. She filled her jerry cans quickly, sealed them and loaded them onto the small wagon. The wagon barely wanted to move. The wheels were rusty, and with four full jerry cans she had to pull hard for the wagon to move.

She saw the photographer approach her again. "Ma'am, can I help you?"

She shook her head 'no,' but the photographer was adamant and reached his hand to the wagon's handle. Aida sighed, "But no photos!"

The photographer laughed and said, "No

problem."

They walked in silence. Knowing the journey she'd have later on, she was grateful for this help, saving her energy for later.

Snowflakes blew on them. The photographer stopped, put the camera in its case on his back, and then hurried to continue walking. Aida said, "Are you sure, I'm fine—"

"I'm certain," the photographer said.

She wanted to be cordial, but she was in no mood to speak. That morning Stella had cried and asked her, "Mama, when will I be able to go to school again?"

The helplessness she felt, not knowing what to tell her daughter, was unbearable.

She led the photographer through the streets, turning left, right, and then reaching her street. He insisted on pulling the wagon all the way to the building. She thanked him.

From the seventh floor, near the window, Zaynab could see her daughter walking along with a stranger. She squinted. From his stride she could see he was a foreigner. She had a premonition. He'd help them.

The photographer pulled the wagon to the building's entrance and said, "I can help you carry the jerrycans to your door."

"No, thank you, sir. You have already helped a lot," Aida said in her limited English.

"It's Edward," the photographer smiled, "not 'sir.'"

Aida smiled and nodded. She took one jerry can in each hand and opened the door to the building. Behind her she saw the foreigner take the other two cans and follow her. She laughed, "Take one, one is enough."

"But I can carry two."

"You'll need one hand to feel your way in the darkness."

Edward was startled when the lady did not take the elevator, but opened a door to a dark stairway. He followed her, the door closing behind them. It was pitch dark. He heard her steps up the stairs. She was right. He needed a free hand to clutch to the railing.

"Sir, leave one jerry can here. I'll get it later."

"It's Edward," he said as he slowly felt his way in the darkness, surprised at how the lady could do it with both her hands taken.

She heard him stumbling on the stairs, nearly falling. She said, "It's 18 stairs each time, count."

"Okay." Edward said. They climbed a couple of floors and he was already tired. The woman kept climbing quickly. He continued, now counting in his head 18 stairs on each floor. It helped.

Then there was finally some light in the hallway. Aida was surprised to see the door to her apartment open. "Mama?" she said, seeing her mother's wheelchair in the door. "You should be in bed!"

"I saw you coming," Zaynab said. "Who is this guest?"

"A foreigner."

"That I see. Where from?"

"America."

Edward could hear the conversation. Now, with the light coming from the door, he rushed and caught up with Aida.

Aida panted, placing the two jerry cans by the door. "Thank you, Edward."

He nodded and placed the can along the other two, smiling at the old lady in a wheelchair at the door, and at the young girl hiding behind her.

Zaynab said to Aida, "Aren't you going to invite him inside?"

Aida whispered, "Mama, I don't know him. He might report to someone of Braunmir's presence. It's dangerous."

Zaynab waved her hand dismissively. "Hospitality is charity, daughter!" she looked at the young man and spoke the only English word she knew. "Welcome, welcome! Welcome!"

As Zaynab rolled her chair away from the door, Aida reluctantly smiled at the stranger. He nodded at her shyly and said, "The other jerry can."

"I'll get it," she said and hurried downstairs.

He tried to protest, but she had already rushed down.

"Welcome," Zaynab repeated, gesturing into the small apartment. Stella giggled at the look of the foreigner. "Stella, get him some water!"

Stella ran to the kitchen and poured water from the nearly-empty bottle. She hurried to hand it to the stranger and then hid behind her grandmother.

Edward noticed the broken window in the kitchen. Zaynab saw his look and pointed at the bullet holes in the wall behind him. He gasped, immediately turning to the window and looking at the hills in the distance. Only then did he realize he was a target, and rushed away from the window and out of the kitchen. Zaynab and Stella looked at him and laughed.

Soon Aida returned with the last jerry can and brought all four into the apartment. "Where is Papa?" she asked Stella.

"He's sleeping."

Aida took her gloves off and watched as the stranger spoke to Zaynab and Stella, neither understanding him.

"They don't understand English," she smiled.

Zaynab protested, "Yes, yes!"

Edward smiled.

Zaynab turned to him and asked in Bosnian, "Are you Christian? Orthodox? Catholic?"

Aida scolded her, "Mama, he doesn't understand you, and it's also impolite to ask a stranger such questions!"

Edward did not understand Zaynab's question. She repeated them, articulating again each word in Bosnian, "Hrišćanin? Pravoslavni? Katolik?"

She looked at Aida, "Translate!"

Aida shook her head "I'm not going to!"

Zaynab tried again, this time in Serbian, while crossing her chest like a catholic.

"Oh!" Edward laughed, "Am I Christian? No."

Stella giggled. After a year and a half of being stranded at home, this was pure entertainment.

Zaynab's eyes grew wide, "A Muslim then?"

Edward smiled and looked down, "No, I am… a…" he hesitated, but saw no reason why to hide. "I am Jewish. I work for the Washington Post."

Zaynab understood. "Jewish? Welcome, welcome!" She turned to Aida, "Bring him some of the Passover bread. It's in the top cupboard."

"Mama, I'm not going to, this is too—"

"Do as I tell you!"

Aida reluctantly reached for the top cupboard and pulled out a box of square Matzah bread. Seeing this, Edward was mind boggled, "Matzah? How come you have it?"

Aida mumbled, "My mother has Jewish friends in the community."

Zaynab urged her, "Now open it! Let him eat!"

"Mama, it's two years old. It must be stale!"

"No, it never goes stale. It's like iron. Open it, open it!"

Aida opened the box and took a piece of the thin unleavened flatbread. It was hard as a rock.

Zaynab urged the guest, "Welcome, welcome," motioning her hand to her mouth for him to eat.

The three of them looked at him as he tried breaking a piece of the flatbread and then put it in his mouth. It was stale, but he smiled.

His smile made all three of them laugh.

For the following hours the stranger was treated like family. They ate together, laughed, and talked. A doctor came at one point to check on Zaynab. Edward also got to meet Aida's husband, Braunmir, who seemed very sick and had difficulty walking. After the doctor left, Zaynab showed the guest her medal and certificate from the Holocaust Museum. His Hebrew wasn't good, but he could read the French on the diploma. Aida told him the story. He was impressed. Here was a WWII hero.

Aida explained to him, "My mother does not like to brag about the past, but she is very proud. We have family in Jerusalem."

"Really?"

"Yes, they invited us to go there now, because of the war."

"And you do not want to go?"

"Oh we do! But now the rabbi says there is a bureaucratic problem. They have given my mother a visa, but not us. And she won't go without us."

That night Edward did not sleep. He helped Aida go back and forth several times to fetch wood and food. Later in the evening he spoke to the rabbi at the synagogue, and spoke by radio to the Head of the Jewish Distribution Committee in Washington.

Unable to fall asleep, Edward got up and wrote the following article. Two days later it was printed, with pictures, in the Washington Post.

"IN BOSNIA, A HERO ABANDONED

By Edward Serotta, January 12, 1994

Zaynab Hardaga is a 77-year-old Muslim woman living in Sarajevo. She has a letter from the Foreign Ministry of Israel asking all those who come in contact with her to aid her in any way possible. The Jewish community sends a doctor several times a week to look in on her. The American Joint Distribution Committee, which aids Jewish communities in need throughout the world, makes sure her family receives food packages regularly. And recently a Jewish woman in the neighborhood knitted a bright pink sweater for her 10-year-old granddaughter.

During World War II, Mrs. Hardaga learned a costly lesson from her father. "You do not abandon your friends," he told her. This was his explanation for why the family was hiding and protecting a Jewish man during the Nazi occupation of Bosnia. Later her father gambled with his own life to aid a Jewish family in need. Someone informed on him, and Zaynab's father lost his gamble and his life.

In 1985, Zaynab and her sister were flown to Israel, and at the Museum of the Holocaust became the first Muslims to receive a Righteous Gentile Award, the honor given to those non-Jews who heroically rescued Jews from certain death. Her sister has since died, and Zaynab now shares an unheated seventh-floor apartment with her daughter Aida, son-in-law Branumir and granddaughter Stella.

As Zaynab has but one leg, her life is reduced to the one room where the family keeps a wood-burning stove. She does not have much, but among the items she holds dearest are her medal from Israel, a scrapbook of pictures from that trip and the citation from the Jerusalem Holocaust Museum. She has held this paper and looked at it so many times that its edges are frayed and brown.

Her daughter Aida faces the pitch-black stairwell several times a day, and does so alone, as Branumir suffers from multiple sclerosis. She lugs sacks of wood, containers of water and boxes of food. Her kitchen window faces the Serb-held mountainside. Snipers take an occasional pot shot, and one window in her kitchen was blown out. Two bullet holes decorate the walls.

The Israeli government recently vowed to

fulfill its promise never to forget by offering to bring the 77-year-old woman to Israel to live. Yet for some reason Israeli authorities have not approved the immigration of Mrs. Hardaga's family, and she refuses to leave her 36-year-old daughter, Aida, her son-in-law, Branumir, and her 10-year-old granddaughter, Stella, behind in Sarajevo.

I met Aida, Zaynab's daughter, on the street one morning during a snowstorm. In this dying city with no running water and precious little gas or electricity, Aida was dragging a wagon of plastic jerry cans filled with water, wheeling it around a mortar crater where five neighbors had been killed the previous week.

She used to work in an office. Now she was lugging two heavy jugs up seven flights of stairs in her pitch-black building. She rested a moment, then went back down to haul up the rest.

"I have to get wood now," she said, glancing at her watch. Then she headed downstairs again. Two hours later, after dragging up a 30-pound sack of chips, boards and branches, she went out for the third time to pick up a package of food from the Jewish community center down the street.

By 2 p.m. Aida had returned and was starting to prepare lunch. These days she uses her kitchen only during daylight hours because Serb snipers have twice targeted its windows after dark. The bullets ricocheting off the kitchen walls interrupted her cooking and rushed her screaming from the kitchen.

While the snow swirled outside, Aida's mother, sat in the unheated living room as the Jewish community's doctor checked her blood pressure.

Aida's husband, Branumir, has multiple sclerosis and could only manage a weak smile.

After the fire was ready in the oven, Aida placed a bread-cake in it to bake. As she stirred a rice and potato dish at the stove, she explained the family's desperate situation.

"We have been asking to leave for months," she said. "But my mother will not go without us, and she shouldn't have to."

She turned away from the stove and faced me. "Look, I'm used to working," she said. "I love to work and I will do anything, anything at all. The only thing I insist on is that I keep my family together. I'm sorry. I don't think that's too much to ask. I'm just asking for the smallest of chances. Do you know of anyone who might help us?"

The Joint Distribution Committee's president, Milton Wolf, monitors Zaynab's condition by radio every week from New York. "Mrs. Hardaga will die if she remains there," he said. She has an invitation from the Israeli government to go and live in that country, but for reasons no one understands, her family does not. And, adds Wolf, "as far as we know, the Bosnian government has not okayed their names for the next convoy out of Sarajevo, but we're trying like hell."

Wolf sighs. "I wonder if anyone has thought of the obvious," he said. "While it's nice to commemorate a hero, the problem is she is alive now, and the woman who would not abandon the Jews should not be expected to abandon her family. Not in Sarajevo."

CHAPTER 41

Weeks passed, and it seemed like nothing changed. Winter was relentless. Zaynab commented that she did not remember it being so snowy since World War Two. She mumbled over food, "Allah is upset with us. Upset with us humans disappointing Him."

One day terrible news came from Mostar. After kicking the Serbs out several months earlier, the Muslims and the Croats began fighting. After Muslims attacked several Croat outposts, Croats aimed at destroying the historical Mostar Bridge.

"They took the bridge down," Aida said to her mother.

"The Mostar Bridge? Impossible! It's hundreds of years old! It's as sturdy as a rock!"

"I'm sorry, Mama. They did. The bridge is gone."

"What has become of us, Aida? What?"

One day in early February they heard a knock on the door. Edward, the American photographer, was breathless.

"What happened?" Aida asked.

"They got you the visas! Everything is arranged," he said, panting, "The convoy will leave tomorrow morning. You should get ready."

Aida was unsure for a moment whether he was serious. "How do you know?"

"The rabbi told me just now and asked me to rush to you. They received the list from Israel this morning. Your names are there, all four of you."

Zaynab, pushing her wheelchair toward the door, understood. "This is a blessing from Allah," she said as tears began to fill her throat. She reached her hand to kiss the messenger. Edward leaned down to kiss the old lady. She grabbed his face firmly and kissed him several times on each cheek, "You are a blessing from Allah!"

The following morning, February 5th, 1994, on the frozen streets of Sarajevo, Zaynab, Aida, Braunmir and Stella left their shattered apartment building and trudged through the cold streets of Sarajevo, assisted by Edward and three volunteers from the synagogue, pushing Zaynab and Braunmir's wheelchairs. As Zaynab's chair rolled over the icy road, she looked at her abandoned city. Her beloved city. The city she was born into just as the First World War ended. Now she was leaving it in the middle of another war.

Tears streamed on her cheeks as she saw the closed flower shop, the closed grocery store, the closed bank, the square, the old clock tower in the distance along with the minaret of Sarajevo's tallest mosque, not far away from the tall tower of the Old Orthodox church.

The group walked quickly, one volunteer pulling the two suitcases on a small wagon, another pushing Braunmir's wheelchair, while Edward pushed Zaynab's wheelchair. Aida held firmly to Stella's hand. She could not believe it was happening. In her nightmares she had imagined the building would fall, like the famous Oriental Institute that fell a week earlier, burning thousands of ancient manuscripts. Or like the Residence of the President, which was destroyed, or the National Library, or the Olympic games stadiums, or any other of many other buildings that came down around them.

But now Aida was walking to freedom. It felt unreal. She clutched her daughter's hand even harder.

In the street of the synagogue stood a row of six buses. Aida had not seen buses in nearly two years. All were either burned or broken. These looked new. How did they arrange for them to enter the besieged city? How did the Serbian Army let them pass?

Aida noticed her older sister and brother running toward them. Aisha and Salih, both in their fifties, were very emotional. They kissed Aida, Braunmir and Stella, and then both knelt by Zaynab. Tears poured as Zaynab hugged them both close to her chest. "You should come with us!"

Aisha wiped her tears, shaking her head. Over the

past few weeks, when the possibility of going to Israel became a real option, both Aisha and Salih, along with their spouses, children and grandchildren, chose to stay in Sarajevo. Aisha looked at her mother and said, "You go. Take care of yourself, Mama. We will be alright."

Zaynab protested, "I can ask them to wait with the buses, and you can bring everyone here!"

Aisha whispered something to her mother while looking at Aida and Braunmir and Stella. Zaynab nodded. She grabbed Aisha's arm and they embraced and cried together.

As they all walked toward the buses, the rabbi noticed them and exclaimed, "Here you are!" He shook his head in disbelief as he saw Zaynab, "Mrs. Hardaga! I am so sorry for all the time this took..."

"Don't be sorry, Rabbi!" Zaynab said, her eyes still wet from crying, "Allah will bless you for all your help!"

Salih and Aida helped Zaynab out of her wheelchair and up the stairs of the bus. She had a reserved seat in the front. Four seats were saved for her and her family. The bus was already full. War-worn people who had braved the siege for the past two years. Most of them were Jewish. Only a few were not, those with extreme humanitarian stories, most of them requiring emergency medical treatment. On the six buses, the 294 people were but a token in comparison to the thousands remaining.

Edward took pictures of the departing family, who had hosted him several times over the past weeks.

Zaynab turned to him, "You are coming too, right?"

Aida hurried to translate.

Edward smiled, "No, I am staying here. I have work to do."

Zaynab shook her head. She saw in his eyes that he was resolved. "Come here," she said.

He reached over to her and she put her hand on his head, "May Allah bless you, protect you, guard you, save you from ill wills, and bring you back home safe and sound. Amen."

Edward, twinkle in his eyes, said, "Amen."

The bus driver was about to pull out. Edward left the bus after saying goodbye to Aida, Braunmir and little Stella. Two UN officials climbed aboard. Zaynab waved to Edward, to Aisha and Salih, when she suddenly noticed the rabbi was left behind. She shouted to the driver, "Stop, stop, the rabbi!"

The rabbi climbed aboard to reassure the old lady, "I am staying here, Mrs. Hardaga."

"But… this is foolishness!"

"Like your father did foolish things to save people's lives, so must I."

"And your family?" Zaynab asked, concerned.

"They are all in Vienna now. I'm alone here."

Zaynab shook her head and put her hand on his head, reciting a long prayer. The driver and the UN officials became impatient.

Finally, the rabbi thanked her and disembarked.

As the buses pulled out of the street, the rabbi turned to Salih and Aisha, "She's quite something, your mother."

Salih smiled and said, "Oh, yes she is."

The bus made its way out of the quiet streets, in which many of the roads were damaged by shells.

Soon, exiting the city, the buses was held at a checkpoint. They waited there for over an hour. The UN officials collected all the IDs and passports and brought them over to the men behind the cement barricade, but the men were in no hurry to let the bus convoy through.

The French UN official, climbing back onto the bus, cursed under his breath.

Everyone in the bus became impatient. Seeing the armed men through the windows—knowing these same men were possibly the men who shot shells at their houses, who terrorized their city, who were responsible for the death of so many—seeing these men through the window brought a hushed cry of dismay through the bus.

One Jewish lady sitting across from Zaynab muttered, unaware of Braunmir sitting behind her, "Oh, those filthy Serbs, may they burn in hell!"

Zaynab, upon hearing her, smiled, "Madam, they are not to blame."

"Not to blame? These people are ruthless!"

"These people," Zaynab whispered, "are the sons and grandsons of the Serbs who were gunned down during the War. These are the people whose fathers were prosecuted without trials in the concentration camps. Jasenovac alone had more Serbs killed there than Jews."

The woman's eyes widened. "I didn't know that."

Zaynab smiled at her. "No one is to blame. Even the perpetrator was once a victim."

The lady nodded, tears welling in her eyes.

Seconds later the UN official came, the pile of passports in his hand. He told the driver, "We got a green light. Now get us out of here. Fast."

CHAPTER 42

As the airplane landed in the Tel Aviv airport, the passengers, mostly Jewish refugees from Sarajevo, began singing the old Jewish song, "We have brought peace onto you," or in Hebrew, *Hevenu Shalom Aleychem.* Zaynab, exhausted from all the traveling, shed a tear.

From the airplane's window Aida noticed a throng of people along with camera crews. "Look, Stella," she said, "look at all the people waiting for us."

What Aida did not know was that many of the people outside were waiting specifically for them. Articles about the Muslim woman from Sarajevo who had saved a Jewish family in the Holocaust made the local news. It even reached the office of the Prime Minister, who had given the order to bring the woman to Israel along with any family member she wanted.

The flight attendant smiled seeing all the people singing in the airplane. She brought Zaynab her wheelchair and helped her into it. Zaynab and her family were the first to exit the airplane, and were met, to their astonishment, by a roaring applause from the people on the tarmac.

Among them was a 56-year-old woman who had known Zaynab long before Aida was born. She rushed up the stairway and greeted Zaynab, "Auntie!"

"Tova!" Zaynab said and clutched firmly Tova's face, kissing her again and again. "My Tova!"

Tova, tears in her eyes, hurried to embrace Aida, "You must be Aida, welcome!"

Aida, who was a little anxious about landing in the foreign land, was soothed by Tova's words, spoken in her mother tongue.

Tova hurried to kiss Stella and Braunmir. Cameras flashed. Four men were brought to help carry Zaynab with her wheelchair down the stairs into the tarmac, but Zaynab, perhaps filled with adrenaline from the reception, insisted on standing, and along with Aida on her side, and while holding firmly to the railing, made her way slowly down the stairs to the sound of camera flashes and people cheering. She felt at home.

That same day in Sarajevo, a shell landed in the market, killing 68 people and wounding a dozen others. The market massacre, as it came to be known, was broadcast on the television in Tova's apartment, after her new guests arrived.

Tova hurried to grab the remote control, wishing to turn the television off. "You should not watch this now that you are here!"

Braunmir shook his head. "Let us watch. It's our home."

Reluctantly, Tova put down the remote. The pictures were horrifying. A market in ruins, and people screaming.

The family had not watched television in nearly two years and the pictures brought immense pain. Zaynab was worried about the children she left behind. Should she have forced them to come? She remembered Aisha's whisper: "Take Aida and her family. For mixed couples it is hell here now. We are fine. We have the mosque and the community. We cannot leave them."

Now, in Tova's apartment in Jerusalem, Stella began crying watching the TV. "Mama, I don't want to return!"

Aida stroked her daughter's hair. "You won't need to, baby. We are safe now."

Going to sleep on her newly-made bed, Zaynab Hardaga, exhausted from the long day, was unable to fall asleep. She whispered in her head the first Surah of the Qur'an and then added, "God, my God. My father said I had brought luck, that my birth had ended the First World War. If you need, take me, but bring peace to my people. Please Allah. Please, remember me. Do not forsake thy servant. Bring peace. Bring us peace."

The Ministry of Interior gave Zaynab's family an apartment in Jerusalem. Braunmir, Aida and Stella received Israeli citizen's IDs through the mail. Zaynab's ID, however, was held in the Prime Minister's office. Prime Minister Yitshak Rabin instructed his assistants, "I want to give her the ID myself."

A small ceremony was planned, and two weeks after her arrival Zaynab, along with Aida, Braunmir and Stella, arrived at the Prime Minister's office, overseeing the entire city of Jerusalem. Prime Minister Rabin walked toward Zaynab as she entered the office. "Here is our hero!"

Zaynab, after the translator explained this to her, hurried to adjust her head covering modestly, "No, sir, not a hero. I did what you would have done as well."

It was a Friday, and the Prime Minister was weary from a long week. He told the translator, "Tell her I asked for the meeting with her to be the last thing for this week, to leave me with a good taste for the weekend, with hope."

The translator interpreted as they walked toward the reception room where the small ceremony was to be held. Zaynab took Rabin's hand, "You should always have hope."

Rabin looked at her. These were difficult days for him. Trying to push for peace with the Palestinians proved to be a difficult task, especially given internal

Israeli opposition.

A short ceremony was held, and cameras flashed as Rabin handed Zaynab her blue Israeli ID. Aida, in the front row, was immensely proud of her mother. Her mother was a hero. She was younger than Aida when she decided to hide Joseph's family, and to later bring him potatoes when he was doing forced labor. In her generosity she planted the seeds of the survival of her own family decades later.

Zaynab, holding her new ID, said to the translator, "Please thank the Prime Minister."

Rabin, upon hearing the translation, laughed, "No, it is you, Mrs. Hardaga, that we should be thanking."

After the ceremony ended, Zaynab grabbed Rabin's arm, "You do peace," she whispered. The translator hurried to huddle near the two of them. "You bring peace, I tell you! Ignore what they say. Peace is possible. The world needs a peaceful Jerusalem, a peaceful Holy Land!"

Rabin nodded, listening to the translator and looking at the old lady's deep brown eyes. She held to his arm tightly. He nodded again.

"Promise me!" she said.

He nodded, his eyes becoming moist. "I promise."

Braunmir seemed to be doing better. Medications were available in Israel, and with the help of doctors specializing in Multiple Sclerosis, they were able to keep his physical decline in check. Zaynab's health, however, slowly deteriorated. Doctors hovered over her, and they were able to prolong her life only for a few more months.

Her last days were spent in constant prayer, and gratitude for God for all that she had been given in life. She thanked God for a thriving family, three children, eight grandchildren, two great grandchildren, and wonderful memories. She prayed for peace. And she thought a lot of her late husband, Mustafa, and how she would join him in heaven. She thought too of her mother Aisha, and of her father Ahmed. How she had missed them all these years. She was ready to leave.

Nine months after her arrival in Israel, on October 23rd, 1994, Zaynab Hardaga, age 77, took her last breath. At her bedside was her daughter Aida, her son-in-law Braunmir, her granddaughter Stella, and her Jewish niece Tova. In Sweden her granddaughter and her family lit candles for their Nana's departure. In Sarajevo, her daughter and son, along with their children, received the news and began the Hiddad mourning.

On Zaynab's request, she was buried in an old cemetery overlooking the Jerusalem hills, not far from the tree she planted a decade earlier in the memory of her father.

Soon after Zaynab's death, the leaders of the Muslims, Croats and Serbs, finally met together in Dayton, Ohio, under American leadership. The subsequent peace agreement ended, among other atrocities, the siege of Sarajevo. The Dayton Accords are respected to this day.

EPILOGUE

In the Holy Land, on a hill outside Jerusalem, there is a small cemetery facing the Jerusalem hills. If you visit this cemetery, your eyes may notice a small grave with many flowers on it. People from around the world come and pay homage to the woman buried there, leaving behind flowers and notes of gratitude. There is no name on the grave, only five words: "Mother. Righteous Among the Nations."

* * *

THE END

PHOTOGRAPHS

Zaynab Sadik (later Hardaga) as a child. c. 1925

Ahmed Sadik. c. 1925

Zaynab Hardaga, standing, with her son Salih in her arms, and her daughter Aisha standing near her. On the carpet, Tova Kabilio. Photograph taken in the Hardaga back yard during WWII, c. 1941.

Sarajevo, 1941. The veiled woman on the right is Zaynab Hardaga. She is holding the arm of Rebecca Kabilio. Rebecca is holding the hand of Zaynab's first born, who is holding the hand of Tova Kabilio. On the left, veiled, is Zaynab's sister in law, Bahriya Hardaga. It is said that Rebecca, under the new laws, had to wear an armband with a star of David, identifying herself as Jewish. She felt embarrased to walk the streets that way, and Zaynab offered to have her own veil cover the armband so that no one in the street could see. Photo courtsey of the Yad Vashem Holocaust Meuseum, Jerusalem.

For more photographs please visit the online book companio in the following page.

CLAIM YOUR GIFT!

Thank you for purchasing this novel. For a special behind-the-scenes e-book, including historical background on which *After the storm* was based please visit:

https://books.click/Storm

* * *

This e-book companion includes group discussion ideas, unique photographs and much more!

JOIN OUR ONLINE BOOK CLUB!

Book club members receive free books and the hottest pre-release novels. To join our exclusive online book club and discuss *After the storm* with likeminded readers, please visit:

Books.click/MoringBookclub

* * *

We look forward to see you in our bookclub family!

RATE THIS BOOK!

We thank you for taking a quick moment to rate this book online. Let others know what you thought at this easy link!

Books.click/StormRating

The author has requested that we include the following personal email address below. Readers are invited to contact author Marcel Moring directly at the following address. The author attempts to answer each and every email from dedicated readers.

AuthorMarcelMoring1@gmail.com

NOVELS BY MARCEL MORING:

My India

The Survivor

The Holocaust

Innocence

The Teacher

After the Storm

The Revenge